See the
Wider picture

Spice shop, Karnataka, India

The colourful piles of powder at the front of the shop are not spices but paint or dye. This is used to dye fabrics for saris, the beautiful costumes worn by Indian women.

Do you know what the powders are made of?

CONTENTS

Contents **3**

0

Welcome to Harlow Mill

0.1

INTRODUCING LEE

Spelling; family members; possessive adjectives;
possessive *'s*; *have got* for possession

VOCABULARY

Family members | Months and dates |
Free time activities | Sports |
Giving opinions | Possessions |
School subjects | Skills and abilities

GRAMMAR

Possessive adjectives | Possessive *'s* |
Have got for possession | There *is/are*
with *some* and *any* | *Can/can't*
for ability | Question words

1 🔊 **1.02 Read the text. Find these people in the photos.**

Dave   Gloria   Ruby   Lee

> This is Lee Marshall. He's fifteen and he's from Harlow Mill, a small town near
> London. He's in Year 10 at Harlow Mill High and he's mad about music. Lee has got a
> sister, Ruby — she's thirteen. He hasn't got a brother. Lee's dad, Dave, is a policeman.
> His mum's name is Gloria and she's an artist. She's from a big family in Jamaica. Lee's
> family have also got some pets — a cat and two guinea pigs. Their cat's name is Elvis.
> The guinea pigs' names are One and Two.

2 Mark the sentences T (true) or F (false). In pairs, correct the false sentences.

1 [F] Lee's surname is Smith.
    Lee's surname is Marshall.
2 [ ] Harlow Mill is in England.

3 [ ] Ruby is Lee's brother.
4 [ ] Lee's dad hasn't got a job.
5 [ ] Lee's mum is Spanish.

3 🔊 **1.03 In pairs, spell the names in Exercise 1. Listen and check.**

4 🔊 **1.04** **I KNOW!** **In pairs, listen and check you understand the words
below. Can you add more words?**

Vocabulary	Family members

aunt   cousin   grandfather   mother   parents   sister   son   wife

5 Look at Lee's family tree and Grammar A. Complete the sentences below with the correct possessive adjectives. Decide who is speaking in each sentence.

Grammar A		Possessive adjectives			
I	you	he	she	we	they
my	your	his	her	our	their

JACK   DIANA

SUE   BOB   GLORIA   DAVE

LEE   RUBY

1 _Gloria_

I've got a husband – _his_ name is Dave.

2 _____

I've got a sister. _Her_ name is Ruby.

3 _Sue_

I've got a brother and a sister – _our_ brother's name is Bob.

4 _Diana_

Jack and I have got three children – _their_ names are Bob, Sue and Gloria.

5 _Bob_

Gloria and I are sisters – _our_ parents' names are Jack and Diana.

6 Add apostrophes (') to the sentences about Lee's family.

Grammar B	Possessive 's
Singular	my brother's laptop, Lee's sister
Regular plural	my parents' car
Irregular plural	the children's mother
Two words	Lee's dad's bike, Dave and Gloria's house

Lee's sister's name is Ruby. His dads name is Dave. Gloria is Daves wife. Sue is the childrens aunt. Bob is Lee and Rubys uncle. Lees grandparents are Jack and Diana.

7 Complete the dialogues with the correct form of *have got*.

Grammar C	*Have got* for possession
+	**–**
I've got (have got) a sister. He's got (has got) a cat.	I haven't got a brother. He hasn't got a dog.
?	
Have you got a sister? Has he got a brother?	Yes, I have./No, I haven't. Yes, he has./No, he hasn't.

1 A: _Has_ Ruby _got_ a sister?
  B: No, she _hasn't_. But she _has_ a brother.
2 A: _Have_ Jack and Diana _got_ children?
  B: Yes, they _have_. They _have got_ two girls and a boy.
3 A: _Has_ Bob _got_ any sisters?
  B: Yes, he _has_. He _has got_ two sisters.
4 A: _Have_ Lee and Ruby _got_ a cousin?
  B: No, they _haven't got_.

8 In pairs, use these questions to talk about your family. Then tell the class about your partner's family.

- Have you got any brothers and sisters? How old are they?
- What's your mum's/dad's name?
- Where are your parents from?
- Have you got a pet? What's his/her name?

Adam has got a sister. She's ten.

0.2 INTRODUCING AMY

Months and dates; free time activities; giving opinions; sports

1 🔊 **1.05 Read the text and answer the questions in pairs.**

1 Is Amy the same age as Lee?
2 Are they at the same school?
3 Is Amy interested in sport? Which ones?

» **This is Amy Arnold, Lee's best friend.**
She's fifteen and she's also at Harlow Mill High. She hasn't got any brothers or sisters. Amy's birthday is on 15 November – she's a typical Scorpio. Amy is very good with computers and her hobbies are playing computer games, surfing the internet, taking photos, swimming and, in summer, cycling. She has a busy life – she has judo classes two evenings a week after school and she sometimes has training sessions with the school volleyball team too. Amy is a very big fan of Bro, the pop star.

2 🔊 **1.06 Say the dates in full. Listen and check.**

| We write: **15 November** | **Watch** |
| We say: **the 15th of November** | **OUT!** |

1 21/01 = *the twenty-first of January*
2 12/10 =
3 15/02 =
4 22/07 =
5 04/05 =
6 30/08 =
7 31/12 =

3 **When is your birthday? Tell the class. Are there other students with a birthday in the same month as you?**

My birthday is on the eleventh of April.

4 **Read the text about Amy again. What are her hobbies and interests?**

5a 🔊 **1.07 Listen and check you understand the words below.**

Vocabulary A	**Free time activities**

doing nothing   going to the cinema
listening to music   playing computer games
reading books/magazines   surfing the internet
taking photos   tidying your bedroom
visiting relatives   watching TV/DVDs/films on YouTube

5b 🔊 **1.08 Listen to Amy and Lee. What is Lee's favourite free time activity?**

6 **CLASS VOTE** **Say which two free time activities from Exercise 5 are your favourites.**

My favourite free time activities are … and …

7 🔊 **1.09 Study Vocabulary B. Listen and repeat. In pairs, say what you think about the activities in Exercise 5.**

Vocabulary B	**Giving opinions**

I think reading is ┌ exciting/fun/great/interesting.
                     ├ OK.
                     └ boring/terrible.

I think doing nothing is boring.

8 🔊 **1.10 I KNOW!** **Work in pairs. How many sports can you add to Vocabulary C in three minutes? Compare with another pair.**

Vocabulary C	**Sports**

basketball   cycling   football   running
swimming   tennis   volleyball

9 **In your opinion, which sports in Exercise 8 are fun and which are boring?**

I think basketball is fun.

10 **Tell the class about your partner's favourite sports and free time activities. Use your partner's answers to Exercises 6 and 7 to help you.**

Marta's hobbies are taking photos and reading books. Her favourite sport is …

0.3 AMY'S HOME

Possessions; *there is/are* with *some/any*; articles

1 🔊 **1.11 Read about Amy's bedroom. Mark the sentences T (true) or F (false).**

Amy's house is in a quiet street in Harlow Mill, quite far from the town centre. There aren't any shops but it's quite near Amy's school. Amy's bedroom isn't very big but it's her favourite place in the house. There's a bed, a chair, a wardrobe and a big mirror. There is a table but the bed is Amy's favourite place to work! Amy's room is very untidy. There are always some clothes on the floor … and there are often arguments about this!

1 [T] Amy's hometown is Harlow Mill.
2 [F] Amy's family's house is in the centre of town.
3 [T] It isn't far from the school.
4 [F] Amy's bedroom is quite small.
5 [F] Amy hasn't got a desk.

2 🔊 **1.12 Listen and check you understand the words below. In pairs, underline the things you can see in the photo.**

Vocabulary	Possessions

bike   book   camera   computer game   dictionary
DVDs   guitar   headphones   helmet   keys   laptop
MP3 player   mobile (phone)   pencil case   photo
poster   rucksack   sports bag   sunglasses
trainers   TV set   watch

3 In pairs, use the Vocabulary box to tell your partner three things you have/haven't got/would like to have.

I've got a bike. I haven't got a guitar. I'd like to have a laptop.

4 Complete the sentences about Amy's room.

Grammar A	*There is/are* with *some/any*	
	Singular	**Plural**
+	There's (there is) **a** bed.	There are **some** clothes.
–	There isn't **a** desk.	There aren't **any** shops.
?	Is there **a** chair?	Are there **any** books?

1 There *is* a chair in Amy's room.
2 There _isn't_ a TV.
3 There _is_ some posters on the wall.
4 There _is_ _a_ desk.
5 There _isn't_ _a_ camera.
6 There _are_ _any_ books.

5 Use *there is/are* to write three sentences about your bedroom. Compare with a partner.

There are two posters in my bedroom.

6 In pairs, ask and answer questions about your bedrooms. Use the items from the Vocabulary box or your own ideas.

A: *Are there any photos on the wall?*
B: *Yes, there are./No, there aren't.*

7 🔊 **1.13 Complete the text with *a* or *the*. Listen and check.**

Grammar B	Articles

- The first time we talk about a person/thing, we use **a**.
  There's a café near my house.
- If we talk about the person/thing again, we use **the**.
  The café is popular on Sunday mornings.
- If it's clear what person/thing we're talking about, we use **the**.
  My house is also near the swimming pool.

My flat is in ¹**a** street in ² _the_ centre of town. ³ _the_ street is very busy, day and night. There's ⁴ _a_ big supermarket near ⁵ _the_ flat. On Saturday mornings ⁶ _the_ supermarket is always very busy. There's also ⁷ _a_ nice café in my street, near ⁸ _the_ City Stadium. ⁹ _the_ café's quite expensive but it's very popular.

8 Write about the street where you live. Use the text in Exercise 7 to help you.

My house is in a quiet street …

Krystal Ang is fifteen years old. She's got a little sister, Lisa, and a dog called Daisy. Krystal is very artistic – she has extra Art classes and she can draw very well. She's quite musical too – she can play the piano but she can't sing! Amy and Lee are her friends but she's at a different school. She's a very hard-working student and she has extra French lessons after school on Mondays and Thursdays. Her favourite subjects are French and History. Krystal sometimes has problems with Maths but she always has good marks. She's not very sporty but she can play tennis quite well.

1 🔊 **1.14 Read the text. Is Krystal a good student?**

2 🔊 **1.15** **I KNOW!** **In pairs, match school subjects 1-6 with pictures A-F. Can you think of any more subjects? Listen and check.**

1 B Geography
2 A Music
3 F Chemistry
4 E English
5 D Biology
6 C Information Technology

3 Read the text again and answer the questions in pairs.

1 What are Krystal's favourite subjects?
2 What are your favourite subjects?

4 Complete the sentences with *can* or *can't*.

Grammar	*Can/can't* for ability
+	–
I can cook.	I can't sing.
She can draw.	She can't drive.
?	
Can you sing?	Yes, I can./No, I can't.
Can he speak English?	Yes, he can./No, he can't.

1 We can speak French but we **_can't_** speak German.
2 I'm afraid of water because I **can't** swim.
3 My brother can't play the guitar but he **can** play the piano.
4 My parents **can't** drive so I take a bus to school.
5 I **can't** help you – I **can't** speak Italian. Sorry!
6 What a terrible group! The singer **can't** sing!

5a 🔊 **1.16 In pairs, check you understand the verbs and phrases below.**

Vocabulary	Skills and abilities

act   cook   dance   drive a car   play the guitar/piano
repair a computer   speak English/Spanish   swim

5b 🔊 **1.17 Listen to Amy and underline the things in the Vocabulary box that she can do.**

6 In pairs, say which things in the Vocabulary box you can and can't do.

I can't speak Spanish but I can speak English. And you?

7 In pairs, ask and answer the questions.

Can you …

1 study to music?
2 sleep in a chair?
3 run more than two kilometres?
4 do your homework on a bus/in bed?
5 draw people's faces?
6 shoot a basketball?
7 bake a cake?
8 say 'hello' in French or German?
9 read music?
10 play chess?
11 ski?

A: Can you… ?   B: Yes, I can./No, I can't.

8 Tell the class about five things your partner can do and two things he/she can't. Use his/her answers to Exercises 6 and 7 to help you.

And YOU

Revision

1 In groups, do the quiz about Harlow Mill. Use the texts in lessons 0.1–0.4 to help you.

How much can you remember?

1. Where in England is Harlow Mill?
2. What is Lee's cat's name?
3. Who is Diana?
4. What kind of pet has Krystal got?
5. Can Krystal sing?
6. Are there any shops near Amy's house?
7. How old is Amy?
8. What is Lee's dad's job?
9. Has Amy got any brothers or sisters?
10. Where is Lee's mum from?

2 Complete the questions with the words below. Then ask and answer the questions in pairs.

How old   What (4x)   What time
When   Where   Who

1. *When* is your birthday?
2. *Where* are you?
3. *What* are you from?
4. *What* are your parents' names?
5. *Who* is your best friend in your class?
6. *How old* is your favourite possession?
7. *What* is your favourite free time activity?
8. *What* is your favourite song/ track/album ever?
9. *What time* is your first class on Mondays?

3 Complete the questions with *is*, *are*, *can*, *have* or *has*. Then ask and answer the questions in pairs.

1. *Is* there a TV in your bedroom?
2. _____ you got any brothers or sisters?
3. _____ you got any pets?
4. _____ you fifteen?
5. _____ you paint?
6. _____ you sporty?
7. _____ you got a Facebook profile?
8. _____ your teacher got a Facebook profile?
9. _____ you sing?
10. _____ you musical?
11. _____ you play a musical instrument?
12. _____ there a swimming pool near your home?
13. _____ there any shops near your home?

4 Choose four questions from Exercises 2 and 3 that you think are very interesting. Then ask your questions to as many of your classmates as you can.

Time for culture

VOCABULARY
Culture | People | Cultural activities | Likes and dislikes | Age groups | News and entertainment

GRAMMAR
Present Simple: affirmative and negative | Adverbs of frequency | Present Simple: questions and answers

Grammar: He's awesome

Speaking: At the cinema

BBC Culture: Young Dancer Competition

Workbook p. 17

BBC VOX POPS ▶

CLIL 1 > p. 138

Art **1**　　Reading **2**

1.1　VOCABULARY Culture

I can talk about cultural activities, likes and dislikes.

1 🔊 **1.18** What can you see in the photos? In pairs, match photos 1–6 with phrases a–f. Listen and check.

a ⬜5⬜ Is the concert very long?
b ⬜2⬜ It isn't easy to learn the steps.
c ⬜4⬜ I like stories with a happy ending.
d ⬜3⬜ Look at the camera … say 'cheese'!
e ⬜1⬜ I like the colours in that painting but what is it?
f ⬜6⬜ The actors in this movie are terrible!

2 🔊 **1.19** Listen and repeat the words.

Vocabulary A	People		
art	artist	cinema	actor, director
writing	writer	dance	dancer
photography	photographer	music	musician

3 In pairs, make true sentences with the phrases below and the words in Vocabulary A.

artist　_music_　_dancer_
I'm a good …　I'm not a bad …　I'm not a great …

A: *I think I'm a good actor. What about you?*
B: *No, I'm not a great actor but I'm not a bad …*

4 🔊 **1.20** **I KNOW!** Add the words below to the correct category. Listen and check. Can you add more words?

скрипка

~~action films~~　horror films　rock　short stories　techno　violin　Zumba

Vocabulary B	Cultural activities

Types of films: cartoons comedies documentaries fantasy films romantic films science fiction (sci-fi) films ¹*action films* ²*horror film*
Things to read: comics novels graphic novels ³*Short stories*
Types of dance: ballet flamenco salsa ⁴*Zumba*
Musical instruments: drums guitar piano ⁵*rock violin*
Types of music: classical music hip-hop pop traditional
⁶*techno* ⁷*rock*

Photography **3**

Dance **4**

Music **5**

Cinema **6**

[Direct]

5 🔊 1.21 **Listen and choose the correct option.**

Speaking | **Likes and dislikes**

I'm (really) / *not really* interested in modern art.
I *love* / ~~hate~~ reading horror stories.
I (*really like*) / *don't like* taking selfies.
I *love* / *hate* dancing flamenco.
I'm (*into*) / *not into* classical music.
I *like acting* / (*don't like acting*) much.

After these phrases you can use
a verb + *-ing* or a noun.

6 🔊 1.22 **WORD FRIENDS** **Complete the sentences with the words below. Listen and check. Then change the sentences to make them true for you.**

| acting | ~~dancing~~ | drawing | listening |
| playing | reading | taking | watching |

1 I like *dancing* flamenco.
2 I hate _____ to techno.
3 I'm interested in _____ the guitar.
4 I love _____ photos.
5 I'm not into _____ in plays or films.
6 I really like _____ pictures.
7 I'm into _____ comics.
8 I don't like _____ horror films much.

7 🔊 1.23 **Complete the text. Then discuss with a partner. Are your answers the same? Listen and check.**

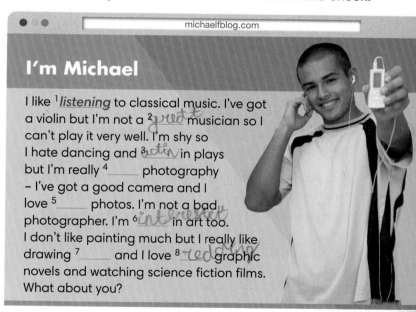

michaelfblog.com

I'm Michael

I like [1] *listening* to classical music. I've got
a violin but I'm not a [2] *great* musician so I
can't play it very well. I'm shy so
I hate dancing and [3] *actin* in plays
but I'm really [4] _____ photography
– I've got a good camera and I
love [5] _____ photos. I'm not a bad
photographer. I'm [6] *interest* in art too.
I don't like painting much but I really like
drawing [7] _____ and I love [8] *reading* graphic
novels and watching science fiction films.
What about you?

8 **In groups, talk about your likes and dislikes. Use Exercise 7 and the Speaking box to help you. Which person in your group has similar likes and dislikes to you?**

And Y?U

A: *Are you into music?*
B: *Yes, I am. I love rock music. I play the guitar. I'm a musician. What about you?*

I can use the Present Simple to talk about habits and routines.

1 🔊 **1.24 Read Rose's blog. Has Rose got the same interests as her sister, Violet?**

roseblog.com

MY SISTER & ME

10 Feb 4:56

We look the same but we don't like the same things.
Violet studies classical music but I study art. She reads novels and poems but I don't read much. And she often watches TV but I never watch TV – it doesn't interest me.
Violet writes poems. I write texts on my phone. I paint pictures. Violet tries to paint but she never finishes her paintings. She doesn't understand art! I love hip-hop. She says that hip-hop annoys her.
Our friends don't understand. 'You don't like the same things!' they say. 'But you always go out together! Why?'
'We have some fantastic arguments!' I say.

added by Rose   Tweet 🐦 13   Like 2

2 Find more examples of the Present Simple in the text in Exercise 1.

Grammar	Present Simple: affirmative and negative
+	**–**
I love hip-hop.	I don't watch TV.
She writes poems.	She doesn't like music.
She often goes out.	
She studies art.	

Adverbs of frequency (*always*, *usually*, *often*, *sometimes*, *never*) go before the verb but after *to be*.

GRAMMAR TIME ▶ PAGE 118

3 In pairs, say how Rose and Violet are different.
Rose studies art but Violet studies music.

4 Add adverbs of frequency to make these sentences true for you. Compare with a partner.

1 I write poems. *I sometimes write poems.*
2 My mother reads novels.
3 My teacher draws pictures on the board.
4 We (my friends and I) go dancing.
5 My classmates listen to classical music.

5 🔊 **1.25 Complete the text with the correct form of the verbs in brackets. Listen and check.**

I ¹*live* (live) in a village so I ² _don't go_ (not go) to the cinema very often. My brother often ³ _watches_ (watch) films on TV but I ⁴ _prefers_ (prefer) playing games with my friend, Dylan. He usually ⁵ _win_ (win) but he ⁶ _don't win_ (not win) every game. We ⁷ _don't_ (not play) very often on school days but we ⁸ _plays_ (play) a lot at weekends.

6 Correct the sentences.

1 Taylor Swift plays the drums in a group.
   Taylor Swift doesn't play the drums. She sings.
2 One Direction play classical music.
3 Director Tim Burton makes documentaries.
4 J.K. Rowling acts in films.
5 Daniel Radcliffe and Emma Watson paint pictures.

7 🔊 **1.26 Complete the text with the words below. There is one extra word. Listen and check.**

~~dancing~~   doesn't   ~~don't~~   ~~go~~
sometimes   loves

I love ¹*dancing*! I ² _go_ to dance classes with my friend, Kay. We do hip-hop — it's great! — and we ³ _sometimes_ do Zumba but not very often. I ⁴ _doesn't_ like salsa much but Kay ⁵ _loves_ it.

8 [VOX POPS ▶ 1.1] In pairs, use the phrases below to say what you do in your free time. Tell the class about you and your partner.

And YOU

see action films   read film reviews
listen to rap music   read comics   take photos

I often listen to rap music but Jo prefers pop.

I can find specific detail in an article and talk about age groups.

1 CLASS VOTE How many hours of TV do you usually watch after school?

- ☐ I never watch TV.
- ☐ Under one hour
- ☑ One–two hours
- ☐ More than two hours

2 Read the first paragraph of the text. What do you think these phrases mean?

- a a couch potato
- b to have square eyes

3 🔊 1.27 Read the rest of the text. Match headings a–e with paragraphs 1–4. There is one extra heading. Listen and check.

- a A global change
- b Surprising statistics
- c TV is cool again
- d Too much TV?
- e A new obsession

4 🔊 1.28 How do you say the words below in your language?

Vocabulary	Age groups
adults kids middle-aged (people) pensioners teenagers	

5 Use the words in the Vocabulary box to make sentences about the people below.

1 Jon and Cara are sixteen. *They're teenagers.*
2 Wendy is eight and Peter is five.
3 Bob and his wife are seventy-nine.
4 Emma and Dom aren't children.
5 Dick and Helen are both fifty-two.

6 Read the text again. Mark the sentences ✓ (right), ✗ (wrong) or ? (doesn't say).

1 ☐ Parents and teachers agree that teenagers watch too much TV.
2 ☐ Middle-aged people watch more TV than teenagers.
3 ☐ Pensioners watch six hours of TV a week.
4 ☐ Teenagers don't watch TV because they prefer to be outside in the fresh air.
5 ☐ Teenagers in Britain usually have a TV in their bedroom.

7 The survey shows British people watch a lot of TV. What about you and your family?

I don't watch TV very often but my sister watches TV all evening.

Where are all the couch potatoes?

1 Too much TV

Parents and teachers always say that teenagers are 'couch potatoes' and spend all their time in front of stupid TV programmes. But is it true that young people have 'square eyes'? Do they really watch a lot of TV?

2 Surprising statistics

The results of a recent survey show that people in Britain typically watch twenty-seven and a half hours of TV every week – almost four hours a day! But there is some surprising news – young people don't watch as much TV as adults. For example, middle-aged adults (aged forty-five to sixty-five) watch about five hours a day. But young people aged twelve to seventeen only watch about two and a half hours a day. And a typical pensioner watches about six hours a day!

3 A new obsession

Studies in countries such as the USA and Australia suggest the same: kids today spend less time in front of their TV sets than young people in the 1980s.

4 A global change

Teenagers today don't often sit with their families on the living-room couch. So where are they? Do they perhaps spend all their free time in the fresh air, away from the TV? The simple answer is no, they don't. The favourite free time activity of British teenagers is now surfing the internet – typically about thirty-one hours a week! The couch potato is alive and well – he's just back in his bedroom.

I can ask and answer questions about habits and routines.

VIDEO   HE'S AWESOME (Part 1)

Lee: Hey, Amy. Do you want to hear my new song?

Amy: Yes, I do, but not right now, Lee. There's a Bro concert on TV.

Lee: What time does it start?

Amy: Eight o'clock.

Lee: To be honest, I don't really like …

Amy: He's awesome! He plays the guitar and the piano and he's a wonderful singer!

Lee: Does he write his songs?

Amy: No, he doesn't. Do you know what he does in his free time?

Lee: I've no idea. What does he do in his free time?

Amy: He works in a home for sick animals once a week. He lives in a big house in Hollywood with lots of cats and dogs. Animals love him. He's perfect!

Lee: Yeah, right.

Not right now. *To be honest, …* *Awesome!* *I've no idea.* *Yeah, right.*	**O**UT of class

1 ▶ **1.2** 🔊 **1.29** Watch or listen to Part 1. Is Lee a big fan of Bro?

2 Find more Present Simple questions and answers in the dialogue.

Grammar	Present Simple: questions and answers
?	
Do you want to play?	Yes, I do./No, I don't.
Does he write songs?	Yes, he does./No, he doesn't.
Do they like animals?	Yes, they do./No, they don't.
Where does he live?	In Hollywood.
How often do you go there?	Once/Twice/Three times a day. Every Sunday./Often.

GRAMMAR TIME PAGE 118

3 Read the dialogue again and answer the questions.

1 What time does the concert start?

2 What does Amy think of Bro?

3 What instruments does Bro play?

4 Read the dialogue again and find Bro's answers to the questions below.

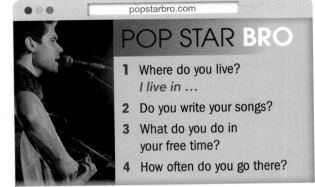

popstarbro.com

POP STAR **BRO**

1 Where do you live? *I live in …*

2 Do you write your songs?

3 What do you do in your free time?

4 How often do you go there?

5 ▶ **1.3** 🔊 **1.30** Make questions in the Present Simple. Watch or listen to Part 2 and answer the questions.

1 Tom Lewis / play music / ?
   Does Tom Lewis play music?

2 what / Tom Lewis / do in his free time / ?

3 how often / he / go there / ?

4 where / Tom Lewis / live / ?

5 Lee / always / listen to Amy / ?

6 what / Amy / want to do / ?

6 In pairs, ask and answer the questions.

1 Who's your favourite actor/pop star? Where does he/she live?

2 What does he/she do in his/her free time?

My favourite actor is Emilia Clarke. She lives in …

7 In pairs, ask and answer questions about the activities below.

watch music videos   make videos play an instrument   take photos   sing change the posters in your room

A: *Do you watch music videos?*

B: *Yes, I do.*

A: *How often do you do it?*

I can identify specific detail in a conversation and talk about media habits.

Newspapers The radio The TV The internet

What type of media do you use:

1 to listen to new music?
2 to watch pop videos?
3 to check news about your favourite celebrity?
4 to check sports results?
5 to see what's on at the cinema?
6 to find information for school projects?
7 to check the news headlines?
8 to check the weather forecast?

1 🔊 1.31 Read the survey. Then listen and match speakers A–E with questions 1–8. There are three extra questions.

A 7 B ☐ C ☐ D ☐ E ☐

2 CLASS VOTE Answer the questions in the survey. What is the most popular type of media in the class?

3 🔊 1.32 In which type of media from the survey can you find these things? Sometimes more than one answer is possible.

Vocabulary	News and entertainment

blog/vlog   current affairs   documentary   game show
film/game reviews   horoscopes   message board
news headlines   phone-in   reality show   soap opera
sports pages   talk show   video clips   weather forecast

4 Use the Vocabulary box to complete the sentences.

1 My dad loves watching *game shows*. He usually shouts out the answers at the TV!
2 The group's _____ is a place on the internet for fans to meet and write about the group.
3 My favourite _____ is on Channel 4 on Mondays. I think the actors are fantastic!
4 I don't often read _____ because my friends tell me which games to buy.
5 My sister often sends me links to funny _____ with cats on the internet.

5 In pairs, take turns to name an example of the types of media in the Vocabulary box.

A: The X Factor.   *B: That's a reality show.*

6 🔊 1.33 Listen and match speakers 1–4 with the type of radio programme they like a–e. There is one extra answer.

1 ☐ Cara   a current affairs
2 ☐ Cara's dad   b Pop Top 20
3 ☐ Rob, Cara's   c sports
      brother   d phone-ins
4 ☐ Cara's mum   e rock music

7a [VOX POPS ▶ 1.4] Complete the sentences to make them true for you. Use the Vocabulary box to help you. Then compare with a partner.

And
Y?U

1 I often read these newspapers/ magazines: _____.
2 My three favourite websites are _____, _____ and _____.
3 My favourite radio station is _____. I usually listen to it when I _____.
4 My favourite types of TV programme are _____ and _____.
5 I watch _____ every week.

7b Tell the class about your partner.

Tara often reads …

I can buy a ticket at the cinema.

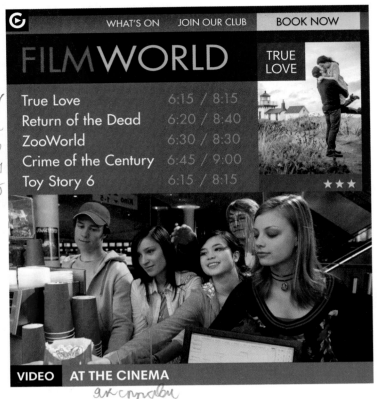

WHAT'S ON   JOIN OUR CLUB   BOOK NOW

FILMWORLD   TRUE LOVE

True Love	6:15 / 8:15
Return of the Dead	6:20 / 8:40
ZooWorld	6:30 / 8:30
Crime of the Century	6:45 / 9:00
Toy Story 6	6:15 / 8:15

★★★

VIDEO   **AT THE CINEMA**

Lee: So, what's on?

Amy: The new Tom Lewis movie, *True Love*. It starts in ten minutes.

Lee: No way! I want to see *ZooWorld*.

Amy: I don't like fantasy films. They're boring.

Lee: Oh, come on, please.

Amy: Oh, OK.

…

Lee: Can I have two tickets for *ZooWorld*, please?

Tess: Sure, which screening?

Lee: The 6.30.

Tess: I'm sorry, it's sold out … Oh, no, hold on! There are two seats.

Lee: Great!

Tess: But they're in the front row.

Amy: Lee, I don't want to sit in the front row!

Lee: OK … I'd like two for *True Love* at 6.15, please.

Tess: Row seven. Is that OK?

Lee: Yes, thanks. How much is that?

Tess: That's twelve fifty, please.

Amy: Here you are.

Tess: Thank you. Enjoy the film!

Lee: Yeah, right.

No way!   *Come on, please!*   *Hold on!*

OUT of **class**

1   **CLASS VOTE**   Look at the cinema programme and say what types of film are on. Which ones would you like to see?
I think True Love is a romantic comedy. I'd like to see it.

2   1.5   1.34   Watch or listen. Answer the questions.

1. Which film do Lee and Amy go to see?
2. What time does it start?
3. How much is each ticket?

3   1.35   Complete the dialogue below with one word in each gap. Listen and check.

Speaking   At the cinema

You need to say:
- What's on?
- Can I have two tickets for *ZooWorld*, please?
- I'd like two for *True Love*, please.
- The 6.15 screening.
- How much is that?
- Here you are.

You need to understand:
- Which screening?
- I'm sorry, it's sold out.
- There are two seats in the front row.
- Row seven. Is that OK?
- That's twelve fifty, please.

Krystal: Can I have two ¹tickets for *True Love*, please?

Tess: Which ²screening

Krystal: The 8.15 screening.

Tess: Here you are… Two tickets in ³row five.

Krystal: How ⁴much is that?

Tess: That's twelve fifty, ⁵please.

Krystal: ⁶Here you are.

Tess: ⁷Can you, enjoy the movie.

4   In pairs, buy tickets for a film from Exercise 1. Use the Speaking box to help you.

And **YOU**

I can write a personal introduction to a webpage.

Lee Marshall
Harlow Mill, near London, England
alternative/lo-fi

About me

1 My name is Lee Marshall and I'm fifteen. I'm English. I live with my parents and my sister, Ruby, in Harlow Mill, near London. I'm in Year 10 at Harlow Mill High School. My favourite subjects are Music, Art and English.

2 I like books and movies but my big passion is music. My favourite band is Arcade Fire – they're from Canada and they're awesome. In my free time, I sing and play the guitar.

3 I make music on my laptop every day and I sometimes write songs. Click on the media player to listen to them and tell me what you think!

1 ▶	NO WAY! 3:20		BUY
2 ▶	COME ON, PLEASE! 4:05		BUY
3 ▶	NOT RIGHT NOW 3:55		BUY
4 ▶	HARLOW MILL BLUES 3:33		BUY

My Friends

1 **CLASS VOTE** Have you got a personal webpage like Facebook or Flickr?

2 In pairs, quickly look at Lee's webpage. Which sentence is not true?

1 There is a photo of Lee on the webpage.
2 You can listen to some of Lee's songs.
3 You can look at Lee's photo gallery.
4 There is some personal information about Lee.
5 You can see some of Lee's friends on his page.

Writing | A personal introduction

1 **Personal details**
My name is ...
I'm ... years old.
I come from ... [place]/ I'm ... [nationality]
I live with my family in/My hometown is ...
I'm in Year ... at ... School.

2 **Interests/Hobbies**
I like/I'm into/I'm mad about ...
I'm interested in/My big passion is ...
My favourite ... is ...
In my free time,/Outside school I ...
I often ...

3 **Routines**
I often/sometimes/usually ...
I ... once a week/every day.

3 In pairs, read Lee's introduction. Tick (✓) the things he writes about.

✓ School	☐ Nationality	✓ Hobbies
✓ Best friend	☐ Name and age	
✓ Family/hometown	☐ Personality	
✓ Interests (books, music etc.)		

4 Look at Lee's profile again. Say how you are similar to or different from Lee.

He's English but I come from Poland.
He's got a sister and I've got a sister too.

5 Look at the Writing box. Complete the sentences to make them true for you. Look at Lee's text to help you.

Writing Time

6 Write a personal introduction for a webpage. Use the Writing box and Lee's text to help you.

Write about:

1 personal details
2 interests and hobbies
3 routines

act /ækt/ v
acting /'æktɪŋ/ n
action film /'ækʃən fɪlm/ n
actor /'æktə/ n
adult /'ædʌlt, ə'dʌlt/ n
art /ɑːt/ n
artist /'ɑːtəst, 'ɑːtɪst/ n
ballet /'bæleɪ/ n
blog /blɒg/ n
camera /'kæmərə/ n
cartoon /kɑː'tuːn/ n
celebrity /sə'lebrəti, sɪ'lebrəti/ n
cinema /'sɪnəmə, 'sɪnɪmə/ n
classical music /'klæsɪkəl 'mjuːzɪk/ n
comedy /'kɒmədi, 'kɒmɪdi/ n
comics /'kɒmɪks/ n
concert /'kɒnsət/ n
current affairs /'kʌrənt ə'feəz/ n
dance /dɑːns/ v
dancer /'dɑːnsə/ n
dancing /'dɑːnsɪŋ/ n
director /də'rektə, dɪ'rektə, daɪ-/ n
documentary /ˌdɒkjə'mentəri/ n
drawing /'drɔːɪŋ/ n
drums /drʌmz/ n
fantasy film /'fæntəsi fɪlm/ n
film/game review /ˌfɪlm geɪm rɪ'vjuː/ n
flamenco /flə'meŋkəʊ/ n

game show /ɡeɪm ʃəʊ/ n
graphic novel /'ɡræfɪk 'nɒvəl/ n
guitar /ɡɪ'tɑː/ n
hip-hop /'hɪp hɒp/ n
hobby /'hɒbi/ n
hometown /ˌhəʊm 'taʊn/ n
horoscope /'hɒrəskəʊp/ n
horror film /'hɒrə fɪlm/ n
horror story /'hɒrə 'stɔːri/ n
interests /'ɪntrəsts/ n
kid /kɪd/ n
media /'miːdiə/ n
magazine /mæɡə'ziːn/ n
message board /'mesɪdʒ bɔːd/ n
middle-aged (person) /ˌmɪdəl 'eɪdʒd 'pəːsn/ adj
modern art /'mɒdn ɑːt/ n
music /'mjuːzɪk/ n
musician /mjuː'zɪʃən/ n
nationality /ˌnæʃə'næləti, ˌnæʃə'nælɪti/ n
news headlines /ˌnjuːz 'hedlaɪnz/ n
novel /'nɒvəl/ n
painting /'peɪntɪŋ/ n
pensioner /'penʃənə/ n
phone-in /'fəʊn ɪn/ n
photographer /fə'tɒɡrəfə/ n
photography /fə'tɒɡrəfi/ n
piano /pi'ænəʊ/ n
picture /'pɪktʃə/ n

play /pleɪ/ n
poem /'pəʊəm, 'pəʊɪm/ n
pop /pɒp/ n
poster /'pəʊstə/ n
(cinema) programme /ˌsɪnəmə 'prəʊɡræm/ n
radio station /'reɪdiəʊ 'steɪʃən/ n
reading /'riːdɪŋ/ n
reality show /ri'æləti ʃəʊ/ n
rock /rɒk/ n
romantic film /rəʊ'mæntɪk fɪlm/ n
row (in cinema) /'rəʊ ɪn ˌsɪnəmə/ n
salsa /'sælsə/ n
science fiction film /ˌsaɪəns 'fɪkʃən fɪlm/ n
screening /'skriːnɪŋ/ n
seat /siːt/ n
sing /sɪŋ/ v
soap opera /səʊp 'ɒpərə/ n
sold out /səʊld aʊt/ adj
sports pages /spɔːts 'peɪdʒ ɪz/ n
story /'stɔːri/ n
survey /'sɜːveɪ/ n
talk show /tɔːk ʃəʊ/ n
techno /'teknəʊ/ n
teenager /'tiːneɪdʒə/ n
traditional /trə'dɪʃənəl/ adj
TV programme /ˌtiː 'viː 'prəʊɡræm/ n
video clip /'vɪdiəʊ klɪp/ n

violin /ˌvaɪə'lɪn/ n
weather forecast /'weðə 'fɔːkɑːst/ n
website /'websaɪt/ n
writer /'raɪtə/ n
writing /'raɪtɪŋ/ n
Zumba /'zumbə/ n

WORD FRIENDS

act in plays/films
be interested in sth
be into sth
be mad about sth
check sports results/the weather forecast/the news
couch potato
dance flamenco
find information
go dancing
happy ending
have square eyes
learn the (dance) steps
listen to (dance) music/ hip-hop
make videos
play the guitar
read comics/film reviews
see what's on (at the cinema)
take photos/selfies
watch music videos/pop videos

VOCABULARY IN ACTION

1 Use the wordlist to find:

1 eight types of film: *horror film, …*
2 eight types of radio/TV programmes:
3 nine things you can read:
4 five types of music:

2 In pairs, say which three things you prefer in each category in Exercise 1.
I prefer horror films, comedies and …

3 Complete the Word Friends. In pairs, say if the sentences are true for you.

1 I'm really *into* poems.
2 I never photo selfies.
3 I'm mad play game shows.
4 I hate films with sad endings.
5 I _____ the weather forecast once an hour.
6 I'm very interested _____ horoscopes.

4 Complete the sentences with the correct form of the word in bold.

1 Banksy is a famous British *artist*. **ART**
2 My sister's a great musician she can play four instruments. **MUSIC**
3 Who is your favourite film actor? **ACT**
4 I want to be a photographer when I leave school. **PHOTOGRAPH**
5 The writer of *The Hunger Games* novels is called Suzanne Collins. **WRITE**
6 I love dancing Zumba. **DANCE**

5a 🔊 1.36 **PRONUNCIATION** Listen to the underlined vowel(s) in each word and decide which sound you hear. Write the word in the correct column.

~~guitar~~ interest media middle-aged reading seat sing teenagers video

1 /iː/	2 /ɪ/
	guitar

5b 🔊 1.37 **PRONUNCIATION** Listen, check and repeat.

Revision

1 Write the correct word for each definition.

1 This person makes films and tells actors what to do. **d** _i r e c t o r_

2 It's something you like doing in your free time.
h _ _ _ _ _

3 It's a big photo or drawing. **p** _ _ _ _ _ _

4 It's a good idea to read one before you see a film. **r** _ _ _ _ _ _

5 This person is aged from thirteen to nineteen.
t _ _ _ _ _ _ _

6 This person doesn't work because of his/her age. **p** _ _ _ _ _ _ _ _ _

2 Complete the Word Friends in the text. Then ask and answer the questions in pairs.

✳ the media and
your parents

Do your parents:

1 listen to the radio? When? Which programmes do they prefer?

2 watch the ¹**n**ews on TV? At what time?

3 watch the weather ²**f**_____ every day?

4 watch documentaries on TV? What about ³**s**_____ operas, ⁴**t**_____ shows, ⁵**g**_____ shows, ⁶**r**_____ shows?

5 buy newspapers or ⁷**m**_____? Which sections do they read first?

SUBMIT >

3 Complete the poem with the words below. There are two extra words.

act ~~go~~ make play potato sing
story take watch write

I want to ¹_go_ dancing and ²_____ the guitar
And then ³_____ a song with my favourite pop star.
I want to ⁴_____ a poem and ⁵_____ in a play
And ⁶_____ some photos of a beautiful ballet.
I don't want to ⁷_____ films on TV all day
Or be a couch ⁸_____, no way!

4 Complete the sentences with the Present Simple form of the verbs in brackets.

1 Beyoncé _lives_ (live) in the USA. She _____ (not live) in England.

2 Jo _____ (go) to dance classes on Fridays.

3 No, I _____ (never/watch) reality shows.

4 My friends _____ (prefer) romantic films. They _____ (not enjoy) science fiction films.

5 Yes, I _____. I _____ (listen) to it every day.

5 Make questions for the answers in Exercise 4.

1 Where … ?
Where does Beyoncé live?

2 When … ?

3 … reality shows?

4 What kind of … ?

5 … to techno?

6 In pairs, use the words in A and B to write five sentences about a classmate. Then ask your classmate questions with *how often* to check.

> **A:** always often sometimes usually
> never once/twice/three times a …

> **B:** act go listen paint play read watch

Lucas always listens to rap music.
A: Lucas, how often do you listen to music?
B: I …

7 Work in pairs. Student A, ask your partner these questions and buy two tickets to see a film. Student B, look at page 131.

Student A
● What's on?
● What time … ?
● … seats / row 7?
● How much …?
● … two tickets / please?

8 🔊 **1.38** Listen, then listen again and write down what you hear.

CULTURE

Why do we dance?

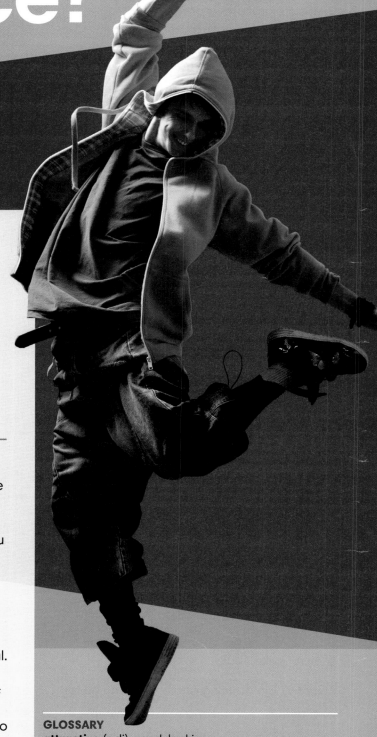

Dancing in the UK

Many of us love dancing or watching dancing. But why do you think we do it? It's strange when you think about it. When we dance, we don't go anywhere and we don't make anything, so what's the reason for it?

Today in the UK dance is very popular. About 5 million people go to dance classes every week. There are many styles but the most popular are street-dancing, ceroc, ballet and salsa.

Street-dancing has got many styles including breaking, hip-hop and popping. It's popular with young people and you have to be very flexible. Some people say we do this kind of dance to show our friends how strong and skilful we are.

Ceroc is a simple version of swing, salsa and jive. You can do ceroc to fast or slow music. It is very popular with middle-aged people because dancing is a good way to keep fit.

Ballet is popular all over the world. There are many spins and jumps in ballet. It's very difficult and you must do a lot of training to be good at it. Ballet usually tells stories and people think it's very beautiful.

Salsa is from Cuba. The word 'salsa' is Spanish for hot and spicy sauce. Salsa dancers have got a lot of passion and energy. People usually dance salsa to fast and fun music. One reason we do this dance is to show how attractive we are to other peope.

So there are many reasons why we dance. Whatever the reason everyone agrees that dancing is great fun.

GLOSSARY
attractive (adj) good-looking
flexible (adj) bends and moves easily
skilful (adj) good at doing something
spicy (adj) a strong, pleasant taste
spin (n) the movement of something turning around very quickly

EXPLORE

1 In pairs, discuss the questions.

1 Do you like dancing? Are you a good dancer?

2 How popular is dancing in your country?

3 Do you know anyone who is a very good (or bad) dancer?

4 Why do you think we dance?

2 Read the text. Mark the sentences T (true) or F (false).

1 ☐F Street-dancing is popular with middle-aged people.

2 ☐F Ceroc is always danced to fast music.

3 ☐F Ballet is from Cuba.

4 ☐ Salsa also means a hot and spicy sauce in Spanish.

3 Work in pairs. Read the text again and find four reasons for why people dance. Are they the same as your ideas in Exercise 1?

The Young Dancer Award

BBC young DANCER 2015

This competition happens every year. Judges choose the best dancers from four sections – ballet, contemporary, hip-hop and South Asian.

A

B

C

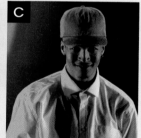

D

E

EXPLORE MORE

4 You are going to watch part of a video from the BBC about a dance competition. Read the advert for the programme. Do you have competitions like this in your country?

5 ▶ 1.6 Watch Part 1 of the video and match photos A–E with the names of the contestants 1–5.

1 ☐A Harry Barnes

2 ☐ Jonadette Carpio

3 ☐ Jodelle Douglas

4 ☐ Sharifa Tonkmor

5 ☐ Kieran Lai

6 In pairs, discuss who your favourite dancer is and why.

7 ▶ 1.6 Watch the video again. Mark the sentences T (true) or F (false). Correct the false statements.

1 ☐ Harry always feels happy.

2 ☐ Jonadette was born in a different country.

3 ☐ Jodelle usually works alone.

4 ☐ Sharifa doesn't plan her dances.

5 ☐ Kieran uses machines when he dances.

8 ▶ 1.7 Watch Part 2 of the video and answer the questions.

1 Who is the winner?

2 Why do the judges like him/her?

3 How does the winner react/feel?

4 What happens next for the winner?

9 Work in pairs. Do you think the winner is the best dancer? Why?/Why not?

Yes, I agree with the result.

No, I don't think so. I think …

YOU EXPLORE

10 **CULTURE PROJECT** In groups, use the language and ideas covered in the lesson to create a digital presentation promoting dance and its benefits.

1 Use the internet to research traditional or popular dances in your country.

2 Write a short script and include some photos or video.

3 Share it with your class.

2

Friends and family

Grammar: Where's Amy?

Speaking: How's life?

BBC Culture: London
Fashion Week

Workbook p. 29

BBC VOX POPS ▶

2.1 **VOCABULARY** Clothes and appearance

I can talk about clothes and appearance.

1 🔊 **1.39** What clothes can you see in the picture? In pairs, find three things below that are NOT in the picture.

Vocabulary A	Clothes and accessories

Clothes and footwear:
boots dress fancy-dress costume hoodie jacket jeans pyjamas
shirt shoes shorts sweater T-shirt tracksuit trainers underwear

Accessories and body art:
baseball cap belt earrings glasses handbag necklace piercings
scarf tattoo

2 **I KNOW!** Work in groups. How many types of clothes, footwear and accessories can you add to Vocabulary A in two minutes? Use the picture to help you.

3 Work in pairs. Copy and complete the tables with clothes, footwear and accessories. Compare with another pair. Have you got the same answers?

Winter	scarf, ...	Parties	
Summer		Sport	

4 **WORD FRIENDS** How do you say the highlighted words in your language?

baggy jeans   leather boots   a woolly hat   a plain T-shirt   a checked shirt
striped pyjamas   a tight skirt   a cotton top with a Batman logo on it

5 🔊 **1.40 Look at the picture on page 22 and choose the correct option. Listen and check.**

1 Tony's jeans are (baggy)/ tight.
2 Leo's shirt is *checked* / *plain*.
3 Jade's got leather *boots* / *shoes*.
4 Eric's got *checked* / *striped* pyjamas.

5 Mia's skirt is *baggy* / *tight*.
6 Angela's got a *plain top* / *top with a Batman logo on it*.
7 Layla's T-shirt is *plain* / *striped*.

6 **In pairs, do the Fashion Quiz. Then look at page 130 and check how similar or different you are.**

I prefer a T-shirt. What about you?

FASHION QUIZ ...

What do you prefer?

1 A shirt, a blouse or a T-shirt?
2 Tight or baggy clothes?
3 Trainers, shoes or boots?
4 Jeans, trousers or leggings?
5 A baseball cap or a woolly hat?
6 A plain top or a top with a logo on it?
7 A striped shirt or a checked shirt?
8 A tracksuit or a football top and shorts?

7 🔊 **1.41 Complete the text with the words below. Listen and check.**

| cap   cotton   earrings   jeans   leather   ~~skirts~~   trainers

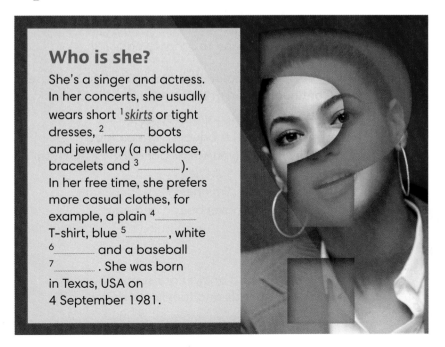

Who is she?

She's a singer and actress. In her concerts, she usually wears short ¹*skirts* or tight dresses, ²_____ boots and jewellery (a necklace, bracelets and ³_____). In her free time, she prefers more casual clothes, for example, a plain ⁴_____ T-shirt, blue ⁵_____, white ⁶_____ and a baseball ⁷_____ . She was born in Texas, USA on 4 September 1981.

8 🔊 **1.42 Listen to six people talking about what they wear. Complete what they say.**

1 When I go to bed, I wear *pyjamas*.
2 When I go to a wedding, I wear …
3 When I play my favourite sport, I wear …
4 When I'm at home, I wear …
5 When I go out with friends, I wear …
6 When I go to a party, I usually wear …

9 [VOX POPS ▶ 2.1]
Complete the sentences in Exercise 8 to make them true for you. Then compare with a partner.

A: What do you wear when you go to bed?

B: I usually wear pyjamas.

I can talk about present activities.

VIDEO   WHERE'S AMY?

Mum: Amy! Are you sleeping?

Amy: No, I'm not.

Mum: What are you doing? Your eggs are getting cold. I hope you aren't talking on that phone again!

Amy: No, I'm getting ready for school. I'm brushing my hair!

Mum: Well, hurry up! We're waiting for you.

Aunty: Is she coming?

Mum: Yes, she is. She's brushing her hair.

…

Amy: Morning!

Aunty: Amy! How's school? How's your boyfriend? Lou, isn't it? Oh dear, you're looking tired this morning. Are you feeling OK?

Amy: Yes, I am. School's fine and *Lee* isn't my boyfriend.

Aunty: Oh, I see … What are you having for breakfast?

Amy: I'm not hungry, Aunty Linda, thanks. Excuse me.

Mum: Amy, where are you going?

Amy: I'm going to school.

Mum: But it's only ten to eight!

Amy: Catch you later, then. See you!

Mum: I don't get it. Why is Amy going to school now?

Catch you later!
See you!   I don't get it.

O UT of class

---

1 CLASS VOTE **Answer the questions.**

- Are you chatty or quiet when you get up?
- Do you like breakfast time? Why?/Why not?

---

2 2.2 1.43 **Watch or listen. Why are the adults shocked?**

3 **Find more examples of the Present Continuous in the dialogue.**

Grammar	Present Continuous
+	**–**
I'm brushing my hair.	I'm not sleeping.
She's coming.	She isn't waiting.
They're eating.	They aren't talking.
?	
Are you coming?	Yes, I am./ No, I'm not.
Is he going?	Yes, he is./No, he isn't.
Are they eating?	Yes, they are./No, they aren't.
Where are you going?	What is she doing?

GRAMMAR TIME   PAGE 119

4 **Make affirmative (✓) and negative (✗) sentences in the Present Continuous.**

1 Amy: sleep ✗   get ready for school ✓
   Amy isn't sleeping. She's getting ready for school.

2 Amy: talk on the phone ✗   brush her hair ✓

3 Mum and Aunty Linda: eat ✗   wait for Amy ✓

4 They: drink coffee ✗   drink tea ✓

5 **Make questions in the Present Continuous. In pairs, look at the photo and try to answer the questions.**

1 Amy / wear / school uniform / ?
   A: Is Amy wearing her school uniform?
   B: Yes, she is.

2 what / they / eat / for breakfast / ?

3 what / mum / do / ?

4 why / Amy / go / to school / early / ?

6 1.44 **Complete the dialogue with the Present Continuous form of the verbs. Listen and check.**

Dad: What ¹*are you doing* (you/do), Lee?

Lee: I ²_____ (eat) a banana for breakfast.

Dad: Why ³_____ (you/eat) a banana? ⁴_____ (you/feel) ill?

Lee: No, I ⁵_____ . I'm fine.

Dad: We ⁶_____ (have) bacon and eggs.

Ruby: Dad? Lee ⁷_____ (eat) fruit! ⁸_____ (he/feel) ill?

7 **In pairs, ask and answer questions about what your friends and family are doing.**

A: What's your mum doing?   *B: She's …*

And YOU

I can find specific detail in a letter and talk about feelings.

TeenLives Magazine

IT'S SO ANNOYING!

Write and tell us about the things that really annoy you.

Bobby Wingate, 15, Hampshire

Dear TeenLives

TOP 3 ANNOYING THINGS THAT PARENTS DO

1 They say the same things again and again

I'm leaving for school when dad says to me, 'Pull up your trousers, son. We can see your underwear.' I answer, 'It's the fashion, dad'. We have this boring conversation every morning.

2 They're embarrassing with your friends

It's Saturday and I'm spending the afternoon with Joel and Harry in the shopping centre. Suddenly I am shocked to see mum and dad outside the supermarket. Dad is wearing his baseball cap and mum is in pink leggings – so embarrassing! They look excited to see us. Dad gives my friends a 'high five' and starts telling one of them his annoying jokes. Mum starts speaking in her high, 'talking to a young puppy' voice. She tells Joel that his piercing is 'totally awesome' and asks where she can get one. She is forty years old.

3 They're always on your Facebook page

It's Sunday morning and I'm adding some great photos from Harry's birthday party to my Facebook page. Suddenly I see there's a new comment next to a funny photo of Harry in his Superman costume. It says, 'OMG, LOL!' I'm annoyed to see the comment is from my mum.

1 In pairs, describe the photo in the article.

2 What can parents do that really annoy their children? Read the letter and check your ideas.

3 🔊 1.45 **Read the letter again. Choose the correct answers.**

1 Bobby's dad
   (a) often talks about Bobby's trousers.
   b likes his son's trousers.

2 Bobby is at the shopping centre
   a with his parents.
   b with his friends.

3 At the shopping centre, Bobby's parents
   a are pleased to see him.
   b are annoyed with him.

4 Bobby's mum
   a speaks with a different voice.
   b hates Joel's piercing.

5 On Sunday, Bobby
   a sees his mum is on Facebook.
   b is writing comments on Facebook.

4 🔊 1.46 **Complete the words below with -ing or -ed.**

Vocabulary	-ing/-ed adjectives

- A person, thing or situation is...
  annoy**ing** bor**ing** excit**ing** embarrass**ing** frighten**ing** interest**ing** irritat**ing** relax**ing** shock**ing** tir**ing** worry**ing**

- You are / get / feel ...
  annoy**ed** bor**ed** excit**ed** embarrass**ed** frighten**ed** interest**ed** irritat**ed** relax**ed** shock**ed** tir**ed** worri**ed**

1 I'm always tir**ed** on Fridays.
2 I like the band but the singer's irritat___ .
3 My phone bill's so high. I'm shock___ .
4 My sister thinks rock music is bor___ .
5 Kerry feels embarrass___ in a skirt – she prefers jeans.

5 🔊 1.47 **Listen. Use the words from the Vocabulary box to comment on what you hear.**

A: I think it's exciting.   B: No, I disagree. I think it's irritating.

6 [VOX POPS ▶ 2.3] **In pairs, use the Vocabulary box to say how you feel when:**

- your team is losing 5:0
- you're not sleeping well
- you make a silly mistake
- it's the last day of school

- you're watching a horror film
- your mum or dad talks to your friends

I feel annoyed/It's annoying when ...

I can talk about what usually happens and is happening around now.

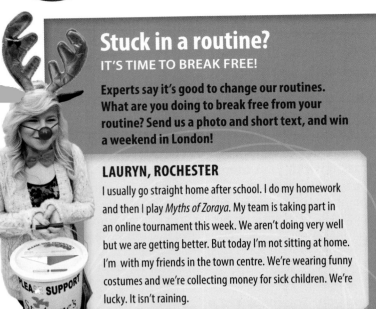

Stuck in a routine?
IT'S TIME TO BREAK FREE!

Experts say it's good to change our routines. What are you doing to break free from your routine? Send us a photo and short text, and win a weekend in London!

LAURYN, ROCHESTER

I usually go straight home after school. I do my homework and then I play *Myths of Zoraya*. My team is taking part in an online tournament this week. We aren't doing very well but we are getting better. But today I'm not sitting at home. I'm with my friends in the town centre. We're wearing funny costumes and we're collecting money for sick children. We're lucky. It isn't raining.

1 🔊 **1.48** **What is Lauryn doing in the picture? Read the text and answer the questions.**

1 What does Lauryn usually do after school?
2 Is her team doing well in the tournament?
3 What is she doing today?

2 **Find two more examples for each rule in the text in Exercise 1.**

Grammar	Present Simple and Present Continuous

- **Present Simple**
  Facts and routines.
  I usually go straight home after school.

- **Present Continuous**
  Things happening at the moment of speaking.
  It isn't raining now.

- **Time expressions:** *now, at the moment, today, these days, this week/month*
  Things happening around now but maybe not at the time of speaking.
  My team is taking part in a tournament this week.

GRAMMAR TIME   PAGE 119

3 **Choose the correct option.**

1 We *study /* are studying Algebra this semester.
2 Leo *saves /* is saving his money to buy trainers.
3 Sam's two so he *doesn't go /* isn't going to school.
4 How often *do you play /* are you playing video games?
5 You *don't watch /* aren't watching this. Can I change the channel?

4 **Make sentences with *but* to describe Paula's usual life and what's happening now.**

Paula usually goes to bed late but tonight she's going to bed early.

Usually	Now
go to bed late	tonight / early
drive to work	today / ride / a bike
not read novels	a great book at the moment
wear jeans	today / go / a wedding / so a dress
eat meat	try to lose weight / so this week / salad

5 **Look at Exercise 4 and make sentences about you.**

6 🔊 **1.49** **Complete the text with the correct form of the words in brackets. Use the Present Simple or the Present Continuous. Listen and check.**

RUSSELL, GLOSSOP

I ¹*always get up* (always/get up) late on Saturdays. I ² _____ (usually/have) breakfast at lunchtime! But this week my parents ³changing (change) the windows and they ⁴putting (put) in a new kitchen. The noise is terrible. So today I ⁵breaking (break) my usual Saturday routine. It's only 9 a.m. but I ⁶don't (not lie) in my bed. I'm with my friend Gareth and we ⁷walking (walk) up a mountain. The sun ⁸shines (shine). It's great! Gareth ⁹doing (do) this every week. Now I understand why.

7 **Complete the sentences with the name of a classmate. Compare in pairs. Then ask your partner if the sentences are true for him/her.**

1 *Ola* doesn't like dancing.
2 ____ always arrives late.
3 ____ laughs a lot.
4 ____ is learning to play an instrument.
5 ____ is working hard these days.
6 ____ isn't wearing jewellery today.

A: Do you like dancing?   B: No, I don't.

I can identify specific detail in a conversation and talk about personality.

1 Tell your partner about the personalities of two people in your family.

My brother is always happy. My cousin is kind.

2 🔊 **1.50** Tick (✓) the positive adjectives and cross (✗) the negative ones.

Vocabulary	Personality adjectives		
✗ big-headed	☐ bossy	☐ chatty	☐ cheerful
☐ hard-working	☐ helpful	☐ moody	
☐ outgoing	☐ quiet	☐ rude	☐ untidy

3 🔊 **1.51** Match the words below with their opposites from the Vocabulary box. Listen and check.

selfish   lazy   polite   shy   talkative   tidy

selfish ≠ helpful

4 🔊 **1.52** Malcolm, Tyler and Frank all like Sandra. Read their opinions and complete each gap with a word from the Vocabulary box. Listen and check.

Malcolm

Sandra is my kind of girl. She loves going out with friends and having fun. She's ¹_____ .

Tyler

Sandra's always so positive about everything. She's always smiling. She's ²_____ .

Frank

I like being with Sandra. She's friendly, interesting and she loves to talk. She's ³_____ .

5 🔊 **1.53** Listen to five dialogues. Choose the correct answers.

1 How much is the blue skirt?
   a £15   ⓑ £20   c £25
2 The speakers are in a
   a park.   b shopping centre.
   c restaurant.
3 What time does the concert start?
   a 6.45   b 7.15   c 7.45
4 What's the weather like?
   a It's sunny.   b It's raining.   c It's cold.
5 What are the speakers doing?
   a eating lunch   b studying
   c playing a game

6 🔊 **1.54** Listen to three dialogues. Mark the sentences T (true) or F (false).

1 ☐T☐ Frank is using his phone during the meal.
2 ☐ Frank's brother is eating with them.
3 ☐ Sandra wants to walk fast in the park.
4 ☐ Malcolm thinks he's good at sport.
5 ☐ Tyler knows Sandra very well.
6 ☐ Sandra gets annoyed with her father.

7 Read the descriptions from Sandra's diary and choose three adjectives from Exercises 2 and 3 for each person.

WED 27

My friends

1 Frank doesn't speak much. – *quiet*
   His face goes red when he speaks to girls.
   He can never find anything in his room.

2 Malcolm thinks he's wonderful.
   He always tells people what to do.
   He often insults them too.

3 Tyler always says 'please' and 'thank you'.
   He studies a lot and has a part-time job.
   He often helps his friends with schoolwork.

8 In pairs, choose three adjectives from the Vocabulary box to describe:

And YOU

- your personality
- your partner's personality
- the personality of the perfect friend
- the personality of a famous person you like/don't like

I'm chatty, …

I can give and respond to news.

VIDEO HOW'S LIFE?

Krystal: Hi Amy! What a surprise! What are you doing here?

Amy: I'm having my breakfast.

Krystal: Oh! OK! Daisy and I are having a walk. How are things?

Amy: To be honest, I'm not enjoying life at the moment. My mum's sister is staying with us and she's very talkative. You know me, I'm not a morning person. So breakfast with my aunt is terrible! She talks all the time and asks me hundreds of questions.

Krystal: Oh, poor you!

Amy: Yeah, so I'm buying my breakfast from the café this week.

Krystal: You're kidding! She can't be that bad!

Amy: Hmm, anyway, how's life with you?

Krystal: Fine! My dance classes are going well.

Amy: Cool!

Krystal: We've got a new teacher. She's great, really friendly and cheerful! Her name's Linda.

Amy: Linda?

Krystal: Yes, Linda Young.

Amy: Linda Young! I don't believe it! Your new dance teacher is my Aunty Linda!

Krystal: No way!

*How are things?   How's life?
I don't believe it!*

OUT of class

1 ▶ 2.4 ◀)) 1.55 **Watch or listen. Where is Amy buying her breakfast these days? Why?**

2 **In pairs, complete the Speaking box with the phrases below.**

> You're kidding!   Cool!   Poor you!

Speaking	Giving and responding to news

Giving news
- I'm learning how to …
- I'm spending a lot of time with/in …
- I'm (not) enjoying …
- I'm feeling excited/worried because …
- I'm doing well at …
- I'm listening to … these days.

Responding to news
- Well done!/Good for you!/[1]_____/Awesome!/Great!
- That's terrible!/[2]_____/What a pity!
- [3]_____/No way!/Amazing!

3 ◀)) 1.56 **Choose the correct option. Listen and check.**

1 A: My exams are going well.
   B: _____
   a What a pity!   b That's terrible!   c Well done!

2 A: I'm not sleeping well these days.
   B: _____
   a Poor you!   b Good for you!   c No way!

3 A: I'm learning how to bungee jump.
   B: _____
   a You're kidding!   b That's terrible!   c Well done!

4 A: My phone isn't working.
   B: _____
   a Awesome!   b What a pity!   c Cool!

4 ◀)) 1.57 **Respond to the news. Practise the exchanges with a partner. Use the correct intonation. Listen and check.**

1 I'm writing a novel.
2 I'm so worried about my dog. He's really ill!
3 I'm an uncle!
4 My mum says I can't go out this weekend!

5 **In pairs, give and respond to news about your life. Use the Speaking box to help you.**

A: I'm doing well at school.   B: Great!

I can talk about when something happens.

1 Read the cartoon. How many extra classes does Holly have?

2 ☐ **I KNOW!**   How many examples of prepositions can you find in the cartoon in thirty seconds?

Language	Prepositions of time

IN
- years: *in 2015*
- months and seasons: *in January, in the winter*
- parts of the day: *in the morning/evening*

ON
- days of the week: *on Wednesday/Fridays*
- dates: *on 3 April*
- a special day: *on Christmas Day*

AT
- holiday periods: *at Christmas*
- clock times: *at 12.15*
- other phrases: *at night, at the weekend*

! *in the evening* but *on Thursday evening*

3 Write the correct prepositions: *in, at* or *on*.

1 *on* Thursday   4 _____ New Year's Day
2 _____ 1980   5 _____ April 2019
3 _____ Easter   6 _____ my birthday

4 🔊 **1.58 Complete the text with *in, at* or *on*. Listen and check.**

I'm studying French at the moment. The class is ¹*on* Mondays ² _____ 7 p.m. ³ _____ the evening. We get a lot of homework ⁴ _____ the weekend but the teacher's great. The course stops ⁵ _____ Christmas and starts again ⁶ _____ 8 January. We want to visit France ⁷ _____ the summer, maybe ⁸ _____ July.

5 🔊 **1.59 Listen to the recorded message and complete the notes about the arts centre.**

Arts centre courses
- *Salsa class – Monday evenings at* ¹ _____
- *Fashion course on* ² _____
- *Theatre group – call Kevin on* ³ _____
- *Computer programming starts on* ⁴ _____ *– costs* ⁵£ _____ *a month.*

Are you enjoying your dance classes?

Yes, I am.

Is she sleeping?

Mrs Smith thinks out of school activities are important. Her daughter Holly is always busy after school. She goes to dance classes every day at 5 p.m.

She has an extra French class on Tuesdays, singing lessons on Wednesdays and Art classes on Thursday nights, after her guitar lesson!

You're not trying very hard today!

Holly usually has a lot of homework but she practises the piano for two hours in the evening. She often goes to bed late at night.

Holly also enjoys art at the weekend.

Yes, mum. I am painting.

6 In pairs, ask and answer the questions.
- What do you do in the evenings after school?
- Which activities in Exercise 5 interest you?

And YOU?

accessories /ək'sesəriz/ n
annoyed /ə'nɔɪd/ adj
annoying /ə'nɔɪ-ɪŋ/ adj
baggy /'bægi/ adj
baseball cap /'beɪsbɔːl kæp/ n
belt /belt/ n
big-headed /ˌbɪg'hedəd, ˌbɪg'hedɪd/ adj
blouse /blaʊz/ n
boots /buːts/ n
bored /bɔːd/ adj
boring /'bɔːrɪŋ/ adj
bossy /'bɒsi/ adj
bracelet /'breɪslət, 'breɪslɪt/ n
breakfast time /'brekfəst taɪm/ n
casual (clothes) /ˌkæʒuəl 'kləʊðz, kləʊz/ adj
chatty /'tʃæti/ adj
checked /tʃekt/ adj
cheerful /'tʃɪəfəl/ adj
Christmas /'krɪsməs/ n
clothes /kləʊðz, kləʊz/ n
cotton /'kɒtn/ adj
dress /dres/ n
earring /'ɪərɪŋ/ n
Easter /'iːstə/ n
embarrassed /ɪm'bærəst/ adj
embarrassing /ɪm'bærəsɪŋ/ adj
excited /ɪk'saɪtəd, ɪk'saɪtɪd/ adj

exciting /ɪk'saɪtɪŋ/ adj
fancy-dress costume /'fænsi dres 'kɒstjʊm/ n
fashion /'fæʃən/ n
fashionable /'fæʃənəbəl/ adj
football top /'fʊtbɔːl tɒp/ n
footwear /'fʊtweə/ n
friendly /'frendli/ adj
frightened /'fraɪtnd/ adj
frightening /'fraɪtn-ɪŋ/ adj
glasses /'glɑːs ɪz/ n
handbag /'hændbæg/ n
hard-working /ˌhɑːd 'wɜːk ɪŋ/ adj
hat /hæt/ n
helpful /'helpfəl/ adj
hoodie /'hʊdi/ n
insult /ɪn'sʌlt/ v
interested /'ɪntrəstəd, 'ɪntrɪstəd/ adj
interesting /'ɪntrəstɪŋ, 'ɪntrɪstɪŋ/ adj
irritated /'ɪrəteɪtəd, 'ɪrɪteɪtəd/ adj
irritating /'ɪrəteɪtɪŋ, 'ɪrɪteɪtɪŋ/ adj
jacket /'dʒækət, 'dʒækɪt/ n
jeans /dʒiːnz/ n
jewellery /'dʒuːəlri/ n
lazy /'leɪzi/ adj
leather /'leðə/ adj
leggings /'legɪŋz/ n
logo /'ləʊgəʊ/ n
moody /'muːdi/ adj

necklace /'nekləs, 'neklɪs/ n
New Year's Day /ˌnjuː 'jɪəz ˌdeɪ/ n
outgoing /ˌaʊt'gəʊɪŋ/ adj
personality /ˌpɜːsə'næləti, ˌpɜːsə'nælɪti/ n
polite /pə'laɪt/ adj
positive /'pɒzətɪv, 'pɒzɪtɪv/ adj
piercing /'pɪəsɪŋ/ n
plain /pleɪn/ adj
pyjamas /pə'dʒɑːməz/ n
quiet /'kwaɪət/ adj
relaxed /rɪ'lækst/ adj
relaxing /rɪ'læksɪŋ/ adj
rude /ruːd/ adj
scarf /skɑːf/ n
school uniform /ˌskuːl 'juːnəfɔːm/ n
season /'siːzən/ n
selfish /'selfɪʃ/ adj
shirt /ʃɜːt/ n
shocked /ʃɒkt/ adj
shocking /'ʃɒkɪŋ/ adj
shoe /ʃuː/ n
shorts /ʃɔːts/ n
shy /ʃaɪ/ adj
skirt /skɜːt/ n
striped /straɪpt/ adj
sweater /'swetə/ n
T-shirt /'tiː ʃɜːt/ n
talkative /'tɔːkətɪv/ adj
tattoo /tə'tuː, tæ'tuː/ n
tidy /'taɪdi/ adj

tie /taɪ/ n
tight /taɪt/ adj
tired /taɪəd/ adj
tiring /'taɪərɪŋ/ adj
top /tɒp/ n
tracksuit /'træksuːt, -sjuːt/ n
trainers /'treɪnəz/ n
trousers /'traʊzəz/ n
underwear /'ʌndəweə/ n
untidy /ʌn'taɪdi/ adj
wear /weə/ v
woolly /'wʊli/ adj
wonderful /'wʌndəfəl/ adj
worried /'wʌrid/ adj
worrying /'wʌri-ɪŋ/ adj

WORD FRIENDS

break free of/ change a routine
brush your hair
collect money (for charity)
do well (at sth)
get annoyed (with sb)
get better (at sth)
get ready (for school)
go out with friends
go to a party/ a wedding
learn how to (do sth)
lose weight
save money (to buy sth)
take part in (an event)

VOCABULARY IN ACTION

1 Use the wordlist to find:

1 ten items of clothing that both men and women wear: *jeans, …*
2 four items of jewellery:
3 three things you wear on your feet:
4 five positive adjectives that can describe people:
5 seven adjectives ending in -ed that describe negative emotions:

2 Use the wordlist to decribe what somebody you know usually wears and what he/she is wearing today.

My best friend/mum/English teacher usually wears …

3 In pairs, say what your opinion is about these things. Use an -ing adjective from the wordlist.

| Christmas   fancy-dress parties   jewellery
| pyjamas   school uniform   selfish people
| summer   tattoos   tracksuits

I think Christmas is exciting. What about you?

4 Complete the Word Friends.

1 I'm learning how **to** kite surf. The instructor says I'm doing _____!
2 Stella wants to take _____ in a half-marathon soon. She's hoping to collect _____ for charity.
3 We're going _____ a party later!

5a 🔊 1.60 **PRONUNCIATION** Listen to the underlined vowel(s) in each word and decide which sound you hear. Write the word in the correct column.

| ~~baggy~~   breakfast   chatty   checked
| dress   fashion   friendly   jacket
| leather   relaxing   sweater   tracksuit

1 /æ/	2 /e/
baggy	

5b 🔊 1.61 **PRONUNCIATION** Listen, check and repeat.

Revision

VOCABULARY

1 Choose the odd one out.

1	dress	(shirt)	skirt	blouse
2	baggy	cotton	woolly	leather
3	plain	striped	checked	tight
4	friendly	outgoing	moody	chatty
5	bossy	helpful	rude	lazy
6	excited	interested	relaxed	frightened

2 Complete the second sentence so that it means the same as the first one. In pairs, say if the sentences are true for you.

1 I'm not interested in fashion.
   I don't think fashion *is interesting*.
2 I get bored when I go shopping for clothes.
   I think shopping for clothes _____.
3 In my opinion, today's fashion is annoying.
   I feel _____ when I see today's fashion.
4 I'm shocked when I see the prices of new clothes.
   I think the prices of new clothes are _____.
5 I think it's relaxing to wear casual clothes.
   I feel _____ when I wear casual clothes.

3 Complete the Word Friends in the text. Use the words in the correct form.

I usually go ¹**out** with friends on Saturday afternoons but not today, because we're going ²**t**_____ a wedding! My brother is ³**g**_____ ready in the bathroom. He's very slow and mum is getting ⁴**a**_____. My sister is ⁵**b**_____ her hair. Dad is ready – he's wearing a white shirt but it's too tight (he really needs to ⁶**l**_____ weight!). Today can only ⁷**g**_____ better!

GRAMMAR

4 Order the words to make questions. Then ask and answer the questions in pairs.

1 at / sitting / home / are / you / ?
   Are you sitting at home?
2 raining / it / is / ?
3 a / are / sweater / you / wearing / ?
4 your teacher / talking / is / ?
5 hard / working / are / you / ?
6 does / lesson / what / time / the / finish / ?
7 sit / you / usually / in / the / do / same / seat / ?
8 usually / give / your teacher / does / a lot of homework / ?

5 Complete the text with the Present Simple or Present Continuous form of the verbs in brackets.

Subject: Not a good start to the holidays!

Hi Lucy,

How are you? My cousins ¹*are visiting* (visit) us at the moment. I ²_____ (not like) it when they visit and unfortunately they ³_____ (come) to stay every summer! Ellen is my age but she ⁴_____ (not like) any of the things I do. Kirsten is nineteen, she ⁵_____ (study) Music and she's very annoying. At the moment I ⁶_____ (sit) in my bedroom and they're downstairs. They ⁷_____ (give) a concert for mum and dad. Ellen ⁸_____ (sing) an old Scottish song. I'm sure my parents ⁹_____ (not enjoy) it because they never ¹⁰_____ (listen) to folk music.

How are things with you? ¹¹_____ (you/go) to your Zumba classes these days?

---

6 Write answers to the questions. Use *at*, *in* or *on* with a time expression. Then compare with a partner.

When do you usually …

- have a shower?
- go on holiday?
- go to bed?
- eat a lot?
- read a book?
- wear shorts?

I usually have a shower in the morning.

SPEAKING

7 Work in pairs. Student A, use the information below to give and respond to news. Student B, look at page 131.

Student A

1 Greet Student B and ask what's new in his/her life.
2 Listen and respond to Student B's news.
3 Give your news:
- you're learning how to make webpages
- you're in love
- your computer isn't working at the moment.

DICTATION

8 🔊 1.62 Listen, then listen again and write down what you hear.

Are hipsters cool?

A DIFFERENT KIND OF FASHION

Hipsters are people, usually under thirty, who want to be different. They like clothes, food and music that is different from most people. They don't want to be fashionable. When lots of people try to dress like hipsters, their look becomes fashionable. Then the hipsters change and wear something else!

Hipsters usually like to live in big cities. There they can find lots of small, unusual shops, art galleries and cafés. In the UK, it's London. In the USA, it's New York City. In Canada, it's Montreal. In Australia, it's Melbourne and in New Zealand, it's Wellington. Where do hipsters like to live in your country?

Right now hipsters like wearing vintage clothes. Hipsters don't think it's cool to wear famous brands, so they like to find old clothes. Perhaps you can find some in your grandparents' attic – lace dresses, granny boots, clothes with flowers on them or old hats.

Hipsters often wear tight jeans in bright colours. They like big glasses too – these are often plastic and rainbow-coloured. Their shirts aren't usually plain – they like checks and flowers. Sometimes they stick on pictures of animals or clever phrases.

Girls can wear very high heels or flat shoes and they carry big bags, so that they can take their tablets, phones and old records (NOT CDs!) with them. Hats and beards are popular for the men.

Hipsters dress in layers. They put clothes on top of other clothes. And a hipster's clothes are usually mismatched – they aren't neat and well-fitting. It's important for the clothes to look lazy – although the hipster sometimes spends a long time getting ready!

Fashion designers often use hipster fashion for ideas for next year's new look. So, today's hipster fashion might be on tomorrow's catwalk!

GLOSSARY
attic (n) a room at the top of a house, just below the roof
_____ (n) high, black footwear for women with shoelaces
_____ (n) a type of material made with a pattern of small holes
_____ (n) a piece of clothing that is between two other pieces
_____ (adj) clothes that do not work well together
_____ (adj) old, but high quality

1 In pairs, discuss the questions.

1 Do you like to wear very fashionable clothes? Why?/Why not?
2 Do you know someone who likes wearing unusual clothes?
3 What is fashionable at the moment?

2 Look at the photo. What do you think a 'hipster' is?

3 Read the article and check your ideas in Exercise 2.

4 Look at the photo again. Can you find any of the clothes and accessories mentioned in the article? Circle the words in the article.

5 Read the article again. Mark the sentences T (true) or F (false).

1 ☐ Hipsters buy fashionable clothes.
2 ☐ Hipsters live in busy areas.
3 ☐ Hipsters usually look very tidy.
4 ☐ Hipster fashion keeps changing.

6 In pairs, discuss if you think it's cool to be a hipster. Why?/Why not?

EXPLORE MORE

7 You are going to watch part of a video from the BBC about London Fashion Week. Read the extract from a magazine below. Do you have big fashion shows in your country?

London Fashion Week

Twice a year, top fashion designers give shows in London. People come to London Fashion Week from all over the world.

8 ▶ 2.5 Watch Part 1 of the video and answer the questions.

1 When is London Fashion Week?
2 Who goes to London Fashion Week? Why?
3 What clothes does the speaker mention?
4 What is the same about all the clothes?
5 What is surprising about the male models?

9 In pairs, discuss the questions.

1 Which clothes in the video did you like? Why?
2 Which clothes did you *not* like? Why?
3 Would you like to wear any of the clothes you saw in the video? Why?/Why not?

10 ▶ 2.5 Watch the video again. Mark the sentences T (true) or F (false). Correct the false sentences.

1 ☐ You can see London Fashion Week on television.
2 ☐ You can't take photographs during the show.
3 ☐ People sometimes write down information about the show.
4 ☐ People are quiet during the show and clap at the end.

11 ▶ 2.6 Watch Part 2 of the video and answer the questions.

1 What do the models need to do before the show?
2 What do they do while they are waiting? Why?

12 Work in pairs. Would you like to be a fashion model? Why?/Why not?

Yes, I'd like to be a model because you wear great clothes.
No, I wouldn't like to be a model because it's tiring.

YOU EXPLORE

13 CULTURE PROJECT In small groups, create a digital presentation about fashion in your country.

1 Use the internet to research fashion trends in your country.
2 Write a short script and include some photos or video.
3 Share it with your class.

3

Animal magic

VOCABULARY
Animals | Animal body parts
Personality | Looking after pets

GRAMMAR
Past Simple: *was/were*
Past Simple: regular verbs

Grammar: Looking after Daisy

Speaking: I don't know how it happened

BBC Culture: Wild at heart

Workbook p. 41

BBC VOX POPS ▶
EXAM TIME 1 > p. 132
CLIL 2 > p. 139

3.1

VOCABULARY Animals

I can talk about animals.

1 🔊 **2.01** In pairs, match the animals in the picture with the words below. Listen and check.

Vocabulary A	Animals			
Pets:	☑ parrot	☐ rabbit	☐ tortoise	
Farm animals:	☐ chicken	☐ cow	☐ donkey	
Wild animals:	☐ bear	☐ chimp	☐ elephant	☐ giraffe
	☐ kangaroo	☐ tiger	☐ zebra	
Insects:	☐ bee	☐ butterfly	☐ fly	

2 🔊 **2.02** **I KNOW!** In pairs, add the animals below to the correct category in Vocabulary A. How many more words can you add in two minutes?

ant cat dolphin duck monkey shark sheep snake spider

3 In groups, think of two or more animals for each category below. Then compare with another group.

1 We can ride these animals. *horse, …*
2 These animals sleep in the winter.
3 People keep these animals for meat.
4 These animals are good at climbing.
5 People use the skin of these animals for clothes or shoes.
6 These animals are good at running.
7 These animals are very dangerous.
8 These animals have sharp teeth and eat meat.

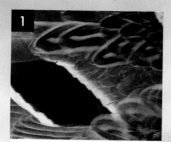

The feathers of a parrot / *a duck*.

The eye of *a tortoise* / *an elephant*.

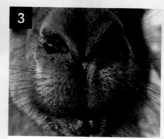

The mouth of a *sheep* / *a kangaroo*.

The claws of *a chicken* / *a parrot*.

The wing of *a fly* / *a bee*.

The tail of *a donkey* / *a monkey*.

The fur of *a chimp* / *a rabbit*.

GUESS THE ANIMAL!

4 🔊 2.03 In pairs, look at the photos and decide which animal you think it is. Listen and check.

5 🔊 2.04 How do you say the words below in your language?

Vocabulary B	Animal body parts
claw feather fur mouth tail wing	

6 In pairs, mark the sentences T (true) or F (false). Check your answers on page 130. Which fact do you find surprising?

7 🔊 2.05 Work in groups. Listen to five descriptions of animals. How quickly can you guess each animal?

8 Choose an animal from Vocabulary A. In pairs, guess your partner's animal by asking questions. You can only answer *yes* or *no*.

A: *Does it live on a farm?*
B: *Yes, it does.*
A: *Does it have a …?*

True or False?

1 ☐ Polar bears have white fur but black skin.
2 ☐ A flamingo's feathers are pink because it eats a special kind of plankton.
3 ☐ Tigers have stripes on their fur but not on their skin.
4 ☐ Bees can beat their wings 200 times a second.
5 ☐ Elephants have a special call that means, 'Danger: Humans!'
6 ☐ For every human in the world, there are about 1.6 million ants.
7 ☐ The tail of a giraffe can grow to over 2.5 metres.
8 ☐ Butterflies can only see the colours red, green and yellow.
9 ☐ A brown bear's claws can grow to over fifteen centimetres.

9 [VOX POPS ▶ 3.1]
In pairs, ask and answer the questions.

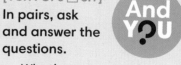
And YOU

- What's your favourite wild animal? Why do you like it?
- Which dangerous wild animals live in your country?
- Are you afraid of any animals? Why?

My favourite wild animal is … because they're cute/ clever/fascinating/funny …

3.2 GRAMMAR Past Simple: *was/were*

I can use *was* and *were* to talk about the past.

1 2.06 **What can you see in the cartoon? Read and listen. What does Kyle say about his brother and sister?**

Zadie: You weren't at home yesterday.
Kyle: I was out.
Zadie: I know that! Were you at the shops?
Kyle: No, I wasn't.
Zadie: Where were you?
Kyle: We were at the zoo.
Zadie: You were at the zoo! Why?
Kyle: It was the twins' birthday.
Zadie: Really? Was it fun?
Kyle: Yes, it was. It was fantastic. There was a great café and there were lots of interesting animals.
Zadie: Were the kids excited?
Kyle: Excited? They weren't excited, they were crazy! The chimps were shocked!

2 **Find more examples of *was/were* in the dialogue in Exercise 1.**

Grammar Past Simple: *was/were*

+	–
I was out. We were at the zoo.	I wasn't at the shops. We weren't at home.

?	
Were you at home?	Yes, I was./No, I wasn't.
Was it boring?	Yes, it was./No, it wasn't.
Were you happy?	Yes, we were./No, we weren't.
Where were they?	

there is (isn't) → there was (wasn't)
there are (aren't) → there were (weren't)
Time expressions: *last night/weekend, yesterday, this morning, two days ago, at ten o'clock*

GRAMMAR TIME PAGE 120

3 2.07 **Complete the dialogue with *was, were, wasn't* or *weren't*. Listen and check.**

Kyle: Where [1]__were__ you yesterday, Zadie?
Zadie: I [2]______ with Midge. We [3]______ at the shops.
Kyle: [4]______ you at the shops in the centre?
Zadie: Yes, we [5]______.
Kyle: [6]______ it busy?
Zadie: No, it [7]______. There [8]______ any people there because the shops [9]______ closed. It [10]______ a public holiday. There [11]______ only one shop open, a newsagent's!

4 **Use the words below and the correct form of *there was/were* to make sentences about the cartoon.**

There were three chimps in a cage.

chimps   not many people   old lion   giraffe
not any bears   monkeys   penguins   gift shop

5 **Complete the table with the places below. In pairs, guess your partner's answers.**

AT home   school   a friend's   a party   the shops   the cinema   the zoo   an aquarium   a concert
IN a pet shop   the classroom   a park   a café

Where	When
	an hour ago
	last weekend
	yesterday at 7 p.m.
	in the summer

A: Were you at the zoo last weekend?
B: No, I wasn't.
A: Were you in a café …?

6 2.08 **Listen and complete the dialogue. Then practise the dialogue in pairs.**

A: Where were you last Saturday? B: [1]______
A: Was it fun? B: [2]______
A: Were there many people there? B: [3]______
A: What was the weather like? B: [4]______

7 [VOX POPS ▶ 3.2] **In pairs, use the questions in Exercise 6 to talk about last Saturday.**

And YOU?

A: Where were you last Saturday?
B: I was at a party.

I can find specific detail in an article and talk about behaviour.

1 In pairs, look at the words and phrases below. Which things do teenagers typically do? What about adults?

belong to gangs   come home late   criticise   feel shy
do dangerous things   eat/drink too much   fight   forget things
ignore advice   make a lot of noise   sleep in front of the TV
study   talk about the past

2 🔊 **2.09** Quickly read the article. What behaviour from Exercise 1 does it mention?

3 Read the text again. Mark the sentences ✓ (right), ✗ (wrong) or ? (doesn't say).

1 [✗] It's impossible to love adolescent dogs.
2 [ ] Young dogs often change their behaviour.
3 [ ] All young elephants live with their families.
4 [ ] Teenage elephants sometimes kill other elephants.
5 [ ] Young sea otters always follow their parents' example.
6 [ ] Dangerous situations can teach a young animal a lot.

adolescent – (n) a teenager;
(adj) describes the time just before
becoming an adult

Watch OUT!

4 🔊 **2.10** Find the words below in the text. Then match the words with sentences 1–5.

Vocabulary	Personality
adventurous aggressive forgetful impulsive lovable	

1 Grandpa often loses his glasses.
   forgetful
2 Harry often buys things he doesn't need.
3 The Smiths love travelling to exotic, dangerous places.
4 Male rabbits often fight when they live together.
5 My puppy is friendly, fun and attractive.

5 In pairs, ask and answer the questions.

And Y?U

1 What do your parents or teachers criticise you for?
2 Do you agree with their opinion?

Those difficult teenage years

When Sally was an adolescent, she was noisy. She was adventurous, lovable and sometimes shy. She was often forgetful too. Sally was my dog.

Adolescent dogs (from six months to a year old) are a little bit like human teens. They explore their world and test their own abilities. They love adventures and they often look for attention. One minute they're tired – then suddenly they're lively and energetic. Sometimes it can be hard for others to understand them.

And dogs aren't the only animals with a 'teenage' time in their lives. Between the ages of ten and twenty, male African elephants leave their family groups and live in large male gangs. These young elephants don't always behave well. They can be noisy and aggressive. They sometimes terrorise other groups and in some cases they kill other animals for sport.

Male sea otters also have a 'teenage' stage. They take risks and ignore their parents' advice. Sometimes they swim near dangerous white sharks and sometimes the sharks eat them. But that doesn't stop other adventurous young otters from playing this dangerous game.

For many animals, the time between childhood and adulthood is difficult. They lose the care and protection which they get from their parents. But they need risk and adventure to learn about the dangers of the world. In other words, impulsive or even crazy behaviour is an important part of an animal's education. It is often the key to success as adults. Just like for humans.

I can use the Past Simple of regular verbs to talk about the past.

VIDEO **LOOKING AFTER DAISY**

Lee: Amy!

Amy: Lee! What's wrong?

Lee: It's Daisy, Krystal's dog! I can't find her.

Amy: Calm down! What's the matter?

Lee: Daisy needed to go outside so we walked to the park and when we arrived there, I decided to take off the leash to let her run around, you know. But then I answered a phone call and then when I finished talking, Daisy wasn't there. I looked everywhere but …

Amy: When did this happen?

Lee: About an hour ago. Some people helped but we …

Amy: Did you go to Krystal's?

Lee: Yes, I did but the dog wasn't there. And then I hurried back here. I didn't know what to do so I phoned you. Krystal gets back from her holiday today! She asked me to look after her dog and I promised to do it but I didn't. Oh!

What's wrong? *Calm down!* *What's the matter?*	**O**UT of **class**

1 ▶ 3.3 ◀)) 2.11 Describe the photo. Why is Lee worried? Watch or listen and check.

2 Find more examples of the Past Simple in the dialogue.

Grammar	Past Simple: regular verbs
+	**–**
I called Amy. She hurried back home. They stopped me.	I didn't call Amy. She didn't hurry back home. They didn't stop me.
?	
Did you phone Amy? When did he arrive?	Yes, I did./No, I didn't.

GRAMMAR TIME ▶ PAGE 121

3 Check you know the meaning of these verbs. Then study the Grammar box and write the Past Simple forms.

carry   change   end   happen   help   invent   like   listen   live   open   start   study   talk   try   use   want   watch   work

4 ◀)) 2.12 Copy the table. Guess which verbs from Exercise 3 go in the columns. Listen and check.

1 helped /t/	**2 carried** /d/	**3 ended** /ɪd/
liked		

5 Complete the text with the Past Simple form of the verbs in brackets.

Lee [1] *asked* (ask) Amy to help him. She [2] _____ (not want) to go out because she [3] _____ (need) to finish some homework. However, Lee was desperate so Amy [4] _____ (agree) to help him. They [5] _____ (decide) to meet at the park. They [6] _____ (shout) Daisy's name and [7] _____ (walk) around the park but the dog wasn't there. Finally, Lee [8] _____ (suggest) calling the police but Amy [9] _____ (not like) that idea.

6 In pairs, make questions from the prompts. Then go to page 130 to find the answers.

1 Lee / call / police / ?
   Did Lee call the police?
2 police / help / them / ?
3 Lee / Amy / go home / ?
4 what / they / do / ?
5 what / they / do then / ?
6 dog / be / there / ?
7 what / Lee / do / ?

7 Make sentences in the Past Simple with the verbs in Exercise 3. In pairs, say if your partner's sentences are true or false.

A: *I talked to a police officer last week.*
B: *False.*

I can identify specific detail in a conversation and talk about pets.

1 🔊 **2.13** **CLASS VOTE** Read the text and decide which of the pets is good for Ali.

2 🔊 **2.14** **WORD FRIENDS** Check you understand these Word Friends. Then listen to Ali talking to a friend. Number the Word Friends in the order you hear them.

When you have a pet, you need to …

- [1] feed it
- [ ] take it for a walk
- [ ] train it
- [ ] take it to the vet's
- [ ] wash it
- [ ] empty its litter tray
- [ ] brush its fur

3 Discuss in pairs. Have you got a pet? If so, who looks after it? Use the Word Friends in Exercise 2 to help you.

We've got a dog. My mum trained it. I usually take it for a walk.

4 🔊 **2.15** Listen to five dialogues. Choose the correct answers.

1 What kind of pet did Ali decide to get?
  (a) a cat   b a dog   c a snake
2 How many animals did Jodie offer Ali?
  a one   b two   c four
3 Ali's dad decided to buy something in a pet shop. How much was it?
  a £15   b £25   c £50
4 What did Ali's dad want her to do?
  a train the cat   b feed it
  c empty its litter tray
5 Ali and her dad looked for Simba. Where was she?

 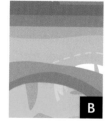 

A   B   C

5 In groups, say which animal you would like as a pet and why. Use the phrases below to help you.

And YOU

It's fun/clean/quiet/boring/dirty/noisy …
You can/can't …
You need to/don't need to …

I'd like to have a fish. They're quiet and they don't scratch the furniture.

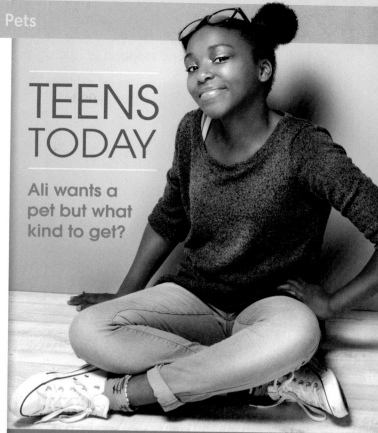

TEENS TODAY

Ali wants a pet but what kind to get?

Ali loves animals but she lives in a small city centre apartment. She's very busy and doesn't have much free time. And she hates getting up early. She doesn't have any problems with allergies.

Dogs are fun. You can play with them and they protect your home but you need to train them and take them for a walk. They're great friends but they feel bad if you don't spend time with them.

A

Cats are cute and clean but they scratch the furniture and bring dead animals into the house. They also give you allergies. They're fun to play with when they're little kittens but they aren't so friendly when they grow up.

B

Snakes are quiet and you don't need to take them for a walk. But you can't play with them much and they eat live animals. They're beautiful but some people are frightened of them.

C

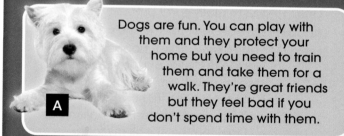

I can make and respond to apologies.

VIDEO **I DON'T KNOW HOW IT HAPPENED**

Krystal: Hi, Lee.
Lee: Oh, hi, Krystal. Are you home already?
Krystal: Yes, we're just back! The holiday was wonderful! So, when can you bring Daisy round? I'm missing her so much.
Lee: Er, I'm really sorry but …
Krystal: Oh no! Don't tell me she's not well!
Lee: I don't know how it happened. We were in the park and Daisy suddenly disappeared. Amy and I looked for her everywhere, in the dark as well, and I even contacted the police but … I feel terrible. It's all my fault.
Krystal: She's lost? I don't believe it! Lee Marshall, you absolute idiot! How could you be so careless! You promised to look after her! Oh, she's here! Daisy! Oh, my baby! Wait! I'm coming! … Lee? Look, I'm sorry I was a bit rude.
Lee: No problem. I totally understand. I'm so glad …
Krystal: Listen, I've got to go now. See you later. Bye!

> *I'm so glad.*
> *I've got to go now.*

OUT of **class**

1 Look at the photos. How do you think Lee and Krystal are feeling? Why?

2 ▶ 3.4 ◀》 2.16 Watch or listen. Check your answers to Exercise 1.

3 Tick (✓) the words and phrases from the dialogue.

Speaking	Apologising

Apologising
- ☐ I'm (really/so) sorry.
- ☐ I didn't realise.
- ☐ I apologise.
- ☐ It's (all) my fault.
- ☐ I feel terrible.
- ☐ It was an accident.

Accepting apologies
- ☐ Never mind.
- ☐ No problem.
- ☐ I totally understand.
- ☐ These things happen.
- ☐ It's not your fault.

Not accepting apologies
- ☐ How can/could you be so careless?
- ☐ You can't be serious!
- ☐ You promised to (look after her).
- ☐ I'm really angry about this!
- ☐ I'll never forgive you!

4 ◀》 2.17 Use the Speaking box to complete the dialogues. Sometimes more than one answer is possible. Listen and check.

1 A: Excuse me. I think you're sitting in my seat.
   B: *I'm so sorry*. I didn't realise!
2 A: _____. I didn't hear you. Could you repeat that?
   B: No problem. It's K-R-Z-Y-S.
3 A: I'm sorry I'm late! My bus didn't arrive on time.
   B: _____. The buses are terrible these days!
4 A: I'm afraid there was an accident with your bike.
   B: What!? _____! I'll never forgive you!

5 In pairs, follow the instructions. Use the Speaking box to help you.

And YOU

1 **Student A:** You borrowed Student B's laptop but you dropped it and it stopped working. Apologise.
   Student B: You don't accept Student A's apology.
2 **Student B:** It was Student A's birthday yesterday. You forgot it. Apologise.
   Student A: It was your birthday yesterday but birthdays aren't very important to you.

I can write a biography.

Steve Irwin

① Steve Irwin was a famous TV presenter and animal expert.

② ③ He was born in Australia in 1962. His parents owned a small zoo. Steve started working with animals when he was nine years old. He didn't go to university but he continued working at the zoo.

④ In 1992 Steve married his girlfriend, Terri. On their honeymoon Steve and his new wife looked for crocodiles for their zoo. They recorded this journey for a TV show, *The Crocodile Hunter*. The show was a big success and people in 120 countries watched their adventures.

Steve died in September 2006 after an attack by a stingray*. The news shocked fans across the world.
*a large sea animal

1 In pairs, ask and answer the questions.
- How often do you watch animal documentaries?
- Do you have a favourite programme about animals?
- Are there any TV presenters in your country who are famous for their programmes about nature and animals? What is your opinion of them?

2 In pairs, look at the photo of Steve Irwin. What do you know about him? Read his biography and answer the questions.
1 What nationality was he?
2 What was his wife's name?
3 What was the name of his famous TV show?
4 How old was he when he died?

3 Look at Steve's biography again. Find all the examples of the Past Simple.

4 Study the Writing box. Which of the phrases can you find in Steve's biography?

Writing	A biography

① Say why the person is/was famous
... is/was a famous ... [job]
... is/was famous for ... [book/film/TV show]
He/She was the first person to ...
He/She discovered ...

② Mention his/her childhood and family
He/She was born in ... [place or year]
His/Her parents are/were ... [job]
They lived in ... [place]

③ Mention his/her early career
He/She studied at ... University.
He/She started working as ... [job]
He/She travelled to ...

④ Mention his/her later life
He/She married ... in ...
He/She worked on ... [book/film/programme]
... [programme/book] was a big success.
He/She died in ...
He/She is still popular today.

5 What do you know about Bear Grylls? Read the fact box and complete it with the Past Simple form of the verbs in brackets.

Who is he?	A famous adventurer, TV presenter, writer
Born	1974
Childhood	His family ¹*lived* (live) in Northern Ireland + England.
Early Career	He ²_____ (study) at London University. He was in the British army for 3 years, and then ³_____ (climb) Mount Everest when he ⁴_____ (be) 23.
Later Life	Bear ⁵_____ (marry) Shara (2000). He ⁶_____ (start) work as a TV presenter in 2005. In 2009, he was appointed the youngest ever Chief Scout in the UK.

Bear Grylls

Writing Time

6 Write a short biography (70–100 words) of Bear Grylls. Use the fact box, the biography of Steve Irwin and the Writing box to help you.

Write about:
① why he is famous
② ③ his childhood and early career
④ his later life

adolescent /ˌædəˈlesənt/ adj
adulthood /ˈædʌlthʊd, əˈdʌlt-/ n
adventurous /ədˈventʃərəs/ adj
aggressive /əˈgresɪv/ adj
animal documentary /ˈænəməl ˌdɒkjəˈmentəri/ n
animal expert /ˈænəməl ˈekspɜːt/ n
ant /ænt/ n
apologise /əˈpɒlədʒaɪz/ v
aquarium /əˈkweəriəm/ n
bear /beə/ n
bee /biː/ n
behave /bɪˈheɪv/ v
behaviour /bɪˈheɪvjə/ n
biography /baɪˈɒgrəfi/ n
butterfly /ˈbʌtəflaɪ/ n
calm down /kɑːm daʊn/ v
career /kəˈrɪə/ n
careless /ˈkeələs/ adj
cat /kæt/ n
chicken /ˈtʃɪkən, ˈtʃɪkɪn/ n
childhood /ˈtʃaɪldhʊd/ n
chimp /tʃɪmp/ n
claw /klɔː/ n
clean /kliːn/ adj
climb /klaɪm/ v
cow /kaʊ/ n

criticise /ˈkrɪtəsaɪz, ˈkrɪtɪsaɪz/ v
crocodile /ˈkrɒkədaɪl/ n
cute /kjuːt/ adj
dangerous /ˈdeɪndʒərəs/ adj
decide /dɪˈsaɪd/ v
die /daɪ/ v
dirty /ˈdɜːti/ adj
discover /dɪsˈkʌvə/ v
dolphin /ˈdɒlfən, ˈdɒlfɪn/ n
donkey /ˈdɒŋki/ n
duck /dʌk/ n
elephant /ˈeləfənt, ˈelɪfənt/ n
energetic /ˌenəˈdʒetɪk/ adj
feather /ˈfeðə/ n
fight /faɪt/ v
flamingo /fləˈmɪŋgəʊ/ n
fly /flaɪ/ v
forgetful /fəˈgetfəl/ adj
forgive /fəˈgɪv/ v
fur /fɜː/ n
giraffe /dʒəˈrɑːf, dʒɪˈrɑːf/ n
grow up /grəʊ ʌp/ v
honeymoon /ˈhʌnimuːn/ n
hurry /ˈhʌri/ v
impulsive /ɪmˈpʌlsɪv/ adj
kangaroo /ˌkæŋgəˈruː/ n
kitten /ˈkɪtn/ n
(dog's) leash /ˌdɒgz ˈliːʃ/ n
lion /ˈlaɪən/ n

lively /ˈlaɪvli/ adj
lovable /ˈlʌvəbəl/ adj
marry sb /ˈmæri ˌsʌmbədi/ v
monkey /ˈmʌŋki/ n
mouth /maʊθ/ n
noisy /ˈnɔɪzi/ adj
parrot /ˈpærət/ n
penguin /ˈpeŋgwən, ˈpeŋgwɪn/ n
pet /pet/ n
pet shop /pet ʃɒp/ n
polar bear /ˈpəʊlə beə/ n
popular /ˈpɒpjələ, ˈpɒpjʊlə/ v
promise /ˈprɒməs, ˈprɒmɪs/ v
quiet /ˈkwaɪət/ adj
rabbit /ˈræbət, ˈræbɪt/ n
ride /raɪd/ v
rude /ruːd/ adj
sea otter /siː ˈɒtə/ n
shark /ʃɑːk/ n
sharp /ʃɑːp/ adj
sheep /ʃiːp/ n
shy /ʃaɪ/ adj
skin /skɪn/ n
snake /sneɪk/ n
spider /ˈspaɪdə/ n
stripe /straɪp/ n
success /səkˈses/ n
tail /teɪl/ n
tiger /ˈtaɪgə/ n

tortoise /ˈtɔːtəs/ n
TV presenter /ˌtiː ˈviː prɪˈzentə/ n
wing /wɪŋ/ n
zebra /ˈziːbrə, ˈze-/ n
zoo /zuː/ n

WORD FRIENDS

be famous for something
belong to a gang
brush a pet's fur
do dangerous things
eat live animals
empty a cat's litter tray
feed a pet
be fun to play with
give you allergies
ignore advice
look after a pet
make a lot of noise
miss sb/sth
protect your home
scratch the furniture
take a dog for a walk
take a pet to the vet's
take risks
train a pet
wash a pet
work on a book/film/ TV programme

VOCABULARY IN ACTION

1 Use the wordlist to find:
1 six animals that can fly: *fly, …*
2 six animals that live in or on water:
3 five animal body parts that people don't have:

2 In pairs, say the names of three animals that you think are:
1 quiet *butterfly, …*   4 cute
2 noisy   5 lively
3 dangerous

3 Complete the Word Friends with the prepositions below. In pairs, say if you agree with the sentences or not.

after for (x2) to (x2) with

1 Tortoises are fun to play *with* .
2 It's difficult to look *after* a cat.
3 You need to take a dog *for* a walk three times a day.
4 It's a good idea to take your pet *to* the vet's every month.
5 It's not good to belong *to* a gang.
6 Leo Messi is famous *for* writing books.

4 Complete the sentences with the correct form of the word in bold.
1 My gran says her *childhood* was very hard – she was often hungry. **CHILD**
2 The teacher was very happy with the *behaviour* of her class. **BEHAVE**
3 It's *dangerous* to ride a bike at night with no lights. **DANGER**
4 Jon Stewart was a famous American TV *presenter*. **PRESENT**

5a PRONUNCIATION Complete the sentences. Use words below that rhyme with the underlined words. There are two extra words.

bear bee ~~fly~~ ~~hurry~~ ~~sharks~~ snake tail wing ~~zoo~~

1 There aren't any <u>sharks</u> in our local <u>parks</u>.
2 A butterfly's *fly* is a beautiful <u>thing</u>.
3 Don't <u>worry</u>, you don't need to *hurry*.
4 It's time for the _____ to <u>take</u> a <u>break</u>.
5 <u>Why</u> didn't the <u>shy</u> _____ say <u>goodbye</u>?
6 Did <u>you</u> lose a <u>blue</u> <u>shoe</u> at the *zoo*?
7 <u>There</u> was a _____ on the <u>chair</u> over <u>there</u>.

5b 2.18 PRONUNCIATION Listen, check and repeat.

Revision

1 Write the names of animals for the definitions.

Animal QUIZ

1. It can fly and it can talk. — *parrot*
2. It's really cute. It's a baby cat. _____
3. It's got eight legs and it eats flies. _____
4. It's got sharp claws and striped fur. _____
5. It's got wings. It can swim but it can't fly. _____
6. It's a big bird with pink feathers and long legs. _____
7. It jumps very well and keeps its baby in a pouch. _____
8. It's from Africa. It eats leaves from the tops of trees. _____
9. It's a dangerous animal with very sharp teeth. It's green. _____
10. It's a farm animal. It's similar to a horse but with long ears. _____

2 Complete the adjectives in the sentences. In pairs, ask and answer the questions.

1. Are you a noisy person or are you **q u i e t**?
2. Do you often forget things? Are you **f _ _ _ _ _ _ _**?
3. Do you do things suddenly without thinking? Are you **i _ _ _ _ _ _ _**?
4. Do you shout at people? Are you **a _ _ _ _ _ _ _**?
5. Do you enjoy taking risks and doing extreme sports? Are you **a _ _ _ _ _ _ _**?
6. Do a lot of people love you and think you're cute? Are you **l _ _ _ _ _**?
7. Do you often make mistakes and have lots of accidents? Are you **c _ _ _ _ _ _ _**?
8. Do you like doing things? Do you have lots of energy? Are you **e _ _ _ _ _ _ _**?

A: Are you a noisy person or are you quiet?
B: I'm a very quiet person. I never make a lot of noise.

3 Complete the Word Friends. Use the words in the correct form. Then, in pairs, say if the sentences are true for you.

1. Animals don't *give* me allergies.
2. We have a cat. I sometimes brush its _____ but I never _____ its litter tray.
3. I never _____ my parents' advice.
4. My dad's a good driver. He never _____ risks.
5. Mum says I'm noisy but I don't think I _____ a lot of noise.
6. We _____ our pet very well – we never give her our food.
7. In the summer holidays I _____ my school friends.

4 Complete the sentences with *was, wasn't, were* or *weren't.*

Dolly the sheep

- Why [1]*was* Dolly famous?
- She [2]_____ the first animal clone in the world.
- [3]_____ Dolly from England?
- No, she [4]_____. She [5]_____ Scottish, from the Roslin Institute near Edinburgh.
- [6]_____ there any other clones at that institute?
- Yes, there [7]_____ but Dolly [8]_____ the first one.
- [9]_____ Dolly's children clones too?
- No, they [10]_____ clones.

5 Complete the text with the Past Simple form of the verbs below.

> not answer   arrive   ask   call   change
> ~~hurry~~   need   study   talk   not want

I [1]*hurried* home yesterday because
I [2]_____ to study for my exams.
I [3]_____ home at ten to six and then
I [4]_____ my clothes. From six to eight
I [5]_____ Biology. Then Jamie [6]_____
me. I [7]_____ to talk to him but he
[8]_____ me lots of questions about the
exam. We [9]_____ for an hour but
I [10]_____ all his questions.

6 In pairs, role play the situations. Student A, look below. Student B, look at page 131.

Student A

1. You argued with Student B. You shouted and called him/her a bad name. You feel bad. Apologise.
2. Student B posted an embarrassing photo of you on the internet. You are angry. Don't accept the apology.

7 🔊 2.19 Listen, then listen again and write down what you hear.

Why do parrots talk?

Pets around the world

For a long time, people used animals for food and for work. Today, many of us keep animals in our homes as pets and people all over the world love dogs and cats. In the UK, there are more than nine million pet dogs! Here are some other popular pets that you might find surprising.

Guatemala

A popular pet in Guatemala is the Macaw parrot. It has colourful feathers and can copy words and sounds. These birds live in the rainforest but there aren't many left now. Because of this, people can only buy them from special places.

China

Chinese people like many different animals but one very popular pet is the goldfish. For Chinese people the colour gold means money and they believe goldfish are lucky. People say that the goldfish has a bad memory – they're very forgetful and can only remember things for five seconds!

Japan

In Japan, they like keeping rabbits. Many Japanese people are vegetarian – they don't eat meat – and rabbits are vegetarian too! They're gentle animals with soft fur but when they're angry or frightened, they get aggressive and tap their feet on the ground loudly! They're also very small, which is important for people who live in a small apartment.

The USA

Snakes are very popular in the USA. They can live up to forty years and people don't need to feed them a lot. They don't usually move very much and some snakes sleep for several months every year. Most pet snakes are born in special centres. They're not dangerous or poisonous – unlike the snakes in the wild!

GLOSSARY
gentle (adj) not strong or violent
in the wild (phr) living free in nature
rainforest (n) a forest with tall trees growing in an area where it is hot and it rains a lot
tap (v) to hit lightly
vegetarian (adj) someone who does not eat meat or fish

EXPLORE

1 In pairs, discuss the questions.

  1 What's your favourite animal? Why?

  2 What are the most popular pets in your country?

  3 Do you have a pet? Would you like one? Why?/Why not?

  4 Do any of your friends have an unusual pet? Can you describe it?

  5 Do you know why parrots talk?

2 Which pets do you think are popular in these countries? Match countries 1–4 with photos A–D.

  1 B Guatemala

  2 A China

  3 C Japan

  4 D The USA

A

B

C

D

3 Read the article and check your ideas in Exercise 2.

4 Read the article again and answer the questions.

Which animals:

  1 can repeat what you tell them?
    parrots

  2 bring you good luck?

  3 are quite rare?

  4 don't eat meat?

  5 are good for small spaces?

  6 are gentle?

5 In pairs, discuss if you would like to have one of these pets. Why?/Why not?

EXPLORE MORE

6 You are going to watch part of a BBC documentary called *Wild at heart*. Read an advert for the programme. Do you like watching documentaries about animals?

Wild at heart

This is part of a series of documentaries about animal behaviour. Why do our pets sometimes do strange things? Are they playing games or is there another reason?

7 ▶ 3.5 In pairs, look at the photos above. What activities do these animals often do? Watch the video and check your ideas.

8 Answer the questions.

  1 How old are the puppies?

  2 How far do hamsters run every day?

  3 How many words can the parrot speak?

9 Work in pairs. Which animal do you think is the most interesting? Why?

10 ▶ 3.5 Watch the video again. Answer the questions.

  1 Why do puppies play?

  2 Why do hamsters run?

  3 Why do hamsters put a lot of food in their mouths?

  4 Why do parrots talk?

11 Work in pairs. Do you think it's a good idea to keep a pet? Why?/Why not?

Yes, because pets are like friends.
No, animals should live in the wild.

YOU EXPLORE

12 CULTURE PROJECT In small groups, create a mini video about pets.

  1 Use the internet to research popular pets in your country.

  2 Find some photos or videos.

  3 Write a short script and record it on your phone.

  4 Share it with your class.

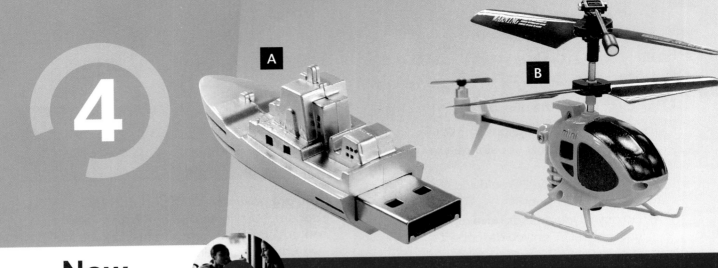

A

B

New technology

C

VOCABULARY
Gadgets and technology | Computer equipment

GRAMMAR
Past Simple: irregular verbs | Verb patterns | Relative clauses

Grammar: Where's my phone?

Speaking: It all went wrong

BBC Culture:
The digital revolution

Workbook p. 53

BBC VOX POPS ▶

COLLECTOR'S CORNER

This week: PRESTON JONES

> I collect USB gadgets – they're small gadgets which you plug into your laptop or tablet. They don't need a battery because they charge from your computer's USB port. There are a lot to choose from and they're usually quite cheap. I've got eighteen different gadgets in my collection but I'm always looking for new ones!

Some USB gadgets are practical. For example, my USB electric gloves. You charge them for two minutes in your USB port and they stay warm for hours. It's very useful when I'm at my keyboard in winter and my hands get cold!

Another useful gadget is my special USB pen drive. It looks like a boat but it's got 32 Gb of memory. I keep all my digital photos on it – I love it.

My favourite gadget is my USB helicopter. It's got a joystick to control it and it really does fly!

D

1 How many gadgets can you see and name in the classroom?

2 2.20 In pairs, ask and answer the questions below.

Vocabulary A Gadgets and technology

CD player digital camera DVD player e-reader games console MP3 player smartphone tablet

Which gadget(s) from Vocabulary A:

- have you got at home?
- do you use every day?
- would you like to have?
- are important to you?

A: *I've got a games console and a DVD player at home. How about you?*

B: *I've got a DVD player but I haven't got a games console. I'd like to have …*

3 WORD FRIENDS **Work in pairs. Which gadgets from Vocabulary A can you use for these activities?**

send instant messages listen to music check emails download files take photos phone a friend play games make video clips watch films surf the internet read a novel

You can send instant messages with a smartphone.

4 **Read the text on page 46. In pairs, answer the questions.**

1 Which gadgets A–D does Preston mention?
2 Which gadget do you think is:

- useful?
- fun?
- a waste of money?

5 2.21 **Find the words below in the text. How do you say them in your language?**

Vocabulary B Computer equipment

battery joystick keyboard memory pen drive USB port

6 I KNOW! **How many words can you add to Vocabulary B in two minutes?**

7 **Choose the correct option.**

1 You can charge this MP3 player from your computer's *keyboard* / *USB port*.
2 Has your phone got enough *photos* / *memory* to download this file?
3 I can play this computer game with my keyboard but it's easier to use a *joystick* / *USB port*.
4 I need to charge the *battery* / *pen drive* on my laptop.
5 I must buy a new *joystick* / *keyboard* – it's hard to type fast on this old one.

8 2.22 **Read the quiz. Then listen and decide which three questions Emily answers. Does she answer *yes* or *no*?**

Do you play **online** games? *adjective*
Do you play **online**? *adverb*

Watch OUT!

ARE YOU A computer freak?

Five or more 'yes' answers means you definitely are!

Do you …

1. enjoy spending time online more than meeting people face-to-face?
2. prefer instant messages to phone calls?
3. often buy gadgets, software or equipment for your computer?
4. often play online games?
5. have more than one email address?
6. know how much memory your computer has?
7. sometimes dream about people or situations from your online life?

9 **In pairs, do the quiz. Are you a computer freak? Tell the class. Use the language in the quiz to help you.**

I think I am a computer freak because I spend all my free time online.

And YOU

I can use the Past Simple of irregular verbs to talk about the past.

VIDEO WHERE'S MY PHONE? (Part 1)

Ruby: Lee! Where's my phone?

Lee: I left it in your room ten minutes ago.

Ruby: No, you didn't!

Lee: Yes, I did!

Ruby: Well, it's not there now! Dad! Lee stole my new smartphone!

Lee: Shut up, Ruby! I didn't steal your phone!

Ruby: You lost it, then! Oh! I only bought it a week ago. It cost a fortune!

Dad: Calm down, Ruby! Lee, did you take your sister's phone?

Lee: No, I didn't! Well, yes, I did. I forgot to top up my phone yesterday so I took Ruby's. I sent Amy *one* text, then before I went to bed, I gave her the phone back. I only had it for five minutes!

Ruby: Where did you put it?

Lee: I put it in the pocket of your jeans.

Ruby: Which jeans?

Lee: Your black jeans. They were on your chair.

Ruby: What!? Oh no! I saw those jeans in the washing machine. Mum!

> *Shut up!   It cost a fortune.*
> *I forgot to top up my phone.*

OUT of **class**

1 In pairs, think of ways you can lose your mobile phone. Then compare your ideas with the class.

You can leave it on the bus.
Someone can borrow it and not give it back.

2 4.1 2.23 Describe the photo. Why are Lee and Ruby arguing? Watch or listen to Part 1 and check your answer.

3 Find the past forms of the verbs below in the dialogue.

Grammar	Past Simple: irregular verbs
+	**–**
You **took** my phone.	I **didn't take** your phone.
?	
Did you **take** my phone?	Yes, I **did**./No, I **didn't**.
Where **did** they **put** it?	

GRAMMAR TIME > PAGE 121

~~buy~~ cost do forget go give have
leave lose put see send steal take

buy – bought

4 Complete the sentences with the Past Simple form of the verbs in brackets.

1 Ruby *bought* (buy) a new phone yesterday.
2 Mum _____ (put) Ruby's blue jeans in the washing machine.
3 Ruby _____ (find) the phone in the jeans.
4 Lee _____ (take) the phone out of the jeans.
5 Ruby _____ (give) mum the phone.
6 Mum _____ (forget) where she put the phone.

5 4.2 2.24 Watch or listen to Part 2. Correct the sentences in Exercise 4.

1 *Ruby didn't buy her phone yesterday. She bought it a week ago.*

6 Write questions in the Past Simple for these sentences.

1 I had toast for breakfast this morning. (What …?)
What did you have for breakfast this morning?
2 I went to France for my holidays. (Where …?)
3 I didn't do anything last weekend. (What …?)
4 I got three presents for my last birthday. (How many …?)
5 I bought my trainers yesterday. (When …?)
6 I left home at 7.30 this morning. (What time …?)

7 [VOX POPS ▶ 4.3] In pairs, ask and answer the questions in Exercise 6. Say if your partner's answers are true or false.

A: *What did you eat for breakfast this morning?*
B: *I ate cold pizza.*
A: *False! You didn't eat cold pizza for breakfast!*

I can find specific detail in a text and talk about using technology.

11 May 1984

Today at school we used a computer with 64 kB of memory! Fantastic!

Later, I told my friend Ian about it. He lives in Wales but we keep in touch on the phone. Unfortunately, my dad asked me to hang up after two minutes. ¹_____ And anyway, my mum needed to use the phone.

I heard a new Michael Jackson song on the radio. It was great! I wanted to hear it again so I listened for hours. I'm glad I didn't give up because they played it again and I recorded it on my cassette player. ²_____ Technology is great!

Tim

1 Do you read or write a regular blog or diary?

2 🔊 2.25 Read Tim's diary and Tina's blog. Complete gaps 1–4 with sentences a–e. There is one extra sentence.

a Now I can listen to it any time I want!

b That's why I didn't finish it.

c Then I played a game on my phone.

d Phone calls are expensive!

e My friend Cara texted me.

3 Read the texts again. Complete the sentences with *Tim* or *Tina*.

1 *Tina* worked with a friend.

2 _____ talked to a friend on the phone.

3 _____ used a computer with very little memory.

4 _____ used a phone to do more than one thing.

5 _____ communicated with friends in different ways.

6 _____ waited a long time to hear some music.

www.tinasblog.com

14 April 2017

When I got home from school, I looked at the time on my smartphone. It was early, so I listened to some songs on headphones and downloaded a new app. ³_____ After that I switched on my tablet computer, checked out my Facebook page and wrote some messages to friends. I also read some of my favourite blogs and watched some videos on YouTube.

⁴_____ She wanted me to help her with her homework. So I called her on Messenger. We looked for some information on Wikipedia together. You can't live today without technology!

4 PHRASAL VERBS Translate the highlighted verbs in the texts into your language. Then use them to complete the questions. Ask and answer the questions in pairs.

1 What was the last gadget you *switched on* last night?

2 Where do you usually _____ information?

3 Did you _____ on anyone yesterday? Why?

4 What was the last YouTube clip that you _____?

5 When did you last _____ because you couldn't do a computer game?

5 Complete the text with the words below. There are two extra words. Then, in pairs, write a similar text about technology today.

64 kB   cassettes   ~~desktop~~   hang   keep   letter   MP4   phone

In 1984 there were only ¹*desktop* computers. They were big and slow with only ²_____ of memory. People contacted their friends by ³_____ and they also talked on the ⁴_____. But they didn't ⁵_____ in touch with their friends very often. People listened to music on the radio, on ⁶_____ and on records.

Today there are desktop computers, laptops and tablets.

6 In pairs, say how you keep in touch with friends. Use the ideas below to help you. Say which way you prefer and why.

chat online   meet in town   call friends
text friends   send emails   visit friends at home
use social networking sites (e.g. Facebook)

I often use Facebook to keep in touch with my friends.

4.4 GRAMMAR Verb patterns

I can make sentences with verbs followed by the *to*-infinitive or the *-ing* form.

1 **How important is your phone to you?**

2 **WORD FRIENDS** **Think about your phone. In pairs, say how often you do these things.**

make phone calls | play games | charge the battery | write/receive texts

I make phone calls once or twice a day.

3 **2.26** **Read the text. Why does Jack think he is addicted to his phone?**

Can you live without your phone?

Jack, 15

I use my phone from the minute I wake up. I don't mind talking to people face to face but I prefer texting friends. I also enjoy following my favourite sports stars on Twitter. But I would like to spend less time on my phone. I don't know why I need to check my Facebook page every few minutes. I try to switch it off sometimes. But I notice that I can't stand being without my phone – for example, when I forget to charge it and the battery dies. I think I'm probably addicted to my phone.

4 **Find examples of the verb patterns in the text in Exercise 3.**

Grammar Verb patterns

- We use ***to*-infinitive** after these verbs: agree, decide, forget, learn, remember, need, try, want, would/'d like
  I try to switch off my phone sometimes.
- We use **verb + *-ing*** after these verbs: can't stand, don't mind, enjoy, finish, hate, keep, like, love, prefer, stop
  I love texting my friends.

GRAMMAR TIME > PAGE 122

5 **Choose the correct option. In pairs, say if the sentences are true for you.**

1 I enjoy *to try* / *trying* new apps on my smartphone.
2 I hate *to be* / *being* without my phone.
3 I would like *to buy* / *buying* a new smartphone.
4 I sometimes forget *to charge* / *charging* my phone.
5 I don't mind *to text* / *texting* but I can't stand *to make* / *making* phone calls.

6 **2.27** **Complete the text with the correct form of the verbs in brackets. Listen and check.**

I can't stand [1] *checking* (check) my phone all the time. That's why at New Year I decided [2] ______ (stop) using it in the evenings. That was six months ago. Sometimes I forget [3] ______ (switch) it off but usually I remember [4] ______ (do) it. I'm never bored in the evenings now. I enjoy [5] ______ (read) and now I'm reading two or three books a month! I'm also trying [6] ______ (learn) to play the guitar – my friend Tom agreed [7] ______ (teach) me. I like [8] ______ (have) a phone but I love [9] ______ (spend) time offline too.

7 **In pairs, complete the text with the correct form of the verbs in brackets. Which app sounds most interesting?**

Abby tells us about her favourite new apps

1 **El Maestro** I really enjoy [1] *drawing* (draw) so I love [2] ______ (use) this app to paint on my tablet. It's fun!

2 **Grunge Guitar Guru** I'm learning [3] ______ (play) the guitar – I want [4] ______ (be) the next Kurt Cobain! This app is like your own personal guitar teacher – it's great.

3 **Chimp Notes** I hate [5] ______ (have) lots of different documents for a project or essay so I use this app when I need [6] ______ (organise) my notes in one place. It's really practical and easy to use.

4 **Internet Lock** This app is useful when you want to stop [7] ______ (waste) time online. It's a shame I keep [8] ______ (forget) that I have this app!

8 **In pairs, ask and answer the questions. Use Abby's review in Exercise 7 to help you.** And YOU

1 What are your favourite apps?
2 Why do you like them and why are they useful?

My favourite app is … It's fun/easy to use/practical.
I use it when I need/want to …

I can identify specific detail in a conversation and talk about websites.

1 **CLASS VOTE** Which of these websites do you use the most often?

eBay

Google

Wikipedia

YouTube

Facebook

2 Match the websites from Exercise 1 with definitions 1–5.

1 You can buy and sell things on this website. *eBay*

2 On this website you can view and download videos. You can also upload your own videos to share them with other people.

3 You can use this to search the web for other websites that interest you.

4 With this website you can keep in touch with friends and chat online.

5 On this website you can read articles and click on links to find out more information.

3 🔊 2.28 **WORD FRIENDS**
Complete the text with the correct form of the highlighted verbs from Exercise 2. Listen and check.

I needed to find a program for making films so I ¹*searched* **the web** and found one. I ² _____ **on the link** and saw it was free so I ³ _____ **the program**. After I finished making my film, I wanted to ⁴ _____ **it with other people** so I ⁵ _____ **my video clip to YouTube**. In the first week, three hundred people ⁶ _____ **my video** and now some of them want to ⁷ _____ **online** with me.

4 🔊 2.29 Listen to a radio interview about YouTube. Complete the notes with one or two words in each gap.

YouTube

● It started in ¹*February 2005*.

● The first video was ² _____ long.

● In ³ _____ Google bought it for $1.65 billion.

● Every ⁴ _____ people watch hundreds of millions of hours of videos.

● Every minute people upload ⁵ _____ hours of videos.

● There are YouTube websites in more than ⁶ _____ languages.

5 🔊 2.30 Listen to the second part of the programme. Choose the correct answers.

1 *Upload* is a
   a computer program.   ⓑ radio programme.
   c website.

2 Alex likes YouTube because
   a he likes watching famous people.
   b it's always funny.
   c it shows many different kinds of videos.

3 How many reasons does Alex give for liking YouTube?
   a two   b three   c four

4 Howard Davies-Carr made a very popular
   a family video.   b music video.   c website.

5 How many times did people watch *Charlie bit my finger* in nine months?
   a 9 million   b 12 million   c over 800 million

6 [VOX POPS ▶ 4.4] In pairs, ask and answer the questions about your favourite websites. Use the Word Friends in Exercise 3.

1 What kind of website is it?

2 What can you do on it?

3 How popular is it?

4 Do you know how and when it started?

5 How often do you visit it?

6 Why do you like visiting it?

My favourite website is … You can use it to …

I can put events in order when talking about the past.

VIDEO   **IT ALL WENT WRONG**

Lee: Hi, Amy.

Amy: Hi, Lee. What's up?

Lee: You know my new song?

Amy: Of course I do. You played it a hundred times last weekend!

Lee: Yeah, anyway, I wanted to make a video of the song and upload it to YouTube but it all went wrong. First, the battery in my camera died after only one minute. Then I couldn't find the charger so I had to buy a new battery. After that my microphone didn't work. I didn't know where to plug it in. In the end it worked and finally, I finished recording the song so then I went online to upload it to YouTube.

Amy: Yeah?

Lee: And my computer crashed!

Amy: Oh no!

Lee: Yeah! Listen, I really need to fix it. Do you fancy coming round tomorrow to give me a hand?

Amy: Yeah, OK.

Lee: Thanks, Amy.

Ruby: Lee, do you know …? Oh! I don't believe it! Mum! Lee's using my phone again!

Lee: Ruby! I can explain. You see, the thing is …

What's up?   Anyway, …
Give me a hand.
Do you fancy (coming)?

OUT of **class**

---

1 WORD FRIENDS   What problems can you get with gadgets and computers? Check if your ideas are in the list. In pairs, say when you last had these technical problems:

- ☐ My computer crashed.
- ☐ My computer got a virus.
- ☐ My internet connection stopped working.
- ☐ I couldn't download a program.
- ☐ I couldn't connect a microphone.
- ☐ The battery in my camera/phone died.

My computer got a virus last weekend.

2 ▶ 4.5 ◀ 2.31 What can you see in the photo? What do you think Lee's problem is? Watch or listen. Tick (✓) the problems in Exercise 1 that Lee had.

3 Underline the words and phrases from the dialogue.

Speaking	Putting events in order

- At first/First/First of all
- Then/Next/After that/Suddenly
- An hour/A few days/Two weeks later
- Finally/In the end

4 ◀ 2.32 Use the Speaking box to complete the story of Lee's dream. Listen and check.

I dreamt that I uploaded the video of my song on YouTube. At [1] *first* , it wasn't very successful. Only three people viewed the video in the first week. But then [2]_____ it became popular. Millions of people saw it. A few days [3]_____ I got a call from a music company and I went to London to make a professional video. That was really successful too. [4]_____ that they asked me to write the music for a Hollywood movie! In the [5]_____ I won an Oscar for the best original song in a film!

5 ◀ 2.33 Dictation. Listen to Amy's side of the story. Listen again and write down what she says.

6 In pairs, use the Speaking box to tell a story. Choose from the ideas below.

- A time when you had technical problems.
- A day when you invited friends to your house.
- A dream you had.

I had a dream. At first, I was on a train and …

I can be specific about people, things and places.

1

This is the scientist who invented a super-intelligent robot.
It's a super-intelligent robot that can do a thousand amazing things.

2

This is a shop where they sell the super-intelligent robot.
These are some things which the robot can do.

3

These are the people that bought the robot.
This is the house where they live.
And these are the things that the robot does.

1 **Look at the cartoons. What is the robot thinking in picture 3? Choose the best caption.**

1 'Why can't humans be more like robots?'
2 'Housework is so much fun!'
3 'I'm super-intelligent and I'm picking up socks. How depressing!'

2 **Find sentences in the cartoon strip for rules 1–3 below.**

Language	Relative clauses

We use relative clauses to say which person, thing or place we are talking about.

1 We use *who* or *that* for people.
   An inventor is a person who/that invents things.
2 We use *which* or *that* for things.
   This is the machine which/that Leonard invented.
3 We use *where* for places.
   This is the university where Leonard works.

3 **Combine the sentences with relative pronouns.**

1 This is a robot. It cleans floors.
   This is a robot which/that cleans floors.
2 She is a woman. She makes things.
3 I bought a clock. It plays music.
4 That's the shop. I bought my gloves there.
5 Is that your friend? She works for Microsoft?
6 Have you got a mouse? You don't need it.
7 This is the town. Marie Curie was born here.

4 **Complete the sentences with *who*, *which* or *where*. Then write the correct word for each definition.**

1 It's a thing **which** you use to charge a phone. **c**_ _ _ _ _ _
2 It's a place _____ you put USB gadgets. USB **p**_ _ _ _
3 This is a person _____ collects things.
   c_ _ _ _ _ _ _ _
4 It's a place _____ you can read information online. **w**_ _ _ _ _ _
5 It's a thing _____ takes photos. **c**_ _ _ _ _
6 This is a person _____ works in a laboratory.
   s_ _ _ _ _ _ _ _

5 **Complete the sentences with *who*, *which* or *where*.**

1 The person **who** I admire the most is …
2 The place _____ I want to live when I'm older is …
3 The next electronic gadget _____ I want to buy is …
4 One place _____ I feel really happy is …
5 The first person _____ I saw this morning was …
6 I'd love to have a robot _____ can …

6 2.34 **Listen and complete the sentences in Exercise 5.**

7 **Complete the sentences in Exercise 5 to make them true for you. Then compare with a partner.**

admire /ədˈmaɪə/ v
after that /ˈɑːftə ðæt/ adv
app /æp/ n
at first /ət fɜːst/ adv
battery /ˈbætəri/ n
blog /blɒg/ n
calm down /kɑːm daʊn/ v
can't stand /kɑːnt stænd/ v
cassette /kəˈset/ n
cassette player /kəˈset ˈpleɪə/ n
CD player /ˌsiː ˈdiː ˈpleɪə/ n
charger /ˈtʃɑːdʒə/ n
check out /tʃek aʊt/ v
collector /kəˈlektə/ n
computer freak /kəmˈpjuːtə friːk/ n
crash (e.g. a computer) /kræʃ/ v
current /ˈkʌrənt/ adj
desktop computer /ˈdesktɒp kəmˈpjuːtə/ n
die (e.g. a battery) /ˈdaɪ/ v
digital camera /ˈdɪdʒətl ˈkæmərə/ n
don't/doesn't mind /ˌdəʊnt dʌz(ə)nt ˈmaɪnd/ v
DVD player /ˌdiː viː ˈdiː ˈpleɪə/ n
e-reader /iː ˈriːdə/ n
electric /ɪˈlektrɪk/ adj
electronic /ˌelɪkˈtrɒnɪk/ adj

email (address) /ˈiː meɪl əˌdres/ n
(computer) equipment /kəmˈpjuːtə ɪˈkwɪpmənt/ n
finally /ˈfaɪnəli/ adv
first (of all) /ˌfɜːst/ adv
fortunately /ˈfɔːtʃənətli/ adv
gadget /ˈgædʒət, ˈgædʒɪt/ n
games console /geɪmz ˈkənsəʊl/ n
give up /gɪv ʌp/ v
hang up /hæŋ ʌp/ v
in the end /ɪn ði end/ adv
instant message /ˈɪnstənt ˈmesɪdʒ/ n
internet connection /ˈɪntənet kəˈnekʃən/ n
invent /ɪnˈvent/ v
inventor /ɪnˈventə/ n
joystick /ˈdʒɔɪˌstɪk/ n
keyboard /ˈkiːbɔːd/ n
(a few weeks) later /ˈleɪtə/ adv
look for /lʊk fə/ v
memory /ˈmeməri/ n
mobile phone /ˈməʊbaɪl fəʊn/ n
mouse (computer) /ˈmaʊs/ n
MP3 player /ˌem piː ˈθriː ˈpleɪə/ n
next /nekst/ adv
online /ˈɒnlaɪn/ adv

online (games) /ˈɒnlaɪn/ adj
pen drive /pen draɪv/ n
plug in/into /plʌg ɪn ɪntə/ v
practical /ˈpræktɪkəl/ adj
print /prɪnt/ v
printer /ˈprɪntə/ n
professional /prəˈfeʃənəl/ adj
record /ˈrekɔːd/ n
record /rɪˈkɔːd/ v
robot /ˈrəʊbɒt/ n
scientist /ˈsaɪəntəst, ˈsaɪəntɪst/ n
smartphone /ˈsmɑːtfəʊn/ n
software /ˈsɒftweə/ n
successful /səkˈsesfəl/ adj
suddenly /ˈsʌdnli/ adv
switch off/on /swɪtʃ ɒf ɒn/ v
tablet (computer) /ˈtæblət/ n
technical (problems) /ˌteknɪkəl/ adj
technology /tekˈnɒlədʒi/ n
then /ðen/ adv
top up (a phone) /tɒp ʌp/ v
unfortunately /ʌnˈfɔːtʃənətli/ adv
USB port /ˌjuː es ˈbiː pɔːt/ n
website /ˈwebsaɪt/ n

charge a phone/battery
chat online
check emails/updates
click on links
connect a microphone
download files/videos
follow somebody (on Twitter)
get a virus (computer)
go wrong
keep in touch (with people)
make phone calls
make videos/video clips
meet (people) face-to-face/ in town
play games
search the web
send emails/instant messages
share files/videos
spend time online/offline
stop working
surf the internet
take photos
text friends
upload files/videos
use social networking sites
visit a website
view videos
visit friends
waste time (online)
write/receive texts

WORD FRIENDS

call/phone a friend

VOCABULARY IN ACTION

1 Use the wordlist to find twelve examples of electronic equipment/gadgets.

CD player, ...

2 In pairs, decide which items from Exercise 1:

1 often have an internet connection *desktop computer*
2 quite often crash/go wrong/stop working
3 can get a virus
4 can help you keep in touch with people
5 you can use to listen to music
6 you are really addicted to

3 Complete the sentences with the correct form of the word in bold.

1 Marie Curie was a great *scientist*. **SCIENCE**
2 Your video clip's great – you did a really _____ job! **PROFESSION**
3 Does anybody remember who was the _____ of the cassette? **INVENT**
4 I wrote you a long email but _____ my computer crashed. **FORTUNATE**
5 The first CD player wasn't very _____. **SUCCESS**

4 Complete the Word Friends. In pairs, say if the sentences are true for you.

1 I got a virus after I clicked <u>on</u> a link.
2 A famous person follows me _____ Twitter!
3 I often _____ the internet for new fashion ideas.
4 I sometimes forget to _____ my phone and the battery dies.

5a 🔊 2.35 **PRONUNCIATION** Listen to how you pronounce the underlined letters in each word and repeat.

/ə/ | <u>a</u>ddress batt<u>e</u>ry cam<u>era</u>
comput<u>er</u> digit<u>a</u>l int<u>er</u>net

5b 🔊 2.36 **PRONUNCIATION** In pairs, practise saying these words with an /ə/ sound. Listen and check.

invent<u>or</u> micr<u>o</u>phone print<u>er</u>
tabl<u>e</u>t vir<u>u</u>s

Revision

1 Match words from A with words from B to make phrases. In pairs, choose four phrases and make sentences.

> **A:** ~~instant~~ digital USB email pen games

> **B:** address console ~~message~~ drive camera port

instant message

2 Complete the words in the text. In pairs, say which course is suitable for:

a someone who wants to spend time away from the internet.

b someone who is interested in making music videos.

c grandparents who want to contact their grandchildren.

New short courses for Autumn 2020

1 **Online Media (6 weeks; £90)**
During this six-week course students have a chance to
¹*take* photos and make video ²**c**_____ . Students also
learn how to ³**s**_____ their videos and ⁴**u**_____ files
and videos to the internet.

2 **Learn to Love Your Computer (4 weeks; £60)**
Do you want to know how to use your smartphone or
computer to keep in ⁵**t**_____ with friends and family?
This four-week course is the answer! Learn how to
⁶**s**_____ emails and messages, ⁷**t**_____ friends, and
chat ⁸**o**_____ .

3 **Vegetable Gardening (8 weeks; £85)**
Do you spend all day surfing the ⁹**i**_____ ? Do you feel
you ¹⁰**w**_____ time online? Are you looking for ways to
¹¹**s**_____ time offline? Try a new skill and meet
¹²**p**_____ face-to-face in the fresh air! PS Only for
people who don't ¹³**m**_____ getting wet or dirty!

---

3 Replace the underlined phrases with the phrasal verbs below.

> hang up plug (sth) into look for ~~check out~~ give up

> *Check out*

1 Wow! <u>Have a look at</u> these games consoles.
2 Don't <u>stop trying</u>. You need practice to become a good photographer.
3 Can you help me <u>try to find</u> my pen drive?
4 He started shouting so I decided to <u>end the phone call</u>.
5 I'm not surprised your printer isn't working. You forgot to <u>connect</u> it <u>to</u> the USB port.

4 Complete the text with the Past Simple form of the verbs in brackets. Use the verb list on page 127 to help you.

Ada Lovelace lived in England in the early 1800s.
She ¹*was* (be) the daughter of Lord Byron, a famous
poet. Ada's mother ²_____ (not want) Ada to be a
poet like her father so she ³_____ (teach) her Maths
and Science. In 1833, Ada ⁴_____ (meet) Charles
Babbage, the inventor of a counting machine (a
primitive computer). In 1843, Ada ⁵_____ (write)
an algorithm for Babbage's machine: perhaps the
world's first computer program. So ⁶_____ (Ada/
have) her father's amazing imagination after all?

---

5 Complete the information about the story in Exercise 4. Choose the correct option.

1 *Ada Lovelace* was the person (who) / which probably became the first computer programmer.
2 _____ was the country *that* / *where* Ada lived.
3 _____ was the poet *who* / *which* was Ada's father.
4 _____ was the early computer *where* / *which* Babbage invented.

6 Complete the sentences with the correct form of the verbs in brackets. In pairs, say which sentences are true for you.

1 I often write emails but forget <u>*to send*</u> (send) them.
2 I would like _____ (spend) more time offline.
3 I don't mind _____ (write) texts.
4 I keep _____ (lose) my phone charger.

7 In pairs, use linking words (*first/then ...*) to tell a story. Student A, look below. Student B, look at page 131. Then swap roles.

Student A Choose a topic:
- A time you nearly gave up – but didn't.
- A time when you didn't finish something because you spent too long online.

8 🔊 **2.37** Listen, then listen again and write down what you hear.

Is there wi-fi in the Sahara?

Strange places around the world to find wi-fi

Today, in the twenty-first century, people can go online nearly everywhere. We don't have to be at home or work or school. There are hotspots in cafés, hotels (even in the Sahara!), shops and hospitals. At the moment there are about 5.8 million hotspots in the world! Although we still can't browse online or check our emails on some planes, in deserts or in some countryside areas, there are some unusual places which do have wi-fi hotspots.

The Moon

Are you surprised? It's true. Scientists put a satellite and receiver near the Moon. No one is using it at the moment. But people might live there and use it in the future? Who knows?

Mount Everest

The highest mountain in the world got wi-fi in 2010. There are hotspots all along the difficult routes up to the top. So, if you want to climb to the very top, the summit, you can take a selfie and share it with your friends!

The North Pole

A Russian team made the difficult journey into the Arctic in 2005. They set up a hotspot at an ice camp eighty kilometres from the Pole. It was the first wi-fi connection in the Arctic.

London black cabs

It usually costs a lot to go online while you're travelling. But now you can do this for free in many London black cabs (taxis). You have to watch a fifteen second advert first but then you get fifteen minutes of free wi-fi to use on your phone, tablet or laptop. Useful for the cabbies too!

Engineers are still working to bring wi-fi to a lot of remote areas all over the world. Small African villages might soon have wi-fi, just like the big hotels!

GLOSSARY
browse (v) to look for information
cabbie (n) a taxi driver
receiver (n) a piece of equipment which receives signals
remote (adj) far away
summit (n) the top of a mountain

EXPLORE

1 In pairs, discuss the questions.

1 What is a wi-fi hotspot?
2 Are there a lot of hotspots in your town/area?
3 How often do you use them?
4 Is there wi-fi everywhere in your country?
5 Which parts of the world do you think *don't* have wi-fi?

2 Read the article and tick (✓) the things 1–7 that we learn about.

1 ☐ hotspots
2 ☐ how hotspots work
3 ☐ possible future hotspots
4 ☐ advertising for hotspots
5 ☐ hotspots on transport
6 ☐ places where there are no hotspots
7 ☐ the cost of hotspots

3 In pairs, discuss what you learned about the items you ticked in Exercise 2.

4 Now answer the question: Is there wi-fi in the Sahara?

EXPLORE MORE

5 You are going to watch part of a BBC programme about the internet. Read an extract from the programme. Do you enjoy watching programmes about technology?

The digital revolution

The internet changed our lives in many ways but 60 percent of the world is still not connected.

EXPLORE MORE

6 ▶ 4.6 Watch Part 1 of the video and answer the questions.

1 Why is today an important day for this small town in Africa?
2 Why is Tim Berners-Lee important?
3 What was his idea?
4 What is he showing people?
5 What is the question the speaker asks?

7 What do you think? Is the internet good or bad for us? In pairs, write a list of good and bad points.

8 ▶ 4.7 Watch Part 2 of the video and check your ideas in Exercise 7. Are your ideas the same as in the video?

9 Mark the sentences T (true) or F (false).

1 ☐ Kudjo is a farmer who grows crops.
2 ☐ Kudjo also teaches his friends about the internet.
3 ☐ He uses the internet to learn the costs of his competitors' crops.
4 ☐ Sir Tim Berners-Lee sold his invention for a lot of money.

10 Work in pairs. Do you think Tim Berners-Lee made the right decision?

Yes, because I believe that everyone should use the internet.
No, it's better if you earn money from your own inventions.

YOU EXPLORE

11 CULTURE PROJECT In small groups, create a digital presentation about an online company.

1 Use the internet to research a new and exciting company that does everything online.
2 Write a short script and include some photos or video.
3 Share it with your class.

5

My home, my town

VOCABULARY
Things in the house | Prepositions of place | Housework | Adjectives to describe a house | Places in town

GRAMMAR
Adverbs of manner | Modal verbs: *can*, *have to* and *must*

Grammar: It's not fair

Speaking: I moved in this morning

BBC Culture:
I want my own room!

Workbook p. 65

BBC VOX POPS ▶

CLIL 3 > p. 140

Unusual rooms

A bathroom

This spacious bathroom has really big windows. But there are no curtains so you can always admire a fantastic view of the Caribbean Sea.

5.1 VOCABULARY Things in the house

I can talk about things in the house.

1 CLASS VOTE Look at the photos. Which room would you most like to visit?

I'd like to visit the …

2 🔊 2.38 Underline the things you can see in the photos.

Vocabulary A	Things in the house

- **kitchen** cooker cupboard fridge oven sink tap
- **bedroom** bed bedside table chair wardrobe
- **bathroom** bath bidet shower toilet washbasin
- **living room** armchair coffee table fireplace sofa
- **different rooms** ceiling curtains desk floor lamp mirror rug switch table wall

3 I KNOW! How many words can you add to Vocabulary A in two minutes?

4 Complete the descriptions of the rooms in the photos with words from Vocabulary A.

A The Caribbean bathroom has a ¹*bath* but no shower. There's a ²_____ and a bidet. There's a mirror on the ³_____ and a ⁴_____ with one tap. On the floor there is a white ⁵_____.

B In the living room in the Ice Hotel, there are two ¹_____ and a round ²_____ in front of the ³_____.

C The aquarium bedroom has a big ¹_____. There is a chair and a low ²_____ near the window and a lamp on the ³_____. There are some orange ⁴_____ at the window.

D In the upside down kitchen, there's a ¹_____ and three ²_____. There's a cooker and an ³_____ for cooking food, a ⁴_____ to keep food cold and lots of ⁵_____ for the plates and glasses.

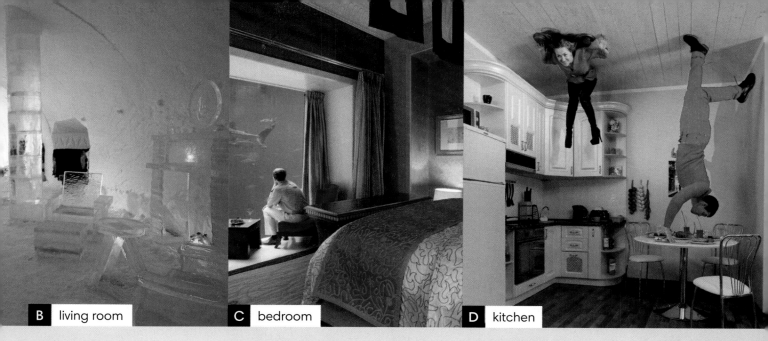

B living room

The armchairs are cold so you need to sit close to the fireplace in the living room of the Ice Hotel near Kiruna, Sweden.

C bedroom

Can't sleep? That's no problem in this underwater hotel bedroom in Dubai. You can get up and watch the fish in the aquarium. It's very relaxing!

D kitchen

No, these people can't fly. They're in the kitchen of the Upside Down House in Moscow, Russia. The furniture is on the ceiling and they are on the floor. Turn the photo round to see!

5 In pairs, think of something from Vocabulary A. Ask ten *yes/no* questions to find out what your partner is thinking of.

A: *Is it usually in the living room?*
B: *Yes, it is.*
A: *Do you sit on it?*

This is my room. There's a ¹wardrobe opposite the bed with lots of clothes in it. There's an armchair ² _____ to the wardrobe and ³ _____ the armchair is my guitar. I love music. There's a poster of my favourite group ⁴ _____ the wall above my ⁵ _____ . I like astronomy too. That's my telescope ⁶ _____ the bed and the armchair. My room isn't very tidy. There are lots of shoes ⁷ _____ the bed. That's my computer on the ⁸ _____ in front ⁹ _____ the wardrobe and that's my games console near the ¹⁰ _____ .

6 2.39 Study Vocabulary B. Look at the rooms again and choose the correct option.

Vocabulary B	Prepositions of place
above behind between in in front of	
near next to on opposite under	

1 There are some drinks *near /(on)* the kitchen table.
2 There's a painting *above / under* the lamp.
3 The bath is *in / next to* the window.
4 The toilet is *between / opposite* the bidet and the washbasin.
5 The coffee table is *behind / in front of* the fireplace.

7 2.40 Look at the picture and complete the text with one word in each gap. Listen and check.

8 In pairs, find four things which are in the same places in your homes. Use Vocabulary A and B to help you.

A: *There's a sofa under the window in my living room.*
B: *No, in my living room the sofa's opposite the window.*

I can describe how people do things.

1 What was the first job you did to help in the house when you were a child?

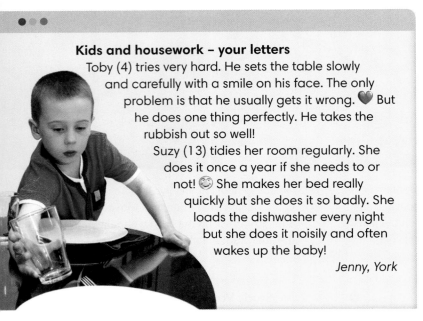

Kids and housework – your letters

Toby (4) tries very hard. He sets the table slowly and carefully with a smile on his face. The only problem is that he usually gets it wrong. 🖤 But he does one thing perfectly. He takes the rubbish out so well!

Suzy (13) tidies her room regularly. She does it once a year if she needs to or not! 😊 She makes her bed really quickly but she does it so badly. She loads the dishwasher every night but she does it noisily and often wakes up the baby!

Jenny, York

2 🔊 **2.41** **WORD FRIENDS** Read the text above. Then complete the Word Friends.

> ¹*make* your bed ² _____ the rubbish out
> ³ _____ your room ⁴ _____ /clear the table
> ⁵ _____ the dishwasher/washing machine
> do the shopping/cooking/ironing
> wash/dry the dishes   vacuum/sweep the floor

3 In pairs, say what housework from Exercise 2 you do or don't do.

I take the rubbish out but I don't do the ironing.

4 Read the text again. Say how the two children do their housework.

Suzy makes her bed quickly.

Grammar	Adverbs of manner

adjective → *adverb*

He is slow. → He does things slowly.
She is noisy. → She does things noisily.

- We use *very*, *really* and *so* before adjectives and adverbs.

He is very/really/so careful.
→ He does things very/really/so carefully.

- Some adverbs are the same as the adjectives: *hard, fast, right, wrong, early, late*
- The adverb for *good* is *well*.

GRAMMAR TIME   PAGE 122

5 Complete the sentences with adverbs from the adjectives in brackets. In pairs, say if the sentences are true for you.

1 I make my bed really *badly*. (bad)
2 My dad doesn't cook very _____. (good)
3 I load the dishwasher very _____. (careful)
4 I tidy my room so _____. (fast)
5 I never arrive _____. (late)
6 I like getting up _____. (early)
7 My parents do the shopping _____. (slow)
8 My grandfather eats very _____. (noisy)

I don't make my bed badly. I make it very well. How about you?

6 In groups, make adverbs from the adjectives below. Then use them to talk about what you did yesterday. Are your partners' sentences true or false?

> good   bad   quick   slow   wrong   hard
> careful   angry   happy   early   late

A: *I sang happily on my way to school.*
B: *I don't believe you. It's false.*

7 🔊 **2.42** Complete the text with one word in each gap. Listen and check.

My mum works ¹*hard* and she's always ² _____ tired when she gets home. So we all help ³ _____ the housework. My brother Tom usually ⁴ _____ the shopping. He can drive so he does it very ⁵ _____ – in under an hour. My sister Bea is the cook because she cooks really ⁶ _____. I set and ⁷ _____ the table and I vacuum the ⁸ _____ every Sunday. I take the rubbish ⁹ _____ too. But I don't ¹⁰ _____ the dishwasher any more because Bea says I don't do it very well.

8 Write a paragraph about who does the housework in your family and how well they do it. Use the text in Exercise 7 to help you.

My parents usually do the cooking. My dad cooks really …

I can find specific detail in a text and describe places.

1 CLASS VOTE Answer the questions. Then say what your favourite film or book about ghosts is.

- Do you believe in ghosts?
- Do you enjoy ghost stories?

2 🔊 2.43 Read the story. Who is the girl in the drawing?

I woke up because I heard a cat. I was surprised because my grandmother doesn't have a cat. It was dark so I switched on the lamp. I listened really carefully but I didn't hear anything. Maybe it was a dream, I thought.

The next night I heard the noise again but this time there was a black kitten on the bed. It jumped to the floor and ran quickly outside. I followed it along the narrow corridor, through the large hall and upstairs into the attic. I switched the light on. The room was very messy. There were old carpets, curtains, chairs and paintings. I looked everywhere but I couldn't find the kitten. It was a mystery.

In the morning I told Gran about the cat.

'Don't be silly, Tom,' she said impatiently.

That night, a girl came to my room. She was beautiful with long brown hair and soft green eyes.

'You have to help me,' she said. She spoke quietly. It was hard to hear her voice.

She took my hand and I followed her to the garden. She pointed to the roof. I looked up. The kitten was near the chimney. When I turned back, the girl wasn't there.

In the morning I told Gran about the girl.

She turned slowly and took an old photo from the wall. It showed a woman sitting in a cosy armchair in an old-fashioned room. At her feet was a small black cat. Next to her was a beautiful girl.

'These people lived here a hundred years ago,' Gran explained. 'They sold the house after something terrible happened.'

'What?' I asked.

'The girl fell from the roof and died. She was only thirteen years old.'

3 Read the story again. Mark the sentences ✓ (true), ✗ (false) or ? (doesn't say).

1 [✗] The story takes place in Tom's house.
2 [ ] The house is near a lake.
3 [ ] Tom heard the cat before he saw it.
4 [ ] Tom knew how the kitten got out of the attic.
5 [ ] Tom's grandmother doesn't like cats.
6 [ ] The girl wanted Tom to help her get the kitten.
7 [ ] The girl in the photo died in an accident.

4 In pairs, find the furniture and rooms in the story.

- Furniture and things in a house: *lamp, …*
- Rooms and parts of a house:

5 🔊 2.44 Match the highlighted words in the story with their opposites below.

Vocabulary	Adjectives to describe a house
bright – ¹*dark*	modern – ⁴_____
small – ²_____	tidy – ⁵_____
wide – ³_____	uncomfortable – ⁶_____

6 Complete the description of the house in the story with words from the Vocabulary box.

My gran's house isn't ¹**modern** like ours, it's really ²_____ . I'm writing this in front of the fire in the living room, it's ³_____ . The house is very ⁴_____ – there are ten bedrooms. It's really ⁵_____ because the curtains are always closed. The corridors are ⁶_____ – you can touch both walls at the same time. Upstairs there is a ⁷_____ attic full of old furniture.

7 🔊 2.45 How do you think the story ends? Choose from endings a–c. Look at page 130 to find out.

a The boy finds the kitten.
b The boy falls from the roof.
c The boy finds out the girl is not a ghost.

8 Use the Vocabulary box to describe your school or bedroom. Compare with a partner.

I think our school is very …
There is/are …

I can talk about permission and obligation.

VIDEO IT'S NOT FAIR

Ruby: What time is it?

Amy: Almost eleven.

Ruby: Cool! I have to go to bed at ten normally!

Krystal: Ten! That's early! I don't have to go to bed until eleven … and I can stay up later at weekends. What time do you have to go to bed, Amy?

Amy: Any time I want.

Ruby: You're lucky! My parents are really strict with me. I have to tidy my room. I have to come home straight after school. I mustn't forget to do my homework. I can't wear make-up. I can't stay out late. But Lee can stay out late …

Krystal: What time does Lee have to come home?

Ruby: He doesn't have to come home until ten! They say it's different for boys! It's not fair!

Amy: Yeah, but you are only thirteen, Ruby. My cousin Meg's thirteen and she has to go to bed at half past nine!

Ruby: Oh!

Cool!   You're lucky!
It's not fair!

OUT of **class**

---

1 5.1 ◄») 2.46 **Look at the photo. What is happening? Watch or listen and answer the questions.**

1 Where are the girls?
2 What are they doing?
3 Why is Ruby not happy?
4 Does Amy agree with Ruby? Why?/Why not?

---

2 **Find more examples of modal verbs in the dialogue.**

Grammar	Modal verbs: *can, have to, must*

Can you stay up late? (= Is it OK?)
I can stay up late at the weekend. (= It's OK.)
I can't stay up late during the week. (= It isn't OK.)

Do I have to go to bed? (= Is it necessary?)
You have to go to bed now. (= It's necessary.)
You don't have to go to bed now. (= It isn't necessary.)

You mustn't leave your clothes on the floor. (= Don't!)

GRAMMAR TIME   PAGE 123

3 CLASS VOTE **Do you think Ruby's parents are strict?**

4 ◄») 2.47 **Choose the correct option. Then listen to Ruby and Krystal and check.**

R: Krystal, ¹*can you* / *do you have to* invite friends to your house any time you want or ²*can you* / *do you have to* ask your parents for permission?

K: I ³*can* / *have to* invite friends round any time I want, Ruby. I ⁴*don't have to* / *mustn't* ask my parents. But if my parents are at home, I ⁵*don't have to* / *can't* take my friends to the living room. We ⁶*have to* / *mustn't* stay in my room or in the kitchen. And if they're watching TV, we ⁷*don't have to* / *mustn't* make a lot of noise.

5 **Complete the sentences to make them true for you. Then compare your answers with a partner.**

How strict are your parents?

1 I *can* stay up late at weekends.
2 I _____ go to bed at _____ o'clock during the week.
3 I _____ get up early at weekends.
4 I _____ eat with my family on weekdays.
5 I _____ go online before I do my homework.
6 I _____ do my homework before I watch TV.
7 I _____ wear any clothes I like.
8 I _____ phone home when I stay out late.
9 I _____ ask my parents for permission to invite friends to my house.

6 [VOX POPS ▶ 5.2] **In groups, ask about the information in Exercise 5. Who has strict parents?**

And Y?U

A: *Can you stay up late at weekends?*
B: *Yes, I can.*
A: *What time do you have to go to bed?*

I can identify specific detail in a conversation and talk about my town.

SURVEY RESULTS

Best things about Keswick
1. Friendly people
2. The beautiful countryside
3. Nice old buildings
4. Great cafés and shops
5. The film festival

Worst things about Keswick
1. Nothing to do in the evenings
2. Not enough shops
3. No public transport in the evenings
4. Too much traffic in the town centre
5. Everybody knows your business

1 **Look at the photos. What do they show? What type of place is Keswick?**

village   small town   city   capital city

2 2.48 **I KNOW!** **Check you understand the words below. How many words can you add in two minutes?**

Vocabulary	Places in town

art gallery café castle church
cinema estate hotel library museum
park police station post office
shopping centre station town hall
tourist information centre

3 **Work in pairs. Give the name of a local place for your partner to guess.**

A: Odeon.   B: That's a cinema!

4 2.49 **Listen to the telephone information line. Complete the gaps with a word or phrase.**

Trip to Keswick

- For maps, leaflets go to the ¹_____ – open every day, in the old ²_____
- Top attraction – ³_____ (the history of pencil making!)
- Small ⁴_____ with a popular arts ⁵_____

5 **In pairs, look at the results of a survey prepared by Keswick teenagers and answer the questions.**

1. What are the three biggest problems for young people in Keswick?
2. What are the three most popular reasons why Keswick is a good place to live?

6 2.50 **Listen and decide which answers from the survey each person mentions. Use one answer twice.**

		LIKES	DISLIKES
1	Declan	*friendly people*	_____
2	Louise	_____	_____
3	Annie	_____	_____
4	Brett	_____	_____

7 2.50 **Listen again and match statements a–e with speakers 1–4. There is one extra statement.**

1 ☐ Declan 2 ☐ Louise 3 ☐ Annie 4 ☐ Brett

a doesn't ride a bike in town any more.
b enjoys riding a bike.
c lived in another town when he/she was younger.
d is planning to live in a different place.
e lives outside the town.

8 [VOX POPS ▶ 5.3] **What are the best and worst things about your town? Tell the class. Use the survey answers in Exercise 5 and the Vocabulary box to help you.**

For me, the best things about our town are the nice old buildings and the music festival. The worst things are …

I can ask for, give and receive advice.

VIDEO **I MOVED IN THIS MORNING (Part 2)**

Krystal:	Hi, Billy.
Billy:	Hi.
Krystal:	Where are you going?
Billy:	I want to explore my new town. Can you give me some advice about what to do?
Amy:	I think you should go for a walk by the canal. It's pretty.
Krystal:	You're kidding, right? That's a terrible idea, Amy. You shouldn't go to the canal, Billy. It's not safe there.
Billy:	Yeah, I don't think that's a good idea. What do you think I should do, Krystal? Where should I go?
Krystal:	Why don't you go to the shopping centre? It's a good place to hang out.
Billy:	That's a good idea, thanks.
Krystal:	We're going there now. Do you want to come?
Billy:	Yeah, why not? OK!

You're kidding, right?
It's a good place to hang out.

OUT of **class**

1 Krystal and Amy meet a new neighbour. In pairs, say what questions you think they ask him.

What's your name?

2 **5.4** 2.51 Watch or listen to Part 1. Complete the information. What questions do the girls ask?

1 **Name:** *Billy Smith*   3 **Age:** _____
2 **Place of birth:** _____   4 **Birthday:** _____

3 5.5 2.52 Watch or listen to Part 2. Which place is Billy going to visit today?

4 2.53 In pairs, complete the dialogues below. Listen and check.

Speaking Advice

Asking for advice
- Where should I ...?
- What do you think I should ...?
- Can you give me some advice about ...?

Giving advice
- You should/shouldn't ...
- Why don't you ...?
- I think/don't think you should ...

Accepting advice
- That's a good idea.
- Thanks for the advice.

Rejecting advice
- That's a terrible idea!
- I don't think that's a good idea.

1 Amy: You ¹*shouldn't* argue with Peter. He gets angry very easily.
  Billy: Thanks ²_____ the advice, Amy.
2 Billy: Can you give me some ¹_____ about how to do better in French?
Teacher: I think you ²_____ do extra homework.
  Billy: That's a good ³_____ . Thanks.
3 Dad: I don't think you ¹_____ stay in bed so late. Why ²_____ you help me wash the car?
  Billy: That's a ³_____ idea! You ⁴_____ take it to the car wash.

5 In groups, write advice for a new student in your town. Use the ideas below to help you.

> how to get to school
> people to hang out with
> clothes to wear/not to wear at school
> places to go to/to avoid   things to do/not to do

You should walk to school. It's not far.

6 Work in pairs. Imagine you are new in town. Ask for advice and respond to the advice you get. Use your ideas from Exercise 5 and the Speaking box to help you.

Where should I meet friends after school?

I can write a personal email.

1 In pairs, ask and answer the questions.

1 How often do you write emails?

2 Who do you write emails to?

2 Read the email. Who wrote it and what is his/her big news?

3 Underline the phrases which are in the email.

Writing	A personal email describing a place

❶ Greeting
Hello/Hi

❷ Ask for/Give news
How are you?/How are things?
I hope you're well.
Everything's fine here./We're all well.
Guess what!/Big news!

❸ Describe the place
The town is called ...
It's in the south of England/near .../not far from ...
It's very big/quite small.
It seems nice/isn't very interesting.
There's a great park./There are some cool shops.
The flat/house isn't very big/modern.
It's on the seventh floor.
It's in a quiet street.

❹ Close your email
It's time to finish.
I have to go now because ...

❺ Closing phrase
See you!/Cheers!/Best wishes,/Love,/
All the best,/Take care!

From: billysmith321@jmail.com
To: coolcal99@jmail.com
Subject: big news!

❶ Hi Callum,

❷ How are things? I hope you're well and that your dad is out of hospital now. Big news! My dad changed jobs so last week we moved to a new flat in a new town!

❸ The town is called Harlow Mill. It's in the south of England, not far from London. It's quite small (about 40,000 people) but it seems nice. There's a canal, a great park and a really cool shopping centre. The flat isn't very big but it's bright and modern. It's on the seventh floor so there's a great view over the park from the living room.

❹ I have to go now because I'm going for a walk along the canal with a girl that I met yesterday! Her name is Krystal and she lives in the flat next door!

❺ All the best,
Billy

4 Find these words in the email. How do you say them in your language? Use them to complete the sentences below.

and ~~but~~ because so

1 My town isn't very big **but** there are lots of things to do.

2 We live in Canada _____ we get a lot of snow in winter.

3 I can walk to school _____ it isn't far.

4 I like the park _____ I like the canal too.

Writing Time

5 Imagine you moved to your home town last week. Write an email to tell your friend about the town:

❶ ❷ greet your friend, ask for and give news

❸ describe the place

❹ ❺ close the email

Use Billy's email and the Writing box to help you.

Connect your ideas with linking words (*and, but, because, so*).	**Watch OUT!**

above /əˈbʌv/ prep
armchair /ˈɑːmtʃeə, ˌɑːmˈtʃeə/ n
art gallery /ɑːt ˈɡæləri/ n
attic /ˈætɪk/ n
balcony /ˈbælkəni/ n
bath /bɑːθ/ n
bathroom /ˈbɑːθrʊm, -ruːm/ n
bed /bed/ n
bedroom /ˈbedrʊm, -ruːm/ n
bedside table /ˈbedsaɪd ˈteɪbəl/ n
behind /bɪˈhaɪnd/ prep
between /bɪˈtwiːn/ prep
bidet /ˈbiːdeɪ/ n
bright /braɪt/ adj
building /ˈbɪldɪŋ/ n
café /ˈkæfeɪ/ n
canal /kəˈnæl/ n
capital city /ˈkæpətl ˈsɪti/ n
carpet /ˈkɑːpət, ˈkɑːpɪt/ n
castle /ˈkɑːsəl/ n
ceiling /ˈsiːlɪŋ/ n
chair /tʃeə/ n
chimney /ˈtʃɪmni/ n
church /tʃɜːtʃ/ n
cinema /ˈsɪnəmə, ˈsɪnɪmə/ n
city /ˈsɪti/ n
coffee table /ˈkɒfi ˈteɪbəl/ n
cooker /ˈkʊkə/ n
corridor /ˈkɒrədɔː, ˈkɒrɪdɔː/ n
cosy /ˈkəʊzi/ adj
countryside /ˈkʌntrisaɪd/ n
cupboard /ˈkʌbəd/ n
curtains /ˈkɜːtənz/ n

dark /dɑːk/ adj
desk /desk/ n
estate /ɪˈsteɪt/ n
fantastic /fænˈtæstɪk/ adj
fireplace /ˈfaɪəpleɪs/ n
flat /flæt/ n
floor /flɔː/ n
fridge /frɪdʒ/ n
furniture /ˈfɜːnɪtʃə/ n
garden /ˈɡɑːdn/ n
hall /hɔːl/ n
hotel /həʊˈtel/ n
in /ɪn/ prep
in front of /ɪn frʌnt əv/ prep
kitchen /ˈkɪtʃən, ˈkɪtʃɪn/ n
lamp /læmp/ n
large /lɑːdʒ/ adj
library /ˈlaɪbrəri, -bri/ n
light /laɪt/ adj
living room /ˈlɪvɪŋ ruːm/ n
messy /ˈmesi/ adj
mirror /ˈmɪrə/ n
modern /ˈmɒdn/ adj
museum /mjuːˈzɪəm/ n
narrow /ˈnærəʊ/ adj
near /nɪə/ prep
neighbour /ˈneɪbə/ n
next to /ˈnekst tə/ prep
old-fashioned /ˌəʊld ˈfæʃənd/ adj
on /ɒn/ prep
opposite /ˈɒpəzət, ˈɒpəzɪt/ prep
oven /ˈʌvən/ n
painting /ˈpeɪntɪŋ/ n
park /pɑːk/ n

police station /pəˈliːs ˈsteɪʃən/ n
post office /pəʊst ˈɒfəs/ n
public transport /ˈpʌblɪk ˈtrænspɔːt/ n
reasonable /ˈriːzənəbəl/ adj
relaxing /rɪˈlæksɪŋ/ adj
roof /ruːf/ n
room /ruːm, rʊm/ n
round /raʊnd/ adj
rug /rʌɡ/ n
shopping centre /ˈʃɒpɪŋ ˈsentə/ n
shower /ˈʃaʊə/ n
sink /sɪŋk/ n
small /smɔːl/ adj
sofa /ˈsəʊfə/ n
spacious /ˈspeɪʃəs/ adj
station /ˈsteɪʃən/ n
street /striːt/ n
strict /strɪkt/ adj
switch /swɪtʃ/ n
table /ˈteɪbəl/ n
tap /tæp/ n
tidy /ˈtaɪdi/ adj
toilet /ˈtɔɪlət, ˈtɔɪlɪt/ n
tourist information centre /ˈtʊərəst ˌɪnfəˈmeɪʃən ˈsentə/ n
town /taʊn/ n
town centre /taʊn ˈsentə/ n
town hall /taʊn hɔːl/ n
traffic /ˈtræfɪk/ n
uncomfortable /ʌnˈkʌmftəbəl, -ˈkʌmfət-/ adj
under /ˈʌndə/ prep

upstairs /ˌʌpˈsteəz/ adv
view (of/over sth) /ˈvjuː/ n
village /ˈvɪlɪdʒ/ n
wall /wɔːl/ n
wardrobe /ˈwɔːdrəʊb/ n
washbasin /ˈwɒʃˌbeɪsən/ n
wide /waɪd/ adj
window /ˈwɪndəʊ/ n

WORD FRIENDS

clear the table
do the cooking
do the housework
do the ironing
do the shopping
dry the dishes
hang out with someone
listen carefully
live next door
load the dishwasher/the washing machine
make your bed
move to a new flat/house/town
set the table
speak quietly
stay out late
stay up late
sweep the floor
switch on a lamp/the light on
take the rubbish out
tidy your room
vacuum the floor
wash the car
wash the dishes

VOCABULARY IN ACTION

1 Use the wordlist to find:

1 six things that you usually find in a bathroom: *mirror, ...*
2 six things that you usually find in a kitchen:
3 eight things that you can find in different rooms:
4 ten public places that are in your town/city:

2 Use the letters to write the words connected with the categories below.

Furniture: h a m i c r a r – *armchair*, e c t a r p – _____, s k e d – _____

Rooms: n i c k e t h – _____, c i t a t – _____, d r e b o m o – _____

City places: s u m e m u – _____, t a n o t s i – _____, s l e c a t – _____

Adjectives: r a k d – _____, s c o y – _____

3 Complete the Word Friends. In pairs, say which things you usually do and when.

1 _sweep_ the floor
2 _____ out late
3 _____ quietly
4 _____ your room
5 _____ out with friends in the park
6 _____ the table
7 _____ the light on

I usually sweep the floor on Wednesdays.

4 🔊 2.54 **PRONUNCIATION** In pairs, find one word in each group that is different from the others. Use the underlined letters to help you. Listen, check and repeat.

1 <u>o</u>ven   <u>u</u>pstairs   <u>u</u>nder   l<u>a</u>rge
2 c<u>a</u>r   r<u>u</u>bbish   c<u>a</u>stle   b<u>a</u>th
3 r<u>u</u>g   p<u>a</u>rk   ab<u>o</u>ve   unc<u>o</u>mfortable
4 sm<u>a</u>ll   fl<u>oo</u>r   w<u>a</u>ll   c<u>o</u>ffee table

Revision

1 Complete the words in the sentences. In pairs, make the sentences true for you.

1 I don't like cities. I prefer the
   c o u n t r y s i d e.
2 I always put my clothes in the
   w _ _ _ _ _ _ _ _.
3 I don't look at myself in the **m _ _ _ _ _ _**
   very often.
4 We haven't got a bath in our bathroom.
   We have a **s _ _ _ _ _ _**.
5 **P _ _ _ _ _ t _ _ _ _ _ _ _ _ _** is expensive
   here so people go by car.
6 The **c _ _ _ _ _ _ _ c _ _ _ _** of my favourite
   country is Dublin.
7 There's one **t _ _ _** for water in our kitchen
   s _ _ _.
8 I often borrow books from the
   l _ _ _ _ _ _.
9 I can't sleep with the **l _ _ _ _** on. So
   I switch it off.

*I don't like the countryside. I prefer city life.
What about you?*

2 Complete the questions with the opposites of the underlined words. In pairs, ask and answer the questions.

1 Is your bedroom <u>messy</u> or <u>tidy</u>?
2 Are the corridors in your school <u>narrow</u> or
   _____?
3 Is your kitchen <u>dark</u> or _____?
4 Is your living room <u>cosy</u> or _____?
5 Do you live in a _____ or big town?
6 Do you prefer <u>modern</u> or _____ buildings?
7 What's on the wall <u>above</u> your bed? And
   what do you keep _____ your bed?

3 Complete the text with one word in each gap. Then write sentences to say what housework from the text you did and didn't do last week.

First, I ¹<u>made</u> my bed. Then I set the ²_____
for breakfast. After eating, I ³_____ the table
and ⁴_____ the dishes. I didn't ⁵_____ the
dishes, I left them in the sink. After that I
loaded the ⁶_____ machine and vacuumed
the ⁷_____. After lunch I did the ⁸_____ at the
supermarket and then I ⁹_____ the ironing. I
don't enjoy doing ¹⁰_____ housework so my
parents were really surprised!

I made my bed every day last week. I didn't ...

4 Complete the questions with the correct form of the words in brackets. In pairs, ask and answer the questions.

1 Do you work very <u>hard</u> (hard) at school?
2 Do you eat _____ (quick) or _____ (slow)?
3 Did you get up _____ (early) last Sunday?
4 Did you sleep _____ (good) or _____ (bad) last
   night?
5 Do you sometimes get up really _____ (late)?
6 Do you usually get Maths problems _____ (right)
   or _____ (wrong)?
7 Do you write text messages _____ (careful)?

5 Choose the correct option.

Dear Mum and Dad,

You ⟨can⟩/ have to come into my room but you
²have to / mustn't knock first.
You ³don't have to / mustn't touch my computer
without permission.
You ⁴can't / have to try to remember my friends' names.
You ⁵can't / have to stay in my room when my friends
are here.
You ⁶don't have to / mustn't bring us drinks but you
⁷can / can't if you like.
You ⁸have to / mustn't ask me to do the housework
when I've got homework.

Love, Teri

PS ⁹Can you / Do you have to call me 'baby' in front of
my friends? It's embarrassing!

6 In pairs, role play the situations. Student A, look below. Student B, look at page 129.

Student A

1 You want to change the decoration in your
   bedroom. Ask Student B for advice. Then accept
   or reject the advice.
2 Give Student B advice for the surprise party he/
   she wants to organise. If he/she rejects your
   ideas, give him/her different advice.

7 🔊 2.55 Listen, then listen again and write down what you hear.

CULTURE

Why are there houses on stilts?

HOUSES AROUND THE WORLD

In the UK, people often live in brick houses with two floors and a garden. In the USA and Australia, people's houses are often made of wood from trees. In some countries, the houses are very different. Is there a reason for this?

Underground houses

People in North Africa and southern Europe started to live in underground houses a long time ago, in the seventh century. Underground houses kept them safe from enemies – people who wanted to hurt them – and the hot sun. Today in Adelaide, South Australia, some people still live in underground houses that miners (people who work underground) made a hundred years ago. Adelaide can get very hot and these houses are nice and cool.

Snow houses

In some very cold parts of the world like the Arctic, Alaska and Greenland, people build their houses from blocks of snow. It's strange but inside the snow walls the temperature can be fifteen degrees when outside it's minus forty!

Stilt houses

In some parts of Asia, South America and West Africa, people live in stilt houses. The stilts lift the houses above the ground or the water. This protects the houses when the sea level rises in bad weather. Sometimes the sea gets very high. On land, the stilts stop animals, like rats and mice, getting into the house. And over or near the water, the stilts stop dangerous animals, like crocodiles.

People everywhere build houses to protect them from different dangers, like the weather, enemies and animals. It seems that the shape and the size of our houses depends on what we need.

GLOSSARY
brick (n) a hard block of material for building walls, houses
enemy (n) someone who wants to harm you
protect (v) to keep something safe
stilt (n) a long stick made of wood

EXPLORE

1 In pairs, discuss the questions.

1 What sort of house do you live in?
2 Are there some unusual houses in your country?
3 Why do you think houses aren't the same in every country?

2 Read the article and match the houses from the text 1–3 with photos A–C.

1 ☐ underground house
2 ☐ snow house
3 ☐ stilt house

3 Read the article again and answer the questions.

Which house:
1 is good when the weather is cold?
2 is good when the weather is hot?
3 is safe from animals?
4 is good for rainy and stormy weather?

4 How do houses in your country protect people from the cold and the heat?

EXPLORE MORE

5 You are going to watch part of a BBC programme about room makeovers. Read an advert for the programme. Do you have programmes like this in your country? Do you watch them?

I want my own room!

Every week the team at *I want my own room!* help kids to design the room of their dreams.

EXPLORE MORE

6 ▶ 5.6 Watch Part 1 of the video. In pairs, answer the questions.

1 What is Freya's hobby?
2 What is Hattie's hobby?
3 What is their mum's hobby?
4 Why do the girls want to change their room?
5 What is Michelle's job?

7 What would you like to change about *your* room?

8 ▶ 5.7 Watch Part 2 of the video. Mark the sentences T (true) or F (false).

1 ☐ The girls paint pictures for the walls.
2 ☐ Their mum throws away everything in the front room.
3 ☐ The girls put photographs on the wallpaper.

9 ▶ 5.8 Watch Part 3 of the video. Tick (✓) things 1–9 which are not in the room. Where are the other things?

1 ☐ a blue cupboard
2 ☐ a red butterfly
3 ☐ an orange wardrobe
4 ☐ a pink blind
5 ☐ a pink and red doorstop
6 ☐ a purple rug
7 ☐ a yellow sofa bed
8 ☐ some black and white cushions
9 ☐ a blue chair

10 In pairs, discuss the questions.

1 What's your favourite thing in the room?
2 What do you not like? Why?

YOU EXPLORE

11 **CULTURE PROJECT** In small groups, prepare a presentation about unusual buildings.

1 Use the internet to research two unusual buildings in your country.
2 Find out why people built them like this.
3 Write a short script and include some photos and videos.
4 Share it with your class.

6

Take care

6.1

VOCABULARY The body

I can talk about the body, injuries and keeping fit.

VOCABULARY
Parts of the body | Accidents and injuries | Keeping fit | Snacks | Sleep | Symptoms and illnesses

GRAMMAR
Countable and uncountable nouns | Quantifiers | Past Continuous and Past Simple | Phrasal verbs

Grammar: What's in your lunch?

Speaking: What's the matter?

BBC Culture: Unusual sports

Workbook p. 77

BBC VOX POPS ▶
EXAM TIME 2 > p. 134

Our amazing bodies!

9

5

8

6

1 *lips*

2

7

4

3

○ It takes seven seconds for food to get from your mouth to your **stomach** – even when you stand on your head!

○ A typical man grows about ten metres of **beard** in his lifetime.

○ In your lifetime, you lose about eighteen kilograms of **skin**.

○ A ballet dancer can stand on her big toe and carry 150 kilograms at the same time.

○ Your **heart** beats about three billion times in your lifetime.

○ Your nose and ears grow all the time!

○ The **muscles** in your eyes are very hard-working – they move about 100,000 times a day.

○ A rugby player uses about 24,000 calories in a game of rugby – that's the energy you get from 200 large bananas!

○ Your **brain** is 80 percent water – that's why it's important to drink a lot of water!

○ A quarter of your **bones** are in your feet.

1 | I KNOW! | In pairs, how many parts of the body can you name in a minute?

2 | I KNOW! | In pairs, use the letters to write the names of the parts of the body.

1 r a m *arm*   5 y e e   9 a r e
2 h o t u m   6 o s e n   10 a r h i
3 t e t e h   7 f o t o   11 c a b k
4 g e l   8 h a d e   12 d a h n

3 🔊 3.01 Match the words below with the parts of the body 1–9 in the photos on page 70. Listen and check.

Vocabulary	Parts of the body

ankle   elbow   eyebrow   finger   knee   lips
neck   shoulder   toes

4 🔊 3.02 Read the information in *Our Amazing Bodies* on page 70 and follow the instructions.

1 Listen and repeat the highlighted words. How do you say them in your language?
2 Which facts do you find interesting?

5 Complete the sentences with the correct form of the words from the text and Exercises 2 and 3.

1 An adult usually has thirty-two *teeth*.
2 The _____ is a symbol of love.
3 _____ can be straight, wavy or curly.
4 Yoga exercises are great for your stomach _____ .
5 I have to be careful in sunny weather – my _____ burns very easily.
6 I never work at my desk – I always sit with my laptop on my _____ .

6 🔊 3.03 Look at the picture and say what you can see. Listen and answer the questions.

1 What type of exercise do Ellen and Owen do?
2 Why are they in the hospital?

7 🔊 3.03 | WORD FRIENDS | Listen again. Choose the correct option.

1 This morning Ellen **hurt** (her back)/ her knee.
2 Last week she fell and **twisted** her knee / her ankle.
3 Owen says it's easy to **break** your arm / your leg when you play rugby.
4 Owen **cut** his knee / his finger.

8 In pairs, say the last time you had one of the injuries from Exercise 7.

A: *I broke my leg on a skiing holiday two years ago.*
B: *I broke my arm when I was a child.*

9 🔊 3.04 Listen and decide who trains harder – Owen or Ellen?

10 🔊 3.04 | WORD FRIENDS | Listen again. Complete the sentences with the words below.

	do (3x) have go (3x) ~~keep~~ play

1 It's important for me to *keep* fit.
2 I _____ **rugby (football/basketball)** every week.
3 I _____ **exercises** at home every morning.
4 I _____ **to the gym** regularly.
5 I _____ **weight training**.
6 I _____ **running (cycling)**.
7 I _____ **yoga (Tai chi)**.
8 I _____ **fitness classes (PE lessons)** every day/week.
9 I _____ **swimming** once a week.

11 In pairs, change the sentences in Exercise 10 to make them true for you.

And Y?U

I don't do exercises at home but I go to the gym once a week.

I can talk about quantities of food.

VIDEO **WHAT'S IN YOUR LUNCH?**

Billy: Ah lunchtime! I'm starving!

Amy: Some crisps and a <u>banana</u>! You never have any healthy food for lunch, some <u>sandwiches</u>, some <u>salad</u> or some <u>soup</u>.

Billy: Bananas are healthy! I don't have any time to make sandwiches – I've always got too many things to do before school!

Amy: Nonsense! It doesn't take much time to make a nice lunch! Today I've got some chicken sandwiches and some delicious Thai soup.

Billy: Amy, how many sandwiches have you got today? I haven't got much food.

Amy: Three! And I want them all! But I've got a lot of soup. Do you want some?

Billy: Yes! Thanks!

Amy: Help yourself. Careful, it's hot … Billy! Are you OK?

I'm starving! *Help yourself.*	**O**UT of **class**

1 🔊 3.05 **CLASS VOTE** Which snacks do you usually eat at school?

Vocabulary	Snacks
cake crisps chocolate bars fruit hamburgers hot dogs nuts salad sandwiches soup	

I sometimes eat crisps but I never eat cake.

2 ▶ 6.1 🔊 3.06 **Describe the photo. Watch or listen. Answer the questions.**

1 Are Billy's lunches usually healthy?
2 What is Amy having for lunch today?

3 **I KNOW!** In pairs, say if the underlined words in the dialogue are countable or uncountable. Then think of more countable and uncountable items of food.

4 Find more quantifiers with nouns in the dialogue.

Grammar	**Quantifiers**
Countable	**Uncountable**
some sandwiches a lot of vegetables too many chips	some salad a lot of fresh fruit too much chocolate
not many things not any sweets	not much time not any bread
how many burgers?	how much salad?

GRAMMAR TIME PAGE 123

5 **Look at what Amy and Billy ate for lunch in one week. Complete the sentences with quantifiers. There is often more than one possible answer.**

Amy – week 1	Billy – week 1
2 apples, 3 kiwi fruit, 4 bananas, 1 orange, 0 chocolate bars, 10 salami sandwiches	1 banana, 7 chocolate bars, 5 packets of crisps, 0 sandwiches

- Amy eats ¹*a lot of* fruit. She doesn't eat ²_____ chocolate bars. She doesn't eat ³_____ oranges.
- Billy eats ⁴_____ chocolate. He doesn't eat ⁵_____ fruit. He doesn't eat ⁶_____ sandwiches.

6 Cross out the incorrect quantifier in each sentence.

1 Adam doesn't eat *any / much / ~~many~~* meat.
2 *A lot of / Some / Too much* salt is bad for you.
3 There's *any / some / too much* sugar in my tea – it's really sweet!
4 Is there *any / many / much* bread on the table?
5 Of course you're not hungry. You ate *how many / a lot of / too many* cakes!
6 There aren't *any / many / some* vegetarian things on the menu here.

7 **In pairs, say how much of these things you eat and drink.**

tea   coffee   water   fruit juice   cola meat   fruit   vegetables   snacks   sweets

I don't drink much coffee. What about you?

I can find specific detail in a text and talk about sleeping habits.

1 CLASS VOTE Do you agree with statements a–c?

a It's hard to get up in the morning.
b I sleep more than my parents.
c I never want to go to bed at 11.00 p.m.

2 🔊 3.07 Read the text. What's Polly's advice a) for weekdays, b) for the weekend?

3 Read the text again. Choose the correct answers.

1 Karl says that last night he fell asleep
  a very quickly.
  (b) after his parents.
  c before his parents.

2 Karl's mother woke him up last Saturday because
  a she needed his help.
  b he wanted to get up early.
  c she thinks it's wrong to stay in bed late.

3 Karl is writing to Polly because
  a he wants to get up early.
  b he disagrees with his parents.
  c he can't sleep.

4 Polly says
  a teenagers need a lot of sleep.
  b adults need a lot of sleep.
  c adults think teenagers are lazy.

5 Teens like staying up late and getting up late because
  a they make hormones differently from adults.
  b they watch too many TV programmes.
  c it's better for their health.

4 WORD FRIENDS Look at the highlighted phrases in the text and complete the Word Friends.

feel tired/¹*sleepy*	get/wake up ⁵_____/late
fall ²_____	sleep ⁶_____/badly
get ³_____ for bed	have a dream
go to ⁴_____/sleep	stay in bed/up ⁷_____

5 Read the Sleep Quiz and choose the correct option.

SLEEP QUIZ

1 What time did you *go)/sleep* to bed last night?
2 What time did you *get / stay* up last Saturday morning?
3 What do you do when you can't *fall / wake* asleep?
4 What do you do to help you *go / wake* up early?
5 How many hours do you usually *fall / sleep* at night?
6 Do you sometimes *feel / stay* up after midnight?
7 Do you ever *feel / go* sleepy in class?
8 Do you often *have / sleep* bad dreams?

Dear Polly,
Last night at ten o'clock I was online when my dad told me to get ready for bed. Two hours later I was in bed with my eyes open. I didn't feel sleepy so I got up. My parents were on the sofa. They always fall asleep in front of the TV. They don't go to bed when they are sleepy so why do I have to go to bed when I'm not sleepy? Then last Saturday my mum woke me up at 11.00 a.m. She says I'm lazy but that's not fair. I always feel tired in the morning but I get up early and work hard all week so why can't I stay in bed at the weekend?

Karl, 15

Hi Karl,
Your parents don't want you to stay up late because they think you need to sleep. And they're right! Teenagers need a lot of sleep. How much? That depends on the person but usually about nine hours a night – that's more than adults!

But it's difficult for teens to wake up early and to go to sleep early. Often they feel lively at night when adults feel sleepy. That's because teenagers' brains produce melatonin* later in the day. When you see bright lights, your brain stops making melatonin. That means you can't sleep well. So during the school week you shouldn't surf the internet or watch too many TV programmes before bedtime. It's better to read or listen to music. And during the day don't drink too much tea or coffee.

Sleep is important for our health. If you don't get much sleep, your memory and concentration suffer. So try to go to bed early during the week but tell your parents you need to stay in bed late at weekends.

Polly
*a hormone which makes you sleepy

6 🔊 3.08 Listen and match speakers A–D with questions from the Sleep Quiz in Exercise 5.

☐ Speaker A   ☐ Speaker C
☐ Speaker B   ☐ Speaker D

7 [VOX POPS ▶ 6.2] In groups, do the Sleep Quiz in Exercise 5. Use the Word Friends in Exercise 4 to help you.

And YOU

A: *What time did you go to bed last night?*
B: *I went to bed early because …*

I can talk about an event in the past and what was happening around it.

ACCIDENTS!

We asked some people to describe accidents they had.
What were you doing when the accident happened?

WAYNE
Yesterday afternoon I was painting the ceiling. My little brother was holding the ladder but he wasn't paying attention.
While I was coming down, the ladder moved and I fell.
I cut my hand, hurt my back and broke my arm.
It was really painful.

 STEPHANIE
My basketball team was playing a match.
We weren't playing well and the other team was really good. They were winning 34–21 when I got the ball. Unfortunately, when I was trying to score a basket, I twisted my ankle and fell. I hit my head and broke my nose. I was lucky I didn't break my neck.

1 What's happening in the photo? Why do you think it's happening?

2 🔊 3.09 Read the text to check your ideas. Then say what happened to Wayne and Stephanie.
Wayne fell off a ladder. He cut …

3 Find more examples of the Past Continuous in the text.

Grammar	Past Continuous and Past Simple
+	–
I was playing.	I wasn't running.
They were playing.	They weren't running.
?	
Were you playing?	Yes, I was./No, I wasn't.
Were they playing?	Yes, they were./No, they weren't.
What was she doing yesterday at 5 p.m.?	

Past Continuous and Past Simple
While/When I was coming down the ladder, I fell.
I was coming down the ladder when I fell.

GRAMMAR TIME   PAGE 124

4 In pairs, ask and answer the questions.
What were you doing …
- at 8.00 p.m. last Friday?
- at 6.00 a.m. this morning?
- last week at this time?
- an hour ago?
- on Sunday at 12.30?
- 24 hours ago?

A: *What were you doing at 8.00 p.m. last Friday?*
B: *I was watching a film. What about you?*

5 Choose the correct option.
1 My cousin (had)/ was having an accident when he rode / was riding a motorbike.
2 My mum hit / was hitting her head when she got / was getting into the car.
3 While my dad played / was playing tennis, he hurt / was hurting his back.
4 When we danced / were dancing, we fell / were falling.
5 I twisted / was twisting my ankle when I ran / was running to school.

6 🔊 3.10 Complete the dialogue with the correct form of the verbs in brackets. Listen and check.

A: What ¹*were you doing* (you/do) when the accident ²_____ (happen)?
B: I ³_____ (drive) my kids to school when they ⁴_____ (begin) to shout. They ⁵_____ (make) a lot of noise so I ⁶_____ (tell) them to be quiet. I ⁷_____ (not look) at the road so I ⁸_____ (not see) the dog. It ⁹_____ (cross) the road. I ¹⁰_____ (drive) into a tree. Fortunately, nobody was hurt.

7 [VOX POPS ▶ 6.3] **Work in groups.** **Describe an accident you had when you were younger. Use the questions below to help you.**
1 How old were you?
2 What were you doing when the accident happened?
3 What happened after that?
4 Were you hurt?

I was ten years old. I was walking to school when …

I can identify specific detail in a conversation and talk about illnesses.

1 Look at the picture. Why is tomorrow a big day for Bridgeton United?

'Bridgeton United five-a-side football team. We're playing in the cup final tomorrow. Come and support us!'

2 🔊 **3.11** How do you say the phrases below in your language?

Vocabulary	Symptoms and illnesses

Symptoms
- feel sick/ill
- have a headache/a stomachache/ a sore throat/a high temperature/a cough
- cough/sneeze

Illnesses
- I've got hay fever/the flu/a cold/a food allergy.

3 🔊 **3.12** What symptoms have the players in the picture got? Complete the sentences. Then listen to Jerry and check.

1 Nathan is *sneezing*.
2 James has got a _____ .
3 Ben has got a _____ throat and a high _____ .
4 Chris has got a _____ .

4 In pairs, say what the symptoms are for these illnesses.

> a cold   hay fever   the flu

When you have a cold, you sneeze a lot and ...

5 Use the Vocabulary box to complete the sentences.

1 If you *sneeze* when you're near flowers, maybe you have _____ _____ .
2 You've got a very _____ _____ – 40° Celsius! I think you have the _____ .
3 I ate too much and now I have a _____ .
4 Please cover your mouth when you _____ !
5 I was shouting and now I've got a _____ _____ .

6 🔊 **3.13** In pairs, answer the questions.

1 Why couldn't Ben play?
2 Why was Nathan sneezing?
3 Why did James have a stomachache?
4 Why couldn't Chris play?
5 What did Tom get at the end?

7 🔊 **3.14** Listen to Jerry talking to a friend about the football match. Choose the correct answers.

1 They played the match on
   (a) Wednesday. b Saturday. c Sunday.
2 While Jerry was visiting friends, he got
   a a cold.   b the flu.
   c hay fever.
3 On the day of the match, Jerry felt
   a great.   b ill.
   c very well.
4 Ben didn't finish the match because he
   a twisted his ankle. b broke his leg.
   c hurt his back.
5 Jerry's team won the match
   a 2–1.   b 3–1.   c 3–2.

8 In pairs, ask and answer the questions.

- How often do you have a cold or the flu?
- Are you allergic to anything?
- What kind of things can give you a headache?

I have a cold once or twice a year.

I can talk about feeling ill and ask about how someone is feeling.

VIDEO **WHAT'S THE MATTER? (Part 1)**

Nurse: William! What's the matter?

Billy: I feel terrible.

Nurse: Mmm, well you haven't got a high temperature. Are you feeling sick?

Billy: No, I'm not. I've got a really bad stomachache.

Nurse: Well, when did you start feeling ill?

Billy: Just after lunch.

Nurse: I see. What did you have for lunch?

Billy: Just the usual – some crisps and a banana. Oh, hold on, and some of Amy's Thai soup …

Nurse: Ah! You're probably allergic to something. Here, have some water. You should drink a lot of water. And perhaps you should make an appointment with your doctor immediately … after school. OK! I think you can go back to class now.

Billy: Oh!

I see. *Just the usual.*	**O**UT of class

1 In pairs, look at the photo. What do you think is happening?

2 6.4 3.15 Watch or listen to Part 1. Why did Billy go to see the school nurse?

3 6.5 3.16 Watch or listen to Part 2. What was Billy's problem?

4 Underline the words and phrases from the dialogue.

Speaking	Health and illness

Asking what the problem is
- What's the matter?/What's wrong?
- How are you feeling?

Talking about symptoms
- I feel sick/ill/terrible.
- I've got a stomachache/a headache/toothache/ a temperature/a sore throat/a cold/the flu.
- My leg/back hurts.

Advice
- Sit down.
- Have some water.
- You should lie down/stay in bed/make an appointment with the doctor/go to hospital.
- You should take an aspirin/a tablet/some medicine.

5 3.17 In pairs, complete the dialogues with one word in each gap. Listen and check.

1 A: What's the _matter_?
  B: I've got a temperature.
  A: I think you should _____ down.
2 A: _____'s wrong?
  B: My leg hurts. Perhaps it's broken.
  A: I think you _____ go to hospital.
3 A: _____ are you feeling?
  B: I've got a really sore throat.
  A: You should make an _____ with the doctor.

6 Suggest what the people should do. Use the Speaking box to help you.

1 Billy's got flu. *Billy should take an aspirin.*
2 Lee's got hay fever.
3 Amy's tooth hurts.
4 Krystal's stomach hurts.
5 Perhaps Ruby's got a broken arm.

7 In pairs, follow the instructions. Use the Speaking box and Exercise 5 to help you.

1 **Student A** – ask how Student B is feeling. Listen and give advice.
2 **Student B** – you feel ill. Tell Student A your symptoms.
3 Change roles.

ENGLISH IN USE Phrasal verbs

I can use phrasal verbs to talk about health.

I'm Eric. Last week I went camping with my sister, Effie. Unfortunately, everything went wrong. First, we left our food in the sun and it went off.

Then I picked up an illness. I felt terrible so we decided to go home.

We got a lift from a farmer on a tractor. But while we were going home, my sister said it was all my fault and we fell out.

1 Look at the cartoons. Which version, A or B, matches the text? Read the information about phrasal verbs to check your answers.

Language	Phrasal verbs

Phrasal verbs are verbs with two parts, e.g. *pick + up*.
Sometimes the meaning of phrasal verbs is clear from the words in them, e.g. *pick up a pencil*.
But often the meaning is not clear:
Eric picked up an illness. = He became ill.
The food went off. = It became bad.
Eric and Effie fell out. = They had an argument.

2 Match the phrasal verbs in sentences 1–9 with meanings a–i.

1 [b] If you want to find out your perfect weight, consult our website.
2 ☐ The doctor told me to take up a sport.
3 ☐ My dad wants to give up smoking.
4 ☐ A: What's going on? B: Nothing much.
5 ☐ Can you give me £10 to top up my phone, please, mum?
6 ☐ Do you get on with your brother?
7 ☐ We often hang out at the shopping centre.
8 ☐ Use your phone to check out what's on at the cinema.
9 ☐ When I was ill, my gran looked after me.

a stop doing something
b discover, learn
c start a hobby/ activity
d have a good relationship
e put money in
f happen
g see, read, consult
h spend time
i take care of

3 🔊 3.18 Complete the text with one word in each gap. Listen and check.

www.dansblog.com

21 March
'It's not easy to keep fit but I know what to do. I should ¹**look** after my body. I shouldn't hang ²_____ at the shops every day. I should go to a gym or take ³_____ a sport. I should ⁴_____ up 'energy' drinks – they aren't good for you. I shouldn't eat fast food. But yesterday I saw a newspaper headline. It said 'Chocolate is good for you!' I checked ⁵_____ the article and I ⁶_____ out some excellent news. Dark chocolate is good for your health. I love dark chocolate.'
Comments (5)

4 🔊 3.19 Use the definitions in brackets to complete the sentences with phrasal verbs. Listen and check.

1 Could you *give up* (stop) eating sweets?
2 What do you do to _____ (take care of) your body?
3 What sport or hobby would you like to _____ (start doing)?
4 How often do you _____ (spend time) in the park with your friends?
5 When you're ill, do you _____ (consult) your symptoms on the internet to _____ (learn) what illness you have?

5 In groups, ask and answer the questions in Exercise 4.

And YOU

A: *Could you give up eating sweets?*
B: *Yes, I could. And you?*

accident /ˈæksədənt, ˈæksɪdənt/ n
ankle /ˈæŋkəl/ n
(doctor's) appointment /ˌdɒktəz əˈpɔɪntmənt/ n
arm /ɑːm/ n
aspirin /ˈæsprən, ˈæsprɪn/ n
back /bæk/ n
beard /bɪəd/ n
body /ˈbɒdi/ n
bone /bəʊn/ n
brain /breɪn/ n
burn /bɜːn/ v
cake /keɪk/ n
calorie /ˈkæləri/ n
check out /tʃek aʊt/ v
chocolate bar /ˈtʃɒklət bɑː/ n
(sports) coach /ˌspɔːts ˈkəʊtʃ/ n
coffee /ˈkɒfi/ n
cola /ˈkəʊlə/ n
cold (illness) /kəʊld/ n
cough /kɒf/ n
cough /kɒf/ v
crisps /krɪsps/ n
delicious /dɪˈlɪʃəs/ adj
ear /ɪə/ n
elbow /ˈelbəʊ/ n
energy drink /ˈenədʒi drɪŋk/ n
exercise /ˈeksəsaɪz/ n
eye /aɪ/ n
eyebrow /ˈaɪbraʊ/ n
fall out /fɔːl aʊt/ v
find out /faɪnd aʊt/ v
finger /ˈfɪŋgə/ n

food allergy /fuːd ˈælədʒi/ n
foot (feet) /fʊt fiːt/ n
match (e.g. football) /ˈmætʃ/ n
fruit /fruːt/ n
fruit juice /fruːt dʒuːs/ n
get on with /get ɒn wɪð/ v
give up /gɪv ʌp/ v
go off /gəʊ ɒf/ v
go on (happen) /gəʊ ɒn/ v
gym /dʒɪm/ n
hair /heə/ n
hamburger /ˈhæmbɜːgə/ n
hand /hænd/ n
hang out /hæŋ aʊt/ v
hay fever /heɪ ˈfiːvə/ n
head /hed/ n
headache /ˈhedeɪk/ n
health /helθ/ n
healthy /ˈhelθi/ adj
heart /hɑːt/ n
hot dog /hɒt dɒg/ n
hurt /hɜːt/ v
illness /ˈɪlnəs, ˈɪlnɪs/ n
knee /niː/ n
leg /leg/ n
lips /lɪps/ n
look after /lʊk ˈɑːftə/ v
meat /miːt/ n
medicine /ˈmedsən/ n
menu /ˈmenjuː/ n
mouth /maʊθ/ n
muscle /ˈmʌsəl/ n
neck /nek/ n
nose /nəʊz/ n

nuts /nʌts/ n
pick up (illness) /pɪk ʌp/ v
salad /ˈsæləd/ n
salt /sɔːlt/ n
sandwich /ˈsænwɪdʒ/ n
shoulder /ˈʃəʊldə/ n
skin /skɪn/ n
sleepy /ˈsliːpi/ adj
snack /snæk/ n
sneeze /sniːz/ v
soup /suːp/ n
stomach /ˈstʌmək/ n
stomachache /ˈstʌməkˌeɪk/ n
sugar /ˈʃʊgə/ n
sweets /swiːts/ n
symptom /ˈsɪmptəm/ n
tablet /ˈtæblət, ˈtæblɪt/ n
take up /teɪk ʌp/ v
tea /tiː/ n
the flu /ðə fluː/ n
toe /təʊ/ n
tooth (teeth) /tuːθ tiːθ/ n
toothache /ˈtuːθeɪk/ n
train /treɪn/ v
vegetable /ˈvedʒtəbəl/ n
vegetarian /ˌvedʒəˈteəriən, ˌvedʒɪˈteəriən/ adj
water /ˈwɔːtə/ n

WORD FRIENDS

cut your knee/finger
do exercises
do yoga/Tai chi
do weight training
fall asleep

feel ill/sick sleepy/terrible/tired
get ready for bed
get up early/late
go running/ cycling/ swimming
go to bed/sleep
go to the gym
good/ bad for you
have an allergy/a cold/a cough/the flu/hay fever/a headache/
a high temperature/sore throat/ stomachache/ toothache
have a dream
have fitness classes/PE lessons
hit your head
hurt your hand/back
make an appointment (with the doctor)
pay attention to sth
play rugby/football/ basketball/tennis
ride a motorbike/bike
score a basket
sleep easily/well/badly
stay up (late)
stay in bed late
take a tablet/some medicine
twist your ankle/leg
wake up early/ late

VOCABULARY IN ACTION

1 Use the wordlist to find:

1 five things you can drink: *cola, …*
2 eight items of food or drink that are bad for you:
3 ten parts of the body that you always have two of:
4 three health problems ending with *-ache:*

2 Complete the phrasal verbs.

1 I often looked *after* my sister when she was little.
2 Sometimes we have terrible arguments and fall _____.
3 Don't eat that salad. I think it's starting to go _____!
4 At New Year I decided to take _____ swimming to keep fit.
5 I usually pick _____ colds from my brother.

3 Complete the sentences with the words below. In pairs, say which sentences are true for you.

| ~~fall~~ fever have ride sleep up

1 I sometimes *fall* asleep in class.
2 I _____ my bike to school every morning.
3 I usually _____ badly on the night before an exam.
4 I usually _____ a cold all winter!
5 I love staying _____ late on Friday night.
6 My family and I always get hay _____ in the early summer.

4 🔊 **3.20** **PRONUNCIATION** Listen to the words below and decide if you hear the underlined letter(s). Then listen again and repeat.

| asp<u>i</u>rin choc<u>o</u>late jui<u>c</u>e <u>k</u>nee mus<u>c</u>le san<u>d</u>wich temp<u>e</u>rature ti<u>r</u>ed vege<u>t</u>able

Revision

1 Write the correct word for each definition.

1 A bad one can wake you up! **d** _r e a m_

2 You do this when you have hay fever.
   s _ _ _ _ _ _

3 This can be high when you have the flu.
   t _ _ _ _ _ _ _ _ _

4 It can stop you eating some foods.
   a _ _ _ _ _ _

5 You take it when you're ill. **m** _ _ _ _ _ _ _ _

6 He/She looks after your teeth.
   d _ _ _ _ _ _

7 This can hurt when you eat too quickly.
   s _ _ _ _ _ _

8 Feeling well, not ill. **h** _ _ _ _ _ _

2 In pairs, read the text and choose the correct option. Do you have anyone in your family like Grandpa George?

Grandpa George never forgot that he was in the army for thirty years. He ¹*fell asleep /* woke up early at the same time every morning, ²*did / made* exercises and he was proud that he could still touch his ³*head / toes*, even when he was seventy. He had five golden rules: don't talk with food in your ⁴*beard / mouth*, don't put your ⁵*elbows / neck* on the table when you're eating, walk with your ⁶*fingers / shoulders* straight, brush your ⁷*hair / teeth* every morning and, most important of all, cut it every two weeks.

3 Complete the Word Friends in the text with the verbs below.

| cut   had (x2)   hit   hurt   ~~twisted~~

Our holiday in the mountains was a disaster. First of all, my mum ¹*twisted* her ankle when we were climbing a mountain – she couldn't walk for days. Granddad ² _____ his back from carrying a heavy rucksack. My sister ³ _____ a very bad stomachache after she ate a sheep's cheese pizza. My dad ⁴ _____ his head every time he stood up in the tent. I ⁵ _____ my finger when I was opening a can of soup. And finally my gran ⁶ _____ a sore throat from shouting at all of us!

4 Choose the correct option.

A: I'm so hungry! Is there anything to eat?
B: Well, we've got ¹*any /* some cheese.
A: Good! Have we got ²*any / some* bread?
B: No, we haven't got ³*any / some*. But we've got ⁴*any / some* eggs.
A: Excellent! How ⁵*many / much* eggs?
B: Four.
A: That's ⁶*not much / not many*!
B: But we've got ⁷*a lot of / any* potatoes.
A: Great! So we can have fried eggs and chips!
B: No, we can't. You need ⁸*a lot of / much* time to cook chips and we don't have ⁹*much / many* time. And you eat ¹⁰*too many / too much* chips! But we have ¹¹*a lot of / too many* vegetables so you can make us a nice vegetable omelette!

5 Complete the text with the Past Simple or the Past Continuous form of the verbs in brackets.

Yesterday I ¹*was studying* (study) in my room when suddenly I ² _____ (hear) a noise from the living room. I ³ _____ (run) into the room and saw that my dad ⁴ _____ (lie) on the floor.
'Are you OK?' I ⁵ _____ (ask) dad.
'My ankle hurts. I think I twisted it!'
'What ⁶ _____ (you/do) ?'
'I ⁷ _____ (look) for a book! I ⁸ _____ (stand) on a chair but I ⁹ _____ (not pay) attention and the chair moved and I fell. My shoulder hurts too! Perhaps it's broken – look!'
His shoulder looked fine. Dad is a hypochondriac.
'What book ¹⁰ _____ (you/look) for?'
'The Book Of Family Health. It's here somewhere.'

6 In pairs, talk about feeling ill. Student A, look below. Student B, look at page 131.

Student A

1 Say hello to Student B. Ask him/her how he/she is feeling. Listen to Student B's news.

2 Give some advice: Take an aspirin./Make an appointment with the dentist.

7 🔊 **3.21** Listen, then listen again and write down what you hear.

CULTURE

Is chess a sport?

Strange sports

Football, tennis, hockey and cricket are all popular sports around the world. But when is a sport not a sport? Most people think that in a sport we must be strong, use our mind and want to win. So what about these activities?

1 Chess boxing

People play chess all over the world. Chess players need to be fit – in body and mind. Sometimes they need to sit and think hard for seven hours a day. In some competitions, they play for eleven days! There's also a hybrid sport called 'chess boxing'. Boxers fight and then play chess! It's popular in Germany, the UK, India and Russia.

2 Makepung

Every summer in West Bali, there are special buffalo races. A team of one man and a pair of buffaloes race against another team. They race over muddy ground for a long time – sometimes five hours. The men often fall off and get dirty. The crowd like that!

3 Haggis hurling

In Scotland, some people like to do haggis hurling. They have to throw a haggis – this is a hard ball of special meat which is a traditional Scottish food. They must throw the haggis a long way and also very carefully. The haggis must not break when it hits the ground. So, you have to be strong but also clever.

What do you think? Are these games or sports? Would you like to see them in the Olympics?!

GLOSSARY
competition (n) an event in which people or teams compete against each other
mind (n) your thoughts
muddy (adj) wet and dirty
race (n) a competition in which people or animals compete to be the fastest and finish first
traditional (adj) existing for a long time

EXPLORE

1 In pairs, discuss the questions.

1 How many sports or games can you name in two minutes?
2 Do you do any sports? Do you do them for fun or for competition?
3 Do you know anyone who is very good at a sport or game?
4 What's the difference between a sport and a game?

2 Read the article and match sports 1–3 with photos A–C.

1 ☐ Chess boxing
2 ☐ Makepung
3 ☐ Haggis hurling

3 Read the article again. Write the name of the game or sport.

1 This only happens at a certain time of year. *Makepung*
2 People do this with something small that we can eat.
3 People sometimes laugh when they watch this.
4 People don't move for a long time in this activity.
5 This is a mixture of two games/sports.

4 In pairs, discuss the final question in the article.

EXPLORE MORE

5 You are going to watch part of a video from a BBC series about unusual sports and games. Read an advert for the programme. Do you know anyone who does an unusual sport?

Unusual sports

People do some very unusual sports and this series shows us just a couple of them.

EXPLORE MORE

6 ▶ 6.6 Watch Part 1 of the video. Mark the sentences T (true) or F (false).

1 ☐ At the World Alternative Games, there are thirty sports.
2 ☐ Backwards running started in the USA.
3 ☐ Backwards running is good for the brain.
4 ☐ Backwards running is a difficult sport.

7 What advice does the speaker give at the end of the video? Why?

8 ▶ 6.7 Watch Part 2 of the video and answer the questions.

1 How and why did wrong pong start?
2 How is wrong pong different from normal table tennis?
3 How many different tables did you see in the video?

9 ▶ 6.8 Watch Part 3 of the video and complete the sentences.

1 This race is called *the wife carrying race*.
2 It started in _____.
3 Usually the man _____.
4 In the race today, for the first time _____.
5 It isn't easy for Steph because _____.

10 Work in pairs. Would you like to try some of these sports? Why?/Why not?

I would like to try wrong pong because I think it's fun.

YOU EXPLORE

11 CULTURE PROJECT In small groups, create a presentation about unusual sports.

1 Use the internet to research unusual sports that people do in your country.
2 Invent a new hybrid sport from two of these sports.
3 Find some photos of the two sports.
4 Write a short description of the new sport.
5 Present your new sport to the class.
6 Vote on the most popular new 'hybrid' sport!

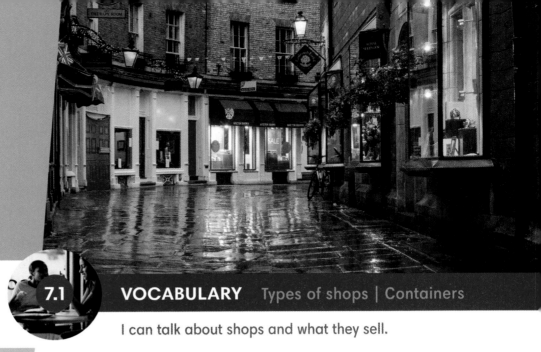

7

Shopping around

VOCABULARY
Types of shops | Containers
Shopping centres | Money

GRAMMAR
Comparatives and superlatives
of adjectives | *going to* and
the Present Continuous

Grammar: Are you coming with us?

Speaking: New shoes

BBC Culture: City shopping

Workbook p. 89

BBC VOX POPS ▶

CLIL 4 > p. 141

7.1 **VOCABULARY** Types of shops | Containers

I can talk about shops and what they sell.

1 In pairs, ask and answer the questions.

1 When was the last time you went shopping?
2 What did you buy?

2 🔊 **3.22** **I KNOW!** How do you say the words below in your language? Can you add more words?

Vocabulary	Types of shops

bakery   bookshop   butcher's   clothes shop   florist's
greengrocer's   newsagent's   pharmacy   shoe shop

I went to the **florist's**. (florist's = place)
The **florist** helped me choose some flowers.
(florist = person)

Watch OUT!

82

3 In pairs, use the clues below and in the picture to label shops A–I with the words from the Vocabulary box. Check your answers on page 130.

- The shoe shop is closed at the moment.
- There's a shop which sells fruit and vegetables between the bookshop and the newsagent's.
- There are a lot of special offers at the clothes shop.
- The shop between the shoe shop and the florist's sells meat.
- The bakery is next to the pharmacy and it's always very busy.

4 Which shops from the Vocabulary box have you got in your neighbourhood? Which shops haven't you got? Discuss in groups.

We've got a bakery but we haven't got a bookshop.

5 WORD FRIENDS How do you say the highlighted words in your language?

> a **bag** of apples   a **bar** of chocolate   a **bunch** of flowers
> a **bottle** of shampoo   a **box** of cream cakes   a **can** of cola
> a **jar** of jam   a **loaf** of bread   a **packet** of crisps

6 🔊 3.23 Listen and complete Jas's shopping list. What did she forget to buy?

> ## Shopping list
> - greengrocer's – apples
> - baker's – ¹ <u>a loaf of bread</u> , cream cakes
> - ² _____ – shampoo
> - newsagent's – crisps, ³ _____ , ⁴ _____
> - florist's – ⁵ _____

7 Choose the correct option.

1 a bottle / (jar) of coffee
2 a bag / can of sugar
3 a jar / bottle of water
4 a bar / packet of biscuits
5 a bunch / box of matches
6 a can / box of lemonade

8 🔊 3.24 Match questions 1–5 with answers a–e. Listen and check.

1 [c] What's its name?
2 [ ] Where is it?
3 [ ] What does it sell?
4 [ ] How often do you go there?
5 [ ] Why do you like it?

a It sells computer games.
b I go there about once a month.
c My favourite shop is called Go2 Games.
d They've got a good choice of games and the people who work there are very helpful.
e It's in the shopping centre in the town centre.

9 [VOX POPS ▶ 7.1] In pairs, ask and answer questions about your favourite shop. Use Exercise 8 to help you.

A: What's your favourite shop?
B: My favourite shop is called …

And YOU?

I can compare things.

1 CLASS VOTE Imagine that you want to buy some headphones. Who do you ask and where do you get information before you buy them?

> friends   magazine   the internet   shop assistant

2  3.25 Check you understand these adjectives. Then read the text. Do people generally have a good opinion of the headphones?

> enjoyable   heavy   low   trendy   (un)comfortable

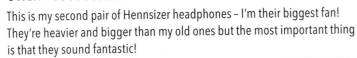

HENNSIZER M13 HEADPHONES

Just £18.99 – lowest ever price

OWEN ★★★★★

This is my second pair of Hennsizer headphones – I'm their biggest fan! They're heavier and bigger than my old ones but the most important thing is that they sound fantastic!

ROSIE ★★★★★

They really are the trendiest headphones! They're comfortable and they look good – my journey to school is definitely more enjoyable these days. One small problem – they're too big for my pocket!

LEAH ★★★★★

You can buy cheaper headphones but they aren't as good as these. They're definitely better than the headphones that came with my MP3 player.

3 Find more examples of comparatives and superlatives in the text in Exercise 2.

Grammar	Comparatives and superlatives of adjectives	
old	older	the oldest
nice	nicer	the nicest
thin	thinner	the thinnest
pretty	prettier	the prettiest
important	more important	the most important
good	better	the best
bad	worse	the worst

They are bigger than my old headphones.
They are not as good as my old headphones.

GRAMMAR TIME   PAGE 125

We don't use *the* after *my/your/their*, etc.
She's my best friend. NOT ~~She's my the best friend.~~

Watch OUT!

4a In pairs, compare phones A–C on page 130. Use the adjectives below or your own ideas. How many sentences can you make in three minutes?

> thin   modern   old   big
> small   ugly   trendy

Phone B is trendier than phone A.

4b In pairs, make sentences with superlatives about phones A–C on page 130.

Phone A is the biggest.

5 Complete the review with the comparatives or superlatives of the adjectives in brackets.

CALLY ★★★★★

My Hennsizer FL40 headphones stopped working. The M13 headphones are ¹**more expensive** (expensive) but I bought them. That was my ²_____ (big) mistake! They're ³_____ (uncomfortable) than my old headphones. I think the quality isn't as good as the FL40 and the sound is ⁴_____ (bad) too. The ⁵_____ (annoying) thing is that the cable is too long! I was ⁶_____ (happy) with my ⁷_____ (cheap) headphones!

6 Rewrite the sentences with *not as … as* and the adjectives in brackets.

1 This laptop is lighter than my old one. (heavy) *This laptop isn't as heavy as my old one.*
2 The prices in the bookshop are higher than on the internet. (low)
3 The MP3 player is cheaper than the iPod. (expensive)
4 The choice of magazines is worse at the supermarket than at the newsagent's. (good)

7 In pairs, ask and answer the questions.

And YOU

- What was the most expensive thing you bought last year?
- What did you buy that was the biggest waste of money? Why?

I can find specific detail in a text and talk about shopping centres.

1 CLASS VOTE Do you prefer to spend your free time in a) the park, b) the shopping centre or c) the town centre?

2 In pairs, answer the questions about shopping centres. Check your answers on page 130.

Why …
1   is there nowhere to sit down?
2   do they play music all the time?
3   is it hard to find the exit?
4   is it a long way from the up escalators to the down escalators?

3 🔊 3.26 Read the text and answer the questions.

1   What was Victor Gruen's profession?
2   When and where did he build Southdale?
3   Was Southdale a success?

4 Read the text again. Mark the sentences ✓ (right), ✗ (wrong) or ? (doesn't say).

1 ✓ Victor Gruen wanted shopping centres to be more than just a place to shop.
2 ☐ Southdale wasn't as nice as other shopping centres.
3 ☐ Southdale was the busiest shopping centre in the USA.
4 ☐ Victor got a pleasant surprise when he went back to Vienna.
5 ☐ His invention didn't do what he wanted.

5 🔊 3.27 Find the words and phrases below in the text. How do you say them in your language?

Vocabulary	Shopping centres

car park   department store   escalator
food court   multi-screen cinema
public toilets   shopper   trolley

6 Use the Vocabulary box to complete the definitions.

1   You put your shopping in it: _trolley_
2   A large shop which sells lots of different things: _____
3   A way to move from one level to another: _____
4   An area with restaurants and bars: _____
5   A place to see films: _____

Who invented the shopping centre?

In 1938, an Austrian architect called Victor Gruen arrived in New York with eight dollars and no English. He started designing shops and quickly became one of the most successful architects in the city.

Victor thought American cities were uglier than European cities like Vienna. He wanted to make them more beautiful. His dream was to make shopping centres like traditional European town centres, lovely places with parks, schools and homes around them. So in 1956, he built Southdale, a shopping centre near Minneapolis. It had the usual shops, department stores, public toilets and a big car park. But Southdale was more pleasant than other shopping centres. All the shops were under the same roof. It was on two levels with escalators to take shoppers and their trolleys up and down. And in the middle was a garden with a café.

Southdale was very popular. Afterwards, most new shopping centres followed the Southdale model. Unfortunately, they didn't become the centre of beautiful new towns. Instead, they were ugly out-of-town buildings with seas of cars around them.

In 1978, Victor went back to Austria but what did he find in Vienna? A large ugly shopping centre with a multi-screen cinema and a food court! It was more popular than the traditional shops and many of them had to close.

Victor Gruen invented the modern shopping centre to make the USA more like Vienna but in the end his invention made Vienna more like the USA.

7 [VOX POPS ▶ 7.2] In groups, ask and answer the questions.

And YOU

● Do you like shopping centres? Why?/Why not?
● How often do you go to shopping centres? Who do you go with?

I can talk about intentions and arrangements.

VIDEO   ARE YOU COMING WITH US? (Parts 1 & 2)

(Part 1)

Lee: Hi, Amy. Listen – it's my mum's fortieth birthday next Tuesday and Ruby and I want to buy her something special. So we're going to take the train to Clearwater shopping centre on Saturday, get mum a present and then we're going to see a film at the Multiplex. Oh, and I'm going to buy some trainers and Ruby's going to buy some posters. Are you going to study again or can you come with us? Hope so! Oh, we're not going to tell anybody – it's a surprise.

(Part 2)

Amy: Hi, Lee.

Lee: Hey, Amy! Are you coming with us tomorrow?

Amy: Yes, but what time are we taking the train? I can't remember.

Lee: We're not taking the train.

Amy: Thanks for telling me!

Lee: Sorry. The bus is cheaper. So we're taking the X4 bus from the bus stop on Mandela Avenue at 10.15. Oh and I checked the films. They're showing *Shrek 8* at the Multiplex at 2.30. Billy's meeting us there.

Amy: Great! See you tomorrow at 10.15!

It's a surprise.
Thanks for telling me!

OUT of **class**

---

1 ▶ **7.3** ◀)) **3.28** Describe the photo. Watch or listen to Part 1. Tick the things Lee and Ruby plan to do on Saturday.

- ☐ take a train
- ☐ watch a film
- ☐ go ice-skating
- ☐ go for a pizza
- ☐ do some shopping

2 ▶ **7.4** ◀)) **3.29** Watch or listen to Part 2. Answer the questions.

1 Is Amy going with Lee and Ruby on Saturday?
2 How are they travelling to Clearwater?
3 What time are they meeting in the morning?

3 ▶ **7.5** ◀)) **3.30** Watch or listen to Part 3. What's the problem? Where's Amy?

4 Find more examples of *going to* and the Present Continuous in the voicemail message and dialogue.

Grammar	**Talking about the future**

Intentions and plans
I'm **going to buy** some trainers.
We're **not going to tell** anybody.
Are you **going to study**?

Arrangements
They're **showing** *Shrek 8* at 2.30.
We're **not taking** the train tomorrow.
Are you **coming** with us?

GRAMMAR TIME   PAGE 125

5 ◀)) **3.31** Complete the sentences with *going to* and the verbs in brackets. Then listen to Ruby and Lee and check.

1 I *'m going to buy* (buy) something to drink.
2 He _____ (come) with me to the shoe shop.
3 _____ (you/come) with us?
4 I _____ (go) to the bookshop first.
5 We _____ (buy) a nice present for mum.
6 I _____ (not spend) all my money.

6 Use *going to* to write three intentions for the near future. Then use the Present Continuous to write about three arrangements for next week. In groups, compare your sentences.

And Y?U

I'm going to start running.
My sister's singing in a concert next week.

I can identify specific detail in a conversation and talk about money.

How important is MONEY to you?

1 One day you get £10 pocket money and earn £20 babysitting. Do you put the money ...
   a in a piggy bank?
   b in your purse/wallet/pocket?

2 You get £50 for your birthday. Do you ...
   a save some and spend the rest?
   b spend it all immediately?

3 You get too much change in a shop. Do you ...
   a keep the money?
   b tell the shop assistant?

4 You need a new pair of jeans. Do you ...
   a wait for the sales?
   b buy the pair you like without looking at the price?

5 Some friends want to borrow £30. Do you ...
   a tell them you never lend money?
   b give them the money and say they can pay you back any time?

> **Watch OUT!**
> **borrow** – take something from someone else and give it back later
> **lend** – give something to someone for some time

1   **CLASS VOTE**   Does money make people happy? Vote *yes* or *no* and then say why.

   A: *Yes, it does because with money you can buy things that make you happy.*
   B: *No, it doesn't. Money can't buy love!*

2   3.32 **Read the quiz. Then listen and circle Greg's answers, a) or b). What does he ask Gemma for at the end?**

3   3.33 **Find the words and phrases below in the quiz. Then, in pairs, complete the sentences.**

Vocabulary	Money		
change	piggy bank	pocket money	price
purse	sales	wallet	

1 My dad has a *wallet* but I keep my money in my pocket.
2 The price of a book is £6.69 and you pay £10. How much _____ do you get?
3 How much _____ do you get a week?
4 Prices are always lower in the summer _____.
5 I have a _____ on a shelf in my room.

4   **WORD FRIENDS**   **Complete the sentences with the highlighted verbs in the quiz.**

1 I think I should *get* more **pocket money**.
2 It's better to _____ **money** than to **spend it**.
3 I sometimes _____ **money** to my friends.
4 When I _____ **money**, I always **pay it back**.
5 Teenagers should work to _____ their **money**.

5 **In pairs, do the quiz. Check your answers on page 130.**

6   3.34 **Listen to a radio phone-in about money. Mark the sentences T (true) or F (false).**

1 ☐T☐ Penny has to work to get pocket money.
2 ☐ She has a lot of money in her piggy bank.
3 ☐ She never buys any clothes in the shops.
4 ☐ She doesn't lend money to her friends.
5 ☐ She thinks it's good to save money before you buy things.
6 ☐ She's saving her money for something special.

7   3.35 **Listen to an interview with an expert on saving money. Choose the correct answers.**

1 Molly thinks Penny
   a is intelligent.
   b should spend more money.
   c isn't telling the truth.
2 Molly thinks it's good to
   a earn more money.
   b make a list.
   c spend nothing.
3 Molly says it's a good idea to
   a stop using your mobile phone.
   b go shopping often.
   c find the lowest prices.

8 **In pairs, discuss the sentences from Exercise 4.**

   A: *Do you think you should get more pocket money?*
   B: *I think ...*

I can shop for clothes and other things.

VIDEO NEW SHOES

Shop Assistant (SA): Can I help you?

Lee: Yes, I'm looking for a pair of trainers.

SA: These ones are on sale.

Lee: How much are they?

SA: Nineteen ninety-nine.

Amy: That's a good price, Lee. You should get them.

Lee: Can I try them on, please?

SA: Of course. What size are you?

Lee: Forty-one.

Two minutes later

Lee: Oh! They're too small … Excuse me! Have you got them in a bigger size?

SA: I think so … Just a second … Here you are.

Two minutes later

Lee: These ones are the right size …

Amy: Great, because I'm fed up! This is the fifth shop we …

Lee: … but I don't like the colour. Excuse me! Have you got these in blue?

Amy: Lee! Are you going to buy them or not?

Lee: Yes! I'll take them. Here you are … Amy! Wait for me!

SA: Don't forget your change!

Just a second. I'm fed up!	**O**UT of **class**

1 ⏵ 7.6 🔊 3.36 In pairs, describe the photo. Is Lee going to buy the red trainers? Watch or listen and check.

2 In pairs, underline ten phrases that are in the dialogue.

Speaking	**Shopping for clothes**
You need to understand	**You need to say**
● Can I help you?	● I'm looking for …
● These ones are on sale.	● How much is it/are they?
● What size are you?	● Can I try it/them on, please?
● The changing rooms are over there.	● It's/They're too big/small.
● Don't forget your change.	● Have you got it/them in a smaller/bigger size/ another colour?
	● I'll take it/the blue one.
	● I'll take them/these ones.

3 🔊 3.37 Complete the dialogue with the phrases from the Speaking box. Listen and check.

Shop Assistant: Hello, can I help you?

Customer: ¹*I'm looking for a T-shirt.*

SA: This one's on sale.

C: ²_____?

SA: Nine pounds ninety-nine.

C: ³_____, please?

SA: Yes, of course. The changing rooms are over there … Oh! It's too big.

C: ⁴_____?

SA: Yes, here you are. … Oh, yes, that's better.

C: ⁵_____.

SA: Great. Don't forget your change. Goodbye.

4 Complete the sentences with *one* or *ones*.

1 Do you want the black shoes or the brown *ones*?
2 This belt is too small. Have you got a bigger _____?
3 I'll take the pink shirt but I don't want the green _____.
4 My headphones aren't as good as these _____.

5 In pairs, buy and sell the things below. Student A is the customer, Student B is the shop assistant. Then change roles. Use the Speaking box to help you.

| a hat   a pair of jeans   a coat/jacket |

A: Good morning! Can I help you?

B: Yes, I'm looking for …

I can write notes and messages to make arrangements.

1 Work in pairs. Choose the best format a–d for your messages in situations 1–4.

1 ☐ You're working on a school project and your bedroom is very untidy. You leave a message asking your mum not to tidy up your papers.

2 ☐ You're meeting a friend but your bus is late. You want to let him/her know.

3 ☐ It's your birthday next week and you decide to invite all your friends to a party.

4 ☐ You need to tell your trainer that you're ill and can't go to judo classes next week.

a a note on a piece of paper
b an update or tweet on Facebook/Twitter
c text or message sent on your phone
d an email

2 Read Lee's messages, A and B. Which one includes an invitation and makes an arrangement? Which one only gives information?

A
> Hi Amy,
> ❶ I'm going into town to buy some guitar strings.
> ❷ Would you like to come?
> ❸ I should be outside the shopping centre at 2.30.
> ❹ Let me know!
> Lee

B
> Hi mum,
> ❶ I'm at the music shop buying some new guitar strings! I should be back about 5.00.
> ❹ See you soon!
> Lee XXX

3 Underline the phrases in the Writing box which are in Lee's messages.

4 Read messages C and D from Amy. Which message is a reply to Lee's invitation? What surprise is Amy planning?

C
> Hi,
> Sorry but I'm really busy right now. Perhaps we could meet tonight? See you soon. Amy XXX

D
> Hi,
> It's Lee's birthday today and I want to organise a surprise party for him at my house. Would you like to come? The party's starting at 7 p.m.
> Love Amy

Writing   Notes (making arrangements)

❶ The information you want the other person to know
I'm having a party.
I'm going into town.
Help! I don't understand my homework.
I'm really ill – I can't come.
The bus is really late ☹

❷ A request, offer or invitation (optional)
Would you like to come?
Can you help?
Perhaps we could meet tomorrow?
Please wait for me.

❸ Arrangements
I should be outside the shop at 2.30.
Let's meet in front of the cinema at 8.00.
The party's starting at 10.00.
I'm planning to be online at 9.00.

❹ Ending
See you there! /See you soon!
Let me know!
I hope you can come/help.

Writing Time

5 Write a note to a friend:

❶❷ say you want to see a film at the cinema this weekend and ask your friend if he/she would like to come
❸ suggest a time/place to meet
❹ close your message

> We often use imperatives (e.g. *Don't call at …/Please come/wait …*) in notes.

Watch OUT!

bakery /'beɪkəri/ n
bookshop /'bʊkʃɒp/ n
busy /'bɪzi/ adj
butcher's /'bʊtʃəz/ n
buy /baɪ/ v
car park /kɑː pɑːk/ n
change /tʃeɪndʒ/ n
changing rooms /'tʃeɪndʒɪŋ ruːmz/ n
cheap /tʃiːp/ adj
closed /kləʊzd/ adj
clothes shop /kləʊðz ʃɒp/ n
comfortable /'kʌmftəbəl, 'kʌmfət-/ adj
cost /kɒst/ v
department store /dɪ'pɑːtmənt stɔː/ n
enjoyable /ɪn'dʒɔɪəbəl/ adj
escalator /'eskəleɪtə/ n
exit /'egzət, 'egzɪt, 'eksət/ n
expensive /ɪk'spensɪv/ adj
florist's /'flɒrɪsts/ n
food court /fuːd kɔːt/ n
generous /'dʒenərəs/ adj
greengrocer's /'griːn,grəʊsəz/ n
headphones /'hedfəʊnz/ n
heavy /'hevi/ adj
interview /'ɪntəvjuː/ n
invention /ɪn'venʃən/ n
invitation /,ɪnvə'teɪʃən, ,ɪnvɪ'teɪʃən/ n
journey /'dʒɜːni/ n
level /'levəl/ n
light /laɪt/ adj
look for /lʊk fə/ v
low /ləʊ/ adj

message /'mesɪdʒ/ n
mistake /mə'steɪk, mɪ'steɪk/ n
model /'mɒdl/ n
modern /'mɒdn/ adj
money /'mʌni/ n
multi-screen cinema /mʌlti 'skriːn ,sɪnəmə/ n
music shop /'mjuːzɪk ʃɒp/ n
neighbourhood /'neɪbəhʊd/ n
newsagent's /'njuːz,eɪdʒənts/ n
nice /naɪs/ adj
note /nəʊt/ n
opinion /ə'pɪnjən/ n
out-of-town /,aʊt əv 'taʊn/ adj
pay /peɪ/ v
penny /'peni/ n
pharmacy /'fɑːməsi/ n
piggy bank /'pɪgi bæŋk/ n
pocket /'pɒkət, 'pɒkɪt/ n
pocket money /'pɒkət 'mʌni/ n
popular /'pɒpjələ, 'pɒpjʊlə/ adj
present /'prezənt/ n
price /praɪs/ n
problem /'prɒbləm/ n
public toilets /,pʌblɪk 'tɔɪləts/ n
purse /pɜːs/ n
quality /'kwɒləti, 'kwɒlɪti/ n
reply /rɪ'plaɪ/ n
sales /seɪlz/ n
sell /sel/ v

shoe shop /ʃuː ʃɒp/ n
shop assistant /ʃɒp ə'sɪstənt/ n
shopper /'ʃɒpə/ n
shopping /'ʃɒpɪŋ/ n
shopping centre /'ʃɒpɪŋ 'sentə/ n
shopping list /'ʃɒpɪŋ lɪst/ n
size /saɪz/ n
sound /saʊnd/ v
special offer /'speʃəl 'ɒfə/ n
supermarket /'suːpə,mɑːkət, 'suːpə,mɑːkɪt/ n
surprise /sə'praɪz/ n
traditional /trə'dɪʃənəl/ adj
trendy /'trendi/ adj
trolley /'trɒli/ n
try (something) on /'traɪ ,sʌmθɪŋ ɒn/ v
tweet /twiːt/ n
uncomfortable /ʌn'kʌmftəbəl, -'kʌmfət-/ adj
update /ʌp'deɪt/ n
voicemail message /'vɔɪsmeɪl 'mesɪdʒ/ n
wallet /'wɒlət, 'wɒlɪt/ n

WORD FRIENDS

a bag of apples/sugar
a bar of chocolate
a bottle of shampoo/water
a box of cream cakes/ matches
a bunch of flowers
a can of cola/lemonade
a good choice

a good/high/low price
a jar of jam/coffee
a loaf of bread
a packet of crisps/biscuits
a piece of paper
be on sale
borrow money from sb
do some shopping
earn money
forget your change
get change
get pocket money
get sb a present
give information
go for a pizza
go ice-skating
go shopping
invite friends to your house
keep money in your pocket, etc
leave a message
lend money to sb/lend sb money
make a list
make an arrangement
meet friends
organise a (surprise) party
pay (sb) back
plan a surprise
save money
show a film
spend money
spend time (doing sth)
take a train
the right size
(a) waste of money

VOCABULARY IN ACTION

1 Use the wordlist to find:
1 four places where you can keep your money: *pocket*, …
2 six containers:
3 ten types of shops:

2 In pairs, complete the words in the text.

I didn't make a ¹*shopping* list before I went to the shops. That was a big ²m_____ . If you don't know what you're going to buy, you buy things you don't need – especially when they are on ³s_____ . In my favourite clothes shop the ⁴p_____ were very low. I tried on lots of things in the ⁵c_____ r_____ . I bought a ⁶t_____ bag and I also bought a birthday ⁷p_____ for my brother.

3 Complete the Word Friends. In pairs, say if the sentences are true for you.

1 I want to <u>earn</u> a lot of money one day.
2 I often _____ parties for my friends.
3 I _____ the train to school.
4 We _____ ice-skating a lot in winter.
5 I'm going to do some _____ after school.

4 🔊 3.38 **PRONUNCIATION** Listen and underline the words in each phrase with a weak sound (/ə/). Listen again and check.

1 make <u>a</u> list (x1)
2 take the train (x1)
3 the right size (x1)
4 a jar of jam (x2)
5 a loaf of bread (x2)

Revision

1 Complete the sentences with one word in each gap.

1 It costs £6.49. You pay £10. How much _change_ do you get?
2 It's not the right _____ . It's too big!
3 I bought a _____ of flowers at the florist's.
4 There's a _____ of chocolate in my bag.
5 Can you get a _____ of cream cakes from the baker's?
6 I got some nice sausages at the _____ .

2a Complete the text with the words and phrases below. There are two extra items.

> car park   department store   ~~escalator~~   exit
> food court   shoppers   public toilets
> multi-screen cinema   trolleys

It wasn't a good shopping trip. Firstly, the ¹_escalator_ wasn't working so we had to use the stairs. We went to all the shops and a big ²_____ but I didn't find anything to buy. There weren't any free tables in the ³_____ so we didn't eat anything. There wasn't anything good on at the ⁴_____ so we didn't see a film. And at the supermarket there weren't any ⁵_____ so we had to carry a heavy basket. Finally, we spent ten minutes looking for our car in the ⁶_____ and then we couldn't find the ⁷_____ !

2b In pairs, check your answers. Then talk about the last time you went to a shopping centre.

I met my friends in front of the shopping centre and we took the escalator to the first floor. Then we …

3 Choose the correct option. Then, in pairs, read the conversation.

A: Let's go ¹_for_ / to a pizza.
B: Good idea but can you ²_borrow_ / lend me five pounds?
A: What? But you ³_borrowed_ / lent ten pounds from me yesterday!
B: I know but I promise to pay you ⁴_back_ / for tomorrow.
A: Why do you always ⁵_earn_ / spend all your money? You should try to ⁶_save_ / spend some money.
B: I haven't got a job so I don't ⁷_earn_ / pay any money and I don't get much ⁸_pocket_ / wallet money. But I ⁹_got_ / made you a present with the money you lent me. Here you are.

4a Compare the shops with the words in brackets and _than_ or _as…as_.

	Ali's	Lido	C2
How big is the shop?	60m²	500m²	3500m²
How much does a typical shopper spend there?	£37.85	£29.49	£33.10
How popular is the shop?	★★★★☆	★★★★☆	★★★☆☆

1 Lido / Ali's (big)
   Lido is bigger than Ali's.
2 Lido / C2 (small)
3 Ali's / C2 (expensive)
4 Lido / C2 (cheap)
5 Ali's / Lido (popular)
6 Ali's / C2 (popular)

4b Write superlative sentences about the three shops with the adjectives in brackets above.

C2 is the biggest shop.

5 Choose the correct option.

1 I'm _winning_ / going to win the Nobel Prize.
2 I'm _lying_ / going to lie down when I get home. I'm really tired.
3 I'm _meeting_ / going to meet some friends at my house tonight. Do you want to come?
4 They're _showing_ / going to show the Lego film on Channel 3 at 6 p.m.

6 In pairs, role play the situations. Student A, look below. Student B, look at page 131.

Student A

1 You go to a sports shop to buy a new tracksuit. You can't decide between a white one and a blue one.
2 You are a shop assistant in a shoe shop. Help Student B buy a new pair of shoes.

7 🔊 3.39 Listen, then listen again and write down what you hear.

Where can you buy a town?

Amazing things sold on eBay

Most people love shopping. It's a popular hobby but our shopping habits don't always stay the same. They change. Today we can buy things in many places and more and more people are buying things online. There are lots of websites where you can buy normal things but if you want something really unusual, go to an online auction site, like eBay. eBay started in the USA but now operates in thirty different countries. It celebrated its twentieth birthday in 2015. Here are some of the amazing things people sold on the site.

Bridgeville

In 2008, the small town of Bridgeville in California was for sale and someone paid 1.25 million dollars for it! It's a very small place and in 2008 it had only thirty people, eight houses, a post office, a café and a cemetery. The town needed a lot of money and work and the new owner sold it again a few years later.

A life

Ian Usher was very sad after his wife left him. He decided to put his whole life for sale on eBay! He sold everything that he had – his house, his car, introductions to his friends and his job. Someone paid 300,000 dollars and Ian started a new life with the money.

A forehead

Kari Smith sold her forehead for advertising space! A company paid her 10,000 dollars to tattoo the name of their company on her forehead!

A yacht

One of the most expensive things for sale on eBay was a big yacht. Roman Abramovich (who owned Chelsea football club) bought it for 168 million dollars. It had a gym, a cinema, a spa and lift.

Have you got something unusual you would like to sell on eBay?

GLOSSARY
auction (n) a public sale where things are sold to the person who offers the most money for them
cemetery (n) a piece of land in which dead people are buried
forehead (n) the part of your face above your eyes and below your hair
introductions (n pl) telling two people each other's names when they first meet and explain who they are
operate (v) to work

1 In pairs, discuss the questions.

1 Do you prefer to buy things online or in shops? Why?

2 Have you got a favourite shopping website or shop?

3 What's the most interesting thing you bought last month?

4 Do you know someone who recently bought something unusual? What did they buy?

2 Read the article. In pairs, answer the questions.

1 How old is eBay?

2 Why was the town for sale again after a few years?

3 Why was the life for sale?

4 How much did the life sell for?

5 Why did a woman sell her forehead?

6 Who bought the yacht?

3 In pairs, discuss the final question in the article.

4 You are going to watch part of a video from the BBC about shopping in different cities. Read an advert for the programme and answer the question.

City shopping

Some big cities have famous places to go shopping. Do you know any? This programme is about some of them.

5 ▶ **7.7** Watch Part 1 of the video. Mark the sentences T (true) or F (false).

1 [F] In Oxford Street, everything costs a lot of money.

2 [ ] People go to a special event in Oxford Street in November.

3 [ ] The air in Oxford Street is very clean.

4 [ ] In Portobello Road, there is a big market every day.

5 [ ] You can buy old clothes in Portobello market.

6 Work in pairs. In your opinion, which is better – a day in Oxford Street or a day in Portobello Road? Why?

7 ▶ **7.8** Watch Part 2 of the video and complete the sentences.

1 The Apple Store on Fifth Avenue is interesting because _____.

2 You might get tired in Macy's because _____.

3 Shibuya Crossing is famous because _____.

4 Trendy young people go to Shibuya because _____.

8 Work in pairs. Imagine you have £4,000 to spend. Will you go to London, New York or Tokyo? Why? What are you going to spend your money on?

9 CULTURE PROJECT In small groups, create a presentation about a shopping area.

1 Use the internet to research a popular city shopping centre or area in your country.

2 Write a short script and include some photos or video.

3 Share your presentation with the class.

I can talk about people and their jobs.

WHAT JOBS ARE GOOD FOR YOU?
Do the flow chart to find out.

Learning to work

VOCABULARY
Jobs | Work and jobs | School and education

GRAMMAR
Will for future predictions | First Conditional | Adjectives with prepositions

Grammar: If you don't study …

Speaking: I'll definitely pass

BBC Culture: The amazing Henn Na Hotel

Workbook p. 101

BBC VOX POPS ▶

START HERE

I want to work indoors.

I prefer an outdoor job.

I want to work in an office

I think office work is boring.

I don't want a dangerous job.

I don't mind danger. I want a challenging job.

I don't want to stay in an office all the time.

I prefer to work in one place.
- accountant
- receptionist
- secretary

- architect
- lawyer
- politician

I want to work with my hands.

I want to travel in my job.

- firefighter
- police officer
- soldier

I want to help people.
- doctor/nurse
- shop assistant
- waiter/waitress

I prefer to work in one place.
- builder
- farmer
- gardener

I prefer to work alone.
- bike courier
- driver
- postman/woman

I want to work with other people.
- journalist
- pilot
- tour guide

I want a creative job.
- artist
- chef
- hairdresser

I want to fix things.
- electrician
- IT specialist
- mechanic

1 🔊 3.40 **I KNOW!** Work in groups. Which jobs below are in the photos? How many more jobs can you think of in two minutes?

Vocabulary	**Jobs**

accountant architect artist bike courier builder chef doctor driver electrician farmer firefighter gardener hairdresser IT specialist journalist lawyer mechanic nurse pilot politician police officer postman/woman receptionist secretary shop assistant soldier tour guide waiter/waitress

2 Follow the job chart to find a good job for you. In pairs, compare your jobs.

A: *What jobs does the flow chart give you?*
B: *Artist, chef or hairdresser.*
A: *What do you think of them?*
B: *I'd like to be a chef because …*

3 In pairs, answer the questions.

1 In your opinion, which job from the Vocabulary box is…

- the most dangerous?
- the easiest?
- the best paid?
- the most stressful?

2 Which job would you most like to have?

4 Find jobs from the Vocabulary box for the people in the sentences below.

He/She …

1 works in a hospital. *doctor/nurse*
2 helps people on holiday. _____
3 draws pictures of buildings for builders. _____
4 makes parks look beautiful. _____
5 answers the phone in an office or a hotel. _____

5 🔊 3.41 **Listen and and guess which jobs from the Vocabulary box each speaker has.**

1 Nicola _____
2 Ruth _____
3 Ewan _____
4 Carrie _____
5 Darren _____
6 Eddie _____

6 🔊 3.42 **Listen to the complete conversations and check your answers to Exercise 5.**

7 WORD FRIENDS Check you understand these Word Friends. Then find jobs from the Vocabulary box for Jane, Brett and Charlotte. There is more than one job for each person.

work from nine to five	be happy at work
work indoors/outdoors	work in a team
get to work on time	work at the weekend
earn (good) money	wear a uniform	work alone

Jane – lawyer, accountant, ….

A Jane, 18

'I want to work from nine to five, and I'd like to work indoors but the most important thing for me is to earn money.'

8 🔊 3.43 **Complete the text with the correct Word Friends. Guess the speaker's job. Listen and check.**

I don't [1]*earn* much money but I don't mind because I'm [2]_____ at work. I really like working in a [3]_____. My workmates are great. I don't work from nine to [4]_____. Sometimes I work during the day and sometimes at night. I have to wear a [5]_____ but that's all right. I look good in it! In my job it's really important to get to work on [6]_____ because people can die if you're late.

9 In pairs, choose a job from the Vocabulary box. Find out your partner's job in ten questions. You can only answer *yes* or *no*.

A: *Do you work indoors?*
B: *Yes, I do.*
A: *Do you wear a uniform?*
B: *No, I don't.*

B Brett, 16

'I want to wear a uniform and work outdoors. I'd like to work in a team too. It's no problem for me to get to work on time.'

C Charlotte, 17

'I want to be happy at work. I enjoy working alone. I don't mind working at the weekend.'

10 Think of people that you know. What jobs do they have? Do they like their jobs? Why?/Why not? Discuss in groups.

And Y?U

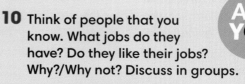

My uncle works in a café. He's a waiter. He loves his job because …

I can use *will* to talk about future predictions.

1 What is your favourite part of the school day? Why?

2 🔊 **3.44** Read the text and tick (✓) the things the writer mentions. Would you like all your lessons at home?

- ☐ break   ☐ classroom   ☐ homework
- ☐ test   ☐ school uniform   ☐ course book
- ☐ timetable

A school day in 2035?

**Higson Corporation Global Schools –
Monday 5 May 2035, 08.57 a.m.**

> Good morning, Emily!
> Your Maths test will start in three minutes. There's an online meeting with your Chinese teacher at 10 a.m. Have a nice day!

Education will be very important in 2035 but children won't go to school. So how will they learn? They will study in their bedrooms at home. Computers will organise the timetable for each day. Pupils will do all their homework and tests online, because we won't have paper course books. They'll only have contact with their teachers through the internet. But will they enjoy their lessons? No, they won't – some things will never change!

3 Find more examples of *will/won't* in the text in Exercise 2.

Grammar	Will for future predictions
+	**–**
I will work **hard.** They will play.	I won't work **hard.** They won't play.
?	
Will you study a lot? Will children play games? How will they learn?	Yes, I will./No, I won't. Yes, they will./No, they won't.

Time expressions:
in 2035/twenty years' time/the next five years/the future
by (= before) 2035/Christmas/my twentieth birthday

I don't think this will happen. NOT ~~I think this won't happen.~~

GRAMMAR TIME ▸ PAGE 126

4 Complete the text with *will* or *won't* and the verbs in brackets.

English ¹*won't be* (not be) so popular in 2035. But Chinese and Portuguese ² _____ (become) very important. Pupils ³ _____ (not learn) with CDs and DVDs: instead pupils ⁴ _____ (chat) to students their age in other countries to practise languages. In the future students ⁵ _____ (not have) the chance to gossip with friends between lessons because everyone ⁶ _____ (learn) at home. So ⁷ _____ students in 2035 _____ (feel) lonely?

5 In pairs, say if and when you think these predictions will come true. Use time expressions with *in* or *by*.

1 Schools will give laptops to all their pupils.
   I think this will happen by 2020.
   I don't agree. I don't think this will happen.
2 Students won't learn languages – everyone will use computers to translate.
3 Many people will decide to study abroad.
4 Students will use the internet in exams.
5 Robots will do all the hard, unpleasant jobs.

6 Tick (✓) the things you think you will do before your twentieth birthday.

- ☐ learn to drive   ☐ get married
- ☐ go to university   ☐ buy a house or flat
- ☐ work or study abroad

7 In pairs, ask and answer the questions in Exercise 6.

A: *Will you learn to drive before your twentieth birthday?*
B: *Yes, I will./No, I won't.*

READING and VOCABULARY First job

I can find specific detail in a text and talk about jobs.

BEYONCÉ CUT MY HAIR

Johnny Depp,
Pen salesman

Some celebrities know what it's like to look for a job and to work from nine to five. For example, did you know that Johnny Depp sold pens in a call centre before he became an actor? It's hard to believe but it's true.

And Johnny Depp is not the only famous person who had a normal job before becoming famous. Model Megan Fox worked as a waitress. Beyoncé helped out at her mother's beauty salon. Jennifer Lopez (JLo) had a temporary job in a lawyer's office. And Tom Cruise had a part-time job delivering newspapers.

Some celebrities had jobs that don't seem surprising. Writer J.K. Rowling was an English teacher. She had a full-time job in a school in Portugal before she wrote about Harry Potter.

But other famous people had more surprising jobs. Brad Pitt, for example, once got a very strange job. He had to dress up as a giant chicken to attract customers to a restaurant! It was better than being unemployed but I'm sure he wasn't upset when he lost that job.

It shows that people with ordinary jobs can become famous. Perhaps your postman will win a TV talent show. Maybe the sales assistant in the games shop will win a Nobel Prize one day. And perhaps that young waitress with a summer job in your local café will become a film star. Who knows?

Beyoncé, Hairdresser's assistant

1 **CLASS VOTE** Which of these famous people is the most popular in the class?

| Johnny Depp   Megan Fox   Beyoncé   Jennifer Lopez
| Tom Cruise   J.K. Rowling   Brad Pitt

2 🔊 3.45 **Read the text. What jobs did the people in Exercise 1 have when they were young?**

Johnny Depp worked in a call centre.

3 Read the text again. Mark the sentences ✓ (right), ✗ (wrong) or ? (doesn't say).

1 ☒ In the writer's opinion famous people don't know about normal people's lives.
2 ☐ Johnny Depp sold the writer a pen.
3 ☐ JLo's mother helped her get a job.
4 ☐ J.K. Rowling taught English when she was younger.
5 ☐ Brad Pitt once had a very unusual job.
6 ☐ The writer is sure the waitress in his local café will become a film star.

4 🔊 3.46 **Find the phrases below in the text. How do you say them in your language?**

| **Vocabulary** | Work and jobs |

Types of jobs
full-time job   part-time job   summer job   temporary job
Work
work in an office   work for a company   look for a job
work as a waitress   be unemployed   get/have/lose a job

5 🔊 3.47 **Use the Vocabulary box to complete the text. Listen and check.**

I don't have a full-time job. I have two ¹*part-time* jobs. In the morning, I work ²_____ the town council. I'm a gardener. And in the evening, I work ³_____ a waiter in a café. It's tiring but I don't want to be ⁴_____. I want to earn more money so I'm ⁵_____ for a new job but it's difficult to ⁶_____ a good job. Last year I had a ⁷_____ job for the summer in a restaurant at the beach. The money was great! Unfortunately, I ⁸_____ my job when autumn came.

6 In pairs, choose three summer jobs you would both like to do in the future.

And YOU

| babysitter   bike courier
| fruit picker on a farm
| lifeguard at a swimming pool
| guide in a local museum
| activity instructor in a summer camp

A: *I'd like to work as a lifeguard at a swimming pool. What about you?*

B: *No, I can't swim very well.*

8.4 GRAMMAR First Conditional

I can use the First Conditional to talk about probability.

VIDEO IF YOU DON'T STUDY … (Part 1)

Mum: Where do you think you're going?

Lee: I'm just going to see Billy and Krystal.

Mum: Oh no, you're not, Lee Marshall! Your end of year tests are starting on Thursday. You can go back to your room and start revising! If you don't study, you won't pass your tests – it's as simple as that! These tests are important.

Lee: Billy's mum lets him go out in the evenings! It's not fair!

Mum: Billy always gets better marks than you. You'll have to repeat the year if you don't get better marks. And if you have to repeat the year, you won't be with your friends at all.

Lee: OK! OK! I get the message!

Mum: I won't tell you again! Oh, and another thing …

It's as simple as that! *I get the message!*	**O**UT of class

1 What's happening in the photograph? What do you think Lee's mum is saying?

2 🔊 3.48 **WORD FRIENDS** How do you say these Word Friends in your language? Listen and tick (✓) the phrases Krystal uses.

☐ study/revise for a test   ☐ get the results of a test
☐ have/take a test   ☐ pass/fail a test
☐ cheat in a test   ☐ get a good/bad mark

3 In pairs, talk about your last big test. What happened? Use Word Friends from Exercise 2.

4 ▶ 8.1 🔊 3.49 Watch or listen to Part 1. Why is Lee's mum angry with him?

5 Find more examples of the First Conditional in the dialogue in Exercise 4.

Grammar	**First Conditional**

if + Present Simple, *will* + verb
If I get a bad mark in the test, my parents will be angry.
You'll have to repeat the year if you don't get better marks.

GRAMMAR TIME   PAGE 127

6 ▶ 8.2 🔊 3.50 **Choose the correct option. Then watch or listen to Part 2 and check.**

Amy: Hi Lee! How's your History revision going?

Lee: Terrible! And I'm really tired now.

Amy: So go to bed! If you ¹(get up)/ 'll get up early tomorrow, you ²feel / 'll feel fresher and you'll remember more.

Lee: Yes, maybe. But I had a great idea. I wrote all the dates for the History test on the back of my ruler! If I ³forget / 'll forget something in the test, I ⁴check / 'll check it on my ruler.

Amy: You can't do that! That's cheating! And I'm sure they ⁵catch / 'll catch you if you ⁶cheat / 'll cheat. And if they ⁷catch / 'll catch you, you ⁸have / 'll have to repeat the year. Don't be an idiot, Lee! Please!

7 Complete the sentences with the correct form of the verbs in brackets.

1 If I *pass* (pass) all my exams, I'll be so happy!
2 If I get good marks, my gran _____ (buy) me a laptop!
3 If Tiggy _____ (get) the results of the test, she'll phone me.
4 My mum won't be pleased if I _____ (not get) a good mark.
5 We'll have to phone the doctor if she _____ (not feel) better soon.
6 If you break it, I _____ (not lend) you anything again!

8 [VOX POPS ▶ 8.3] **Finish the sentences to make them true for you. Then compare with a partner.**

1 If there's nothing good on TV tonight, *I'll read a book.*
2 If I get some money for my birthday, I …
3 If I don't understand my homework, I …
4 If my phone stops working, I …

I can identify specific detail in a conversation and talk about education.

Shetland Islands

Skerries School – the playground at lunchtime

1 In pairs, look at the photo. What do you think is strange about the school?

2 🔊 3.51 In pairs, check you understand the words below. Then listen and check your ideas from Exercise 1.

> gymnasium   library   pupil   science lab
> secondary school   sports field

3 🔊 3.51 Listen again and choose the correct answers.

1 Skerries School
   a has only one classroom.   **b** has a gymnasium.
   c is near a Sports Hall.

2 Pupils at Skerries School
   a start school at half past nine.
   b do the same things as other British pupils.
   c don't have exams.

3 The island
   a is in the North Sea.   **b** has a large town on it.
   c doesn't have an airport.

4 This school year Skerries School
   a doesn't have a teacher.   **b** has only one student.
   c only teaches children from the same family.

4 Work in pairs. Would you like to be the only pupil in your school? Why?/Why not?

5 🔊 3.52 Add the words from Exercise 2 to the correct category. Listen and check.

Vocabulary	School and education
Places of learning	
college primary school [1]*secondary school* university	
People in schools	
classmates form tutor head teacher	
Maths/English teacher [2]_____	
Places/rooms at school	
classroom cloakroom [3]_____ [4]_____	
playground [5]_____ [6]_____ staff room	

6 Complete the sentences with words from the Vocabulary box.

1 Luke was late for school so he had to see the *head teacher*.

2 The _____ is busy on wet days because everyone wants to leave their coats.

3 I changed class last year. My new _____ are a lot nicer.

4 We play football on the school _____ but when it's wet we play in the _____ .

5 The teachers relax in the _____ between lessons.

7 🔊 3.53 **WORD FRIENDS** In pairs, choose the correct option. Listen and check.

1 The best way to revise is to *get* / *make* notes.

2 We *do* / *make* a lot of grammar exercises in English lessons!

3 I'm quite shy so I feel nervous before I *give* / *show* presentations.

4 I always *do* / *make* my homework after I get home from school.

5 It's hard to *draw* / *write* essays in class.

8 In pairs, ask and answer the questions.

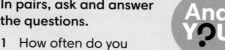

1 How often do you
   ● talk to your head teacher/form tutor?
   ● use the school library/computer room?

2 What are your favourite subjects at school?

I can talk about probability.

VIDEO I'LL DEFINITELY PASS (Part 1)

Amy: Gosh! That was a really difficult test.

Billy: Yes! That last question? What a nightmare! I couldn't remember any of the dates. I probably won't get any points for it!

Amy: I definitely won't! I didn't even answer that question – I didn't have time!

Billy: Oh, don't worry, Amy. You'll probably pass!

Amy: I don't know. I might pass. Fingers crossed! How about you, Lee?

Lee: I thought it was easy! I'll definitely pass! In fact, I think I may get a ten.

Amy: But History's your worst subject. You didn't cheat, did you? Because they'll definitely see from your answers that you cheated!

Lee: No, I didn't cheat!

Billy: So, how did you do it?

Gosh! *What a nightmare!* *Fingers crossed!*	**OUT** of class

1 CLASS VOTE **How do you feel before an important exam?**

☐ relaxed ☐ nervous ☐ frightened

2 Look at the photo. Who do you think looks most relaxed: Amy, Lee or Billy? What do you think they're talking about?

3 8.4 3.54 Watch or listen to Part 1. Then find examples of the phrases below in the dialogue. Who is most confident about passing the exam?

Speaking	Probability

- I will **definitely/probably** pass.
- I **may/might** pass.
- I **definitely/probably** won't pass.

4 8.5 3.55 Why do you think Lee found the test so easy? Watch or listen to Part 2 and check.

5 8.6 3.56 Watch or listen to Part 3. Where would Billy like to go camping this summer?

6 8.6 3.56 Complete the sentences with the words in brackets. Watch or listen to Part 3 again and check.

1 Brighton *will probably be* expensive. (be/will/probably)

2 Billy's uncle _____ them camp on his farm. (let/will/definitely)

3 There _____ space in Amy's tent for Krystal. (be/will/definitely)

4 Krystal _____ to stay in a tent. (want/won't/probably)

5 Krystal _____ to stay in a hotel. (want/might)

6 Lee _____ borrow money for his train ticket. (have to/may)

7 Say if these things will come true in your country in the next ten years. Use the Speaking box to help you.

1 People will stop using banknotes and coins.

2 Food will be cheaper.

3 Our football team will win the World Cup.

4 Newspapers will still be popular.

5 People will live longer.

6 Everyone will use public transport.

People may stop using banknotes and coins.

8 [VOX POPS ▶ 8.7] In pairs, use the Speaking box to say if you think these things will happen to you in the next ten years.

Will you ...

- learn a new language?
- be famous?
- buy a car/motorbike?
- still live in your hometown?
- become a fantastic cook?

I will definitely learn a new language.

I can talk about people's skills and emotions.

1 What can you see in the drawing?

2 Read the teacher's notes and write the names of the children in the drawing.

Bruce is good at counting but he isn't very good at sharing things.

Wendy is fond of talking. She enjoys telling the other children what to do.

Kevin isn't afraid of taking risks and he's really interested in planes.

Hannah is brilliant at drawing but she's hopeless at spelling.

Albert is keen on helping other people. He's always the first to come when someone's in trouble.

Kay is crazy about running. She's the fastest in the class.

3 Find examples of the adjectives with prepositions in Exercise 2.

Language	Adjectives with prepositions

After these phrases we add verb + *-ing*:
(not very) good at, crazy about, keen on,
(really) bad at, afraid of, fond of, hopeless at,
brilliant at, interested in
Bruce is good at counting.
Wendy is fond of talking.

4 In pairs, use the teacher's notes and these jobs to make predictions about the children in the picture.

accountant artist athlete
astronaut doctor nurse pilot
police officer politician

Bruce is good at counting. I think he'll be an accountant.

5 🔊 3.57 Read the text and choose the correct option. Listen and check.

My son loves watching car races on TV but he's afraid ¹*of* / *in* / *on* going fast in the car. He's brilliant ²*about* / *at* / *of* learning languages but he's really bad ³*on* / *to* / *at* remembering people's names. He's keen ⁴*about* / *in* / *on* doing Sudoku puzzles but he's not very ⁵*fond* / *good* / *afraid* at doing Maths problems. He's ⁶*crazy* / *keen* / *brilliant* about playing the guitar but he's hopeless at ⁷*sing* / *singing* / *to sing*. He's ⁸*good* / *keen* / *crazy* at working with his hands and he's fond ⁹*at* / *on* / *of* working in the garden but he thinks he'll work in an office when he's older. I don't understand him.

6 Use the text in Exercise 5 to write a paragraph that an adult you know could write about you.

My daughter is really interested in reading science books but she …

7 In pairs, use the phrases in Exercise 3 and the skills below to ask and answer questions.

And Y?U

learn languages talk do Maths problems
watch car races work with your hands
save money play the guitar dance
read science books drive fast sing
remember things do Sudoku puzzles

A: Are you good at dancing?
B: No, I'm not good at dancing but I'm good at singing.

accountant /əˈkaʊntənt/ n
activity instructor /ækˈtɪvəti ɪnˈstrʌktə/ n
architect /ˈɑːkətekt/ n
artist /ˈɑːtəst, ˈɑːtɪst/ n
astronaut /ˈæstrənɔːt/ n
babysitter /ˈbeɪbiˌsɪtə/ n
beauty salon /ˈbjuːti ˈsælɒn/ n
bike courier /baɪk ˈkʊriə/ n
break (at school) /ˌbreɪk/ n
builder /ˈbɪldə/ n
call centre /kɔːl ˈsentə/ n
celebrity /səˈlebrəti/ n
challenging (job) /ˈtʃæləndʒɪŋ/ adj
chef /ʃef/ n
classmate /ˈklɑːsmeɪt/ n
classroom /ˈklɑːsrʊm/ n
cloakroom /ˈkləʊkrʊm/ n
college /ˈkɒlɪdʒ/ n
(school) computer room /kəmˈpjuːtə rʊm/ n
count /kaʊnt/ v
course book /kɔːs bʊk/ n
creative (job) /kriˈeɪtɪv/ adj
dangerous /ˈdeɪndʒərəs/ adj
doctor /ˈdɒktə/ n
dress up (as) /ˌdres ˈʌp/ v
driver /ˈdraɪvə/ n
education /ˌedjʊˈkeɪʃən/ n
electrician /ɪˌlekˈtrɪʃən/ n
exam /ɪgˈzæm/ n
(on a) farm /fɑːm/ n
farmer /ˈfɑːmə/ n
firefighter /ˈfaɪəˌfaɪtə/ n
form tutor /fɔːm ˈtjuːtə/ n

fruit picker /fruːt ˈpɪkə/ n
full-time (job) /ˌfʊl ˈtaɪm/ adj
gardener /ˈgɑːdnə/ n
gymnasium /dʒɪmˈneɪziəm/ n
hairdresser /ˈheəˌdresə/ n
head teacher /hed ˈtiːtʃə/ n
homework /ˈhəʊmwɜːk/ n
IT specialist /ˌaɪ ˈtiː ˈspeʃələst/ n
journalist /ˈdʒɜːnələst/ n
lawyer /ˈlɔːjə/ n
(school) library /ˈlaɪbrəri/ n
lifeguard /ˈlaɪfgɑːd/ n
look for (a job) /ˌlʊk fə/ v
(Maths/English) teacher /ˈtiːtʃə/ n
mechanic /mɪˈkænɪk/ n
nightmare /ˈnaɪtmeə/ n
nurse /nɜːs/ n
office work /ˈɒfəs wɜːk/ n
ordinary /ˈɔːdənəri/ adj
part-time (job) /ˌpɑːt ˈtaɪm/ adj
pilot /ˈpaɪlət/ n
playground /ˈpleɪgraʊnd/ n
police officer /pəˈliːs ˈɒfəsə/ n
politician /ˌpɒləˈtɪʃən/ n
postman/woman /ˈpəʊsmən, ˈpəʊswʊmən/ n
primary school /ˈpraɪməri skuːl/ n
pupil /ˈpjuːpəl/ n
receptionist /rɪˈsepʃənəst/ n
repeat (a year of school) /rɪˈpiːt/ v
revision /rɪˈvɪʒən/ n

science lab /ˈsaɪəns læb/ n
secondary school /ˈsekəndəri skuːl/ n
secretary /ˈsekrətri/ n
soldier /ˈsəʊldʒə/ n
sports field /spɔːts fiːld/ n
staff room /stɑːf ruːm/ n
stressful /ˈstresfəl/ adj
study /ˈstʌdi/ v
subject /ˈsʌbdʒɪkt/ n
summer job /ˈsʌmə ˌdʒɒb/ n
temporary (job) /ˈtempərəri/ adj
test /test/ n
timetable /ˈtaɪmˌteɪbəl/ n
tour guide /ˈtʊə ˌgaɪd/ n
town council /taʊn ˈkaʊnsəl/ n
translate /trænsˈleɪt/ v
unemployed /ˌʌnɪmˈplɔɪd/ adj
(school) uniform /ˈjuːnəfɔːm/ n
university /juːnəˈvɜːsəti/ n
unpleasant /ʌnˈplezənt/ adj
waiter/waitress /ˈweɪtə, ˈweɪtrəs/ n
well/best paid /ˌwel best ˈpeɪd/ adj
workmate /ˈwɜːkmeɪt/ n

WORD FRIENDS

answer the phone
attract customers
be (really) bad/hopeless at
be afraid of
be crazy about

be fond of
be good/brilliant at
be happy at work
be interested in
be keen on
be late for school/work
be unemployed
become famous
cheat in a test
deliver newspapers
do (grammar) exercises
do homework
earn (good) money
get a good/bad mark
get points (in a test)
get the results of a test
get to work on time
get/have/lose a job
give presentations
go to university
have/take a test/an exam
help people
learn languages
learn to drive
make notes
pass/fail a test/exam
study/revise for a test/exam
wear a uniform
work as a (+ job)
work at the weekend/from nine to five
work for a company
work in a team/alone
work in an office/in one place
work indoors/outdoors
work with your hands
work/study abroad
write articles/essays

VOCABULARY IN ACTION

1 Use the wordlist to find:

1 eight jobs in which you spend a lot of time working outdoors: *builder, ...*
2 four jobs in which you have to be good at counting:
3 five jobs for which you have to wear a uniform:
4 six places where people work:

2 In pairs, say how you feel about the ideas below. Use an adjective and a preposition.

> doing grammar exercises   reading about celebrities
> cheating in tests   giving presentations
> learning languages   wearing a school uniform

- I'm (not) keen/ fond ...
- I'm (really) bad ...
- I'm brilliant/ good ...
- I'm (not) afraid ...

3 Complete the Word Friends.

I spend a long time studying [1]*for* exams. But something always goes wrong on the day I [2]_____ the exam. The worst thing is when I have to [3]_____ an essay. After that there's the horrible wait to [4]_____ the results.

4a 🔊 3.58 **PRONUNCIATION** Listen to the underlined letter(s) in each word and decide which sound you hear.

> <u>ch</u>eat   <u>ch</u>ef   colle<u>g</u>e   electri<u>ci</u>an   dan<u>g</u>erous
> <u>g</u>ymnasium   <u>j</u>ournalist   langua<u>g</u>e   politi<u>ci</u>an
> recep<u>ti</u>onist   <u>s</u>oldier   tea<u>ch</u>er

1 /dʒ/	2 /ʃ/	3 /tʃ/
		<u>ch</u>eat

4b 🔊 3.59 **PRONUNCIATION** Listen and check.

Revision

1 Complete the words in the sentences.

1 My big brother was **u** _n e m p l o y e d_ for six months. But now he's got a **p** _ _ _ - _ _ _ _ job.

2 An expensive **a** _ _ _ _ _ _ _ _ _ is designing the Beckham's new house.

3 I love cooking – I want to work as a **c** _ _ _ when I'm older.

4 I started **s** _ _ _ _ _ _ _ school last week. My form t _ _ _ _ is really nice.

5 During breaks most pupils play outside in the **p** _ _ _ _ _ _ _ _ _ . But one or two pupils prefer reading in the school l _ _ _ _ _ _ .

2 Complete the Word Friends. Use the words in the correct form.

First, I wanted to be a lawyer but you need to study a lot and I'm not crazy about revising for ¹_exams_ . After that I wanted to be a journalist but I realised that I wasn't interested in ²_____ articles. Next I thought about becoming a driver but I couldn't ³_____ my driving test. I started working in a call centre but I really hated answering the ⁴_____ ! It wasn't a surprise when I ⁵_____ my job. After that I was a hotel receptionist for a month but I couldn't get to work ⁶_____ time. Then I worked ⁷_____ a bike courier but found out I don't like ⁸_____ alone. Finally, I have the perfect job – I walk dogs for a living. I love it!

3 In pairs, talk about adults you know and the jobs they have. Why do you think they chose these jobs?

My uncle is a mechanic – he's good at working with his hands.

4 Complete the second sentence so that it means the same as the first one.

1 Helen enjoys working abroad.
Helen is keen _on working abroad_ .

2 Magda loves learning languages.
Magda is crazy _____ .

3 Jack works really badly in a team.
Jack is hopeless _____ .

4 Mary doesn't enjoy working indoors.
Mary isn't interested _____ .

5 Complete the text with *will* or *won't* and the words in brackets. Then, in pairs, write predictions about today's school day.

Our first class today is English. I'm sure we ¹_'ll talk_ (talk) a lot in English and we ²_____ (play) some cool games. Then it's History. ³_____ (we/watch) a film? I hope so! This afternoon isn't so good. Our first class after lunch is Maths. We ⁴_____ (probably/ do) a lot of exercises and I'm sure I ⁵_____ (not understand) anything. After that it's Rugby. I'm sure that somebody ⁶_____ (forget) his rugby boots and Mr Hodd ⁷_____ (shout) at us.

6 Complete the dialogue with the correct form of the First Conditional.

Ann: How are you getting to your job interview?

Bea: By bike. The farm isn't far from town.

Ann: But what ¹_will you do_ (you/do) if the weather ²_____ (be) bad?

Bea: It's OK. If it ³_____ (rain), I ⁴_____ (take) the ten o'clock bus.

Ann: But if the bus ⁵_____ (arrive) late, how ⁶_____ (you/get) there then?

Bea: I ⁷_____ (phone) for a taxi if something ⁸_____ (go) wrong.

Ann: But if there ⁹_____ (not be) a signal, you ¹⁰_____ (not able to phone) for a taxi.

Bea: You worry too much!

7 In pairs, talk about careers. Student A, look below. Student B, look at page 131.

Student A

1 You work in a Student Careers office. Ask Student B what he/she likes doing.

2 Ask Student B about his/her career plans.

3 Give advice: *You definitely/probably won't enjoy being a …/You might be good at …*

8 🔊 3.60 **Listen, then listen again and write down what you hear.**

Will robots do our jobs?

Robots in the future

1 _____

Robots and machines can do a lot of jobs today that people did in the past. Should we be worried because we might lose our jobs? Or should we be happy because they can do jobs we don't enjoy?

2 _____

Technology is progressing very quickly now. Robots and computers can do more and more jobs. 800,000 machines are doing jobs today that people did fifteen years ago and experts say that fifteen million people will lose their jobs in the future.

3 _____

This change started a long time ago. Robots started to build cars in 1961 in the USA and trains without drivers began thirty years ago. At that time, scientists were building robots and machines to do the boring and routine work in manufacturing. Then they started to replace other jobs to make life easier and quicker for people. Today there aren't many secretaries, travel agents, librarians, airport check-in assistants or farm workers. Robots can also do the jobs of receptionists, pharmacists and soldiers.

4 _____

Robots might replace a lot of us in the future but some jobs will always need people. If you have a job which is about looking after people, or talking to people, or finding answers to problems and being creative, you'll be safe. They say that there will always be teachers, bar staff, hairdressers, care workers and top businessmen who make important decisions. Of course, there will be new jobs too because we'll need lots of computer specialists and people to teach everyone to code and design new machines.

But who really knows? There's already a robot bartender in Germany who can mix cocktails and talk to customers! And you can check in to a very unusual hotel in Japan.

GLOSSARY
bartender (n phr) someone who makes and serves drinks in a bar or restaurant
care worker (n phr) someone looks after people who are ill or old
expert (n) someone who knows a lot about something
progress (v) to become better
replace (v) to start doing something instead of someone

1 In pairs, discuss the questions.

1 Write down as many jobs as you can in two minutes.

2 Which of these jobs do you think robots can do now?

3 Which jobs do you think robots will do in the future?

4 Which jobs do you think that robots will not be able to do in the future? Why?

2 Read the article and check your ideas in Exercise 1.

3 Read the article again and match headings A–D with paragraphs 1–4 in the text.

A ☐ Which jobs are in danger?

B ☐ Some questions we need to ask.

C ☐ Which jobs are safe?

D ☐ How big is the problem?

4 Which of the photos below does the text not mention? What do you learn about the others?

 A

 B

 C

 D

5 In pairs, discuss the questions.

1 Who do you think will lose their jobs in the future – people who earn good money or people who don't earn much money? Why?

2 Do you think robots will be good or bad for society in the future? Why?

6 You are going to watch part of a BBC programme about an unusual hotel in Japan. Read an advert for the programme. Do you ever stay in hotels when you're on holiday?

 Click The BBC's technology series tells us about a new hotel in Japan and why it's very special.

7 ▶ 8.8 Watch Part 1 of the video and answer the questions.

1 Why is the Henn Na hotel unusual?

2 Why is the visitor surprised by the second receptionist?

3 Do the receptionists speak English?

4 Why does the visitor laugh when he's at reception?

5 Why does a machine take his photograph?

8 Work in pairs. What do you think his hotel room will be like?

9 ▶ 8.9 Watch Part 2 of the video and check your ideas in Exercise 8.

10 ▶ 8.9 Watch Part 2 of the video again and complete the sentences.

1 It takes a long time to get to his room because _____.

2 There aren't any light switches in the room because _____.

3 The visitor needs to use a book because _____.

4 The visitor has a problem because _____.

11 Work in pairs. Would you like to stay at this hotel? Why?/Why not?

12 **CULTURE PROJECT** In small groups, create a presentation about a robot.

1 Use the internet to research a new and clever robot that works in your country.

2 Write a short script and includes some photos or video.

3 Present your robot to your class.

4 Vote for the cleverest robot.

9

Close to nature

VOCABULARY
Landscapes and natural features | Talking about countries | Phrasal verbs | Outdoor activities | Sporting equipment

GRAMMAR
Present Perfect – all forms | Present Perfect with *just/already/yet*

Grammar: Have you bought the tickets?

Speaking: Can I ask a favour?

BBC Culture: Can you count the fish in the sea?

Workbook p. 113

BBC VOX POPS
EXAM TIME 3 > p. 136
CLIL 5 > p. 142

A

The Aran Islands in the Atlantic Ocean near the coast of Ireland. Most of the population work in farming.

9.1 VOCABULARY Landscapes and countries

I can talk about landscapes, natural features and countries.

1 Look at the photos. Do you have places like this in your country?

2 4.01 Listen and read about the places in photos A–D. Which place would you most like to visit?

I'd like to visit the Sahara.

3 4.02 I KNOW! In pairs, use the letters to write words connected with landscape. Add them to Vocabulary A. Listen and check.

1 c h e a b *beach*	3 k a l e	5 r e v i r
2 d e e r s t	4 i n o m u t a n	6 a s e

Vocabulary A Landscapes and natural features

[1]*beach* cliff coast [2]________ field forest island jungle [3]________ [4]________ ocean rainforest [5]________ rocks [6]________ volcano waterfall

4 How do you say the words in Vocabulary A in your language? Which of the features can you find near your hometown?

5 Work in pairs. Match features 1–4 with photos A–D.

1 ☐ mountains, a lake
2 ☐ rainforest, a river, waterfalls
3 ☐ fields, cliffs, a beach
4 ☐ desert, rocks

6 4.03 Work in groups. Try to match these places with a feature from Vocabulary A. Listen and check.

1 The Sahara	4 The Mississippi	7 The Baltic
2 Loch Ness	5 Great Britain	8 Niagara Falls
3 Mount Everest	6 The Pacific	9 Etna

We think The Sahara is a desert.

B

Karymsky Volcano in east Siberia in Russia is about 6,000 kilometres from Moscow, the capital city.

C

The 'Great Eastern Sand Sea' in the Sahara Desert in Algeria – one of the hottest places on Earth.

D

Iguazu Falls are on the border between Argentina and Brazil. They are seventy metres high and almost three kilometres across. Nearly two million tourists visit them every year.

7 **WORD FRIENDS** In pairs, look at the Word Friends. Then complete the text with the correct prepositions.

in	a forest/a field/a lake/the mountains/the sea
on	a beach/an island/the coast
by	a lake/a river/the sea

We had a fantastic holiday. We stayed ¹*on* the north coast of Spain. We camped ² _____ a field ³ _____ a small river. In the mornings, we swam ⁴ _____ the sea and mum and dad sunbathed ⁵ _____ the beach. On hot days we spent our time ⁶ _____ the mountains.

8 Where is your favourite place in the countryside? Tell the class. Use the Word Friends from Exercise 7.

I love being in the mountains/by the sea.

9 🔊 4.04 How do you say these words in your language?

Vocabulary B	Talking about countries
border capital city country flag	
official language population	

10 🔊 4.05 Listen and answer the questions about Ander's country. Can you guess where he comes from?

1 What is the country's population?
   (about) five million
2 What colours are the national flag?
3 What is the country famous for?
4 Which countries does it share a border with?
5 What is its capital city?
6 What is the official language?

11 🔊 4.06 Listen again. Check your answers to Exercise 10.

12 [VOX POPS ▶ 9.1] In groups, answer the questions in Exercise 10 for your country.

My country's population is about forty million.

I can use the Present Perfect to talk about experience.

1 CLASS VOTE Do you think it's better to go on holiday abroad or to stay in your own country?

2 🔊 4.07 Read the text. How many countries does Todd Morden still have to visit? Which were his favourite places?

Todd Morden is hoping to become the youngest person to visit every country in the world. The twenty-four-year-old Canadian has visited 290 of them and he hasn't finished (there are 321 countries in total)! Planet Discovery talked to Todd.

PD: Tell us about your most exciting experience.
Todd: Where to start? I've swum with dolphins off the coast of Ireland, I've played with bears in Romania and climbed Mount Kilimanjaro.
PD: Have you ever had any bad experiences?
Todd: No, I haven't. Well, I've had some problems with visas. But I've never had any really bad experiences.
PD: Which countries have you enjoyed most?
Todd: I think I've enjoyed Thailand and Libya most – they're so interesting. But in every country people have been nice to me. I've met a lot of very kind people, especially in Africa.
PD: Have you learnt a lot from travelling?
Todd: Yes, I have. I've learnt that people everywhere are good and basically the same!

3 Find all the examples of the Present Perfect in the text.

Grammar	Present Perfect – all forms
+	**–**
I've (have) swum with dolphins.	I haven't visited Africa.
He's (has) visited 290 countries.	She hasn't finished.
They've (have) learnt a lot.	They haven't had problems.
?	
Have you learnt a lot? Yes, I have./No, I haven't.	
Has he enjoyed Libya? Yes, he has./No, he hasn't.	
Have they finished? Yes, they have./No, they haven't.	
Which countries have you enjoyed most?	

GRAMMAR TIME ▸ PAGE 127

4 What are the Past Simple and Present Perfect forms of these verbs? Are they the same or different? Use the verb list on page 129 to help you.

| ~~buy~~ ~~come~~ drink eat forget have look |
| meet see sleep travel visit watch write |

buy – bought, bought (the same)
come – came, come (different)

5 Complete the sentences with the correct Present Perfect form of the verbs in brackets.

1 I *have met* (meet) people from all over the world.
2 My friend, Gill, _____ (write) a blog about his travels.
3 My parents _____ (not visit) the USA but they _____ (be) to Canada.
4 My gran _____ (never leave) her hometown!
5 Brett _____ (not eat) Indian food before.
6 I _____ (spend) a lot of time in London but I _____ (not see) Buckingham Palace.

6 Complete the questions with the correct form of the verbs in brackets. Then ask and answer in pairs. Write down your partner's answers.

1 Have you ever *been* (be) to New York?
2 How many countries have you _____ (visit)?
3 How many times have you _____ (flow) in a plane?
4 Have you ever _____ (eat) something really unusual?
5 Have you ever _____ (swim) in the ocean?
6 Have you ever _____ (climb) a mountain more than 4,000 metres high?

A: *Have you ever been to New York?*
B: *Yes, I have./No, I haven't.*

7 Use your notes from Exercise 6 to tell the class about your partner.

Kasia's never been to New York.

8 Tell the class about a surprising thing you have done in your life. Use the ideas below. Whose fact was most surprising?

And YOU

I've met/seen/won/lived in/been to/played …

I can find specific detail in a text and talk about personal adventures.

Alone in the jungle

It was Christmas Eve. Juliane Koepcke, a seventeen-year-old German girl, was travelling home with her mother for Christmas. They were flying over the rainforest of Peru when suddenly there was a storm and the pilot lost control of the plane. Many of the passengers started crying but Juliane calmly held her mother's hand. After that, the plane blew up. Juliane found herself outside the plane but still in her seat, high above the earth. She fell more than three kilometres. She remembered seeing the rainforest below her but after that she fainted.

The next day Juliane woke up. She had a broken shoulder bone and cuts on her leg. She was completely alone. Although she felt afraid, she knew she couldn't give up. Juliane came to a river and started walking down it – she hoped it would take her to civilisation. She walked for nine days. At night it was very cold and Juliane was wearing only a short dress. She had no food, except one bag of sweets.

On the tenth day, Juliane felt very weak and had to stop walking. But she came across an empty boat and knew that people must be near. She slept near the boat and the next day she heard men's voices. When the men saw the thin, hungry girl they were very frightened. But Juliane knew some Spanish and she told them about the accident. The men took her to a doctor. She later found out that all the other ninety-one passengers on the plane were dead.

This took place forty years ago. There have been two films about Juliane's adventure and many newspapers and magazines have written about her. Juliane has also written a book, 'When I Fell From The Sky'. She now works as a zoologist but has often gone back to the rainforest in Peru. She has tried to have a normal life but she has often asked herself, "Why was I the only person to survive?"

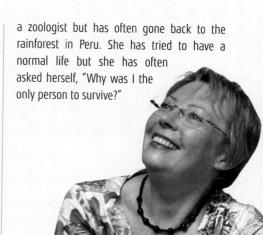

1 🔊 **4.08 In pairs, look at the photo and the title of the article. Answer the questions. Then read the article and check.**

1 What do you think the story is about?
2 Do you think the story has a happy ending?

2 Read the text again. Choose the correct answers.

1 On Christmas Eve, Juliane
   a was travelling to see her mother.
   b was flying to the rainforest.
   c was going home.

2 When the plane hit bad weather,
   a they were over the rainforest.
   b everyone was crying.
   c Juliane started to panic.

3 When Juliane woke up in the jungle, she
   a was in good health.
   b couldn't find any other passengers.
   c had a lot of warm clothes.

4 On the tenth day after the accident, Juliane
   a was very ill.
   b borrowed a boat.
   c spoke to some men.

5 Today Juliane
   a lives in Peru.
   b often thinks about the accident.
   c is afraid of travelling.

3 🔊 **4.09 In pairs, find the phrasal verbs below in the text. Can you guess their meaning from the context? How do you say them in your language?**

Vocabulary	Phrasal verbs
blow up come across find out	
give up go back	

4 Use the Vocabulary box to complete the sentences.

1 I can't answer your question. I _give up_ !
2 It's hard to _____ to school after the summer.
3 I _____ an old diary when I was tidying my desk.
4 Luckily the bomb didn't _____ .
5 I must _____ the train times.

5 [VOX POPS ▶ 9.2] Tell the class about a time when you were completely lost. Use the questions below to help you.

1 What happened?
2 How did you feel?
3 Did you ask for help?

I can use the Present Perfect to talk about recent events.

VIDEO **HAVE YOU BOUGHT THE TICKETS? (Part 1)**

Lee: Hi, Amy! What's up?

Amy: Have you bought the train tickets yet?

Lee: Well, I know exactly what train we want to catch – I've already checked the timetable. But I haven't actually bought the tickets yet … I've bought a map of the Scottish Highlands! … And I've just cleaned both the tents.

Amy: So you haven't started packing yet?

Lee: Give me a break! I've already told you – we haven't bought all the food yet so it's too early to start packing. Anyway, have you heard from Billy yet?

Amy: Yes, I have – he's just phoned to say his uncle will pick us up from the station.

Lee: Great! This'll be a fantastic holiday!

Give me a break!   *Great!*   **OUT** of **class**

---

1 Look at the photo. What are Amy and Lee planning?

2 9.3 🔊 4.10 Watch or listen to Part 1. Check your answer to Exercise 1 and tick (✓) the things Lee has done.

Holiday in Scotland

☐ check train timetable	☐ clean the tents
☐ buy train tickets	☐ buy food
☐ buy a map	☐ pack rucksacks

---

3 Underline other examples of *already*, *just* and *yet* in the dialogue.

Grammar	Present Perfect with *already/just/yet*
+	
I've already checked the timetable. He's just phoned.	
–	
We haven't bought all the food yet.	
?	
Have you bought the tickets yet?	

GRAMMAR TIME ▶ PAGE 128

4 Read the dialogue again. In pairs, write five sentences about what Lee has/hasn't done.

Lee's hasn't bought the train tickets yet.

5 Complete the sentences with *already*, *just* or *yet*.

1 A: *Drek 5* is on TV now. Why don't we watch it?
   B: Sorry but I've **already** seen it twice!

2 Have you finished on the computer _____? I want to check the train timetable.

3 A: You look cold and tired!
   B: Yes, we've _____ been for a long walk.

4 Don't take my plate. I haven't finished _____!

5 Raj has _____ phoned – he's missed the bus!

6 You're slow – Jo has _____ finished the exercise!

6 ▶ 9.4 🔊 4.11 Choose the correct option. Watch or listen to Part 2 and check.

Lee: Hi, mum! Yes, we've ¹*just* / *yet* arrived. No, we haven't seen Billy's uncle ²*already* / *yet*. We've ³*yet* / *just* got off the train. Yeah, everyone's fine. Yes, we've ⁴*already* / *yet* had our sandwiches. Delicious, thanks! The weather's OK – it hasn't rained ⁵*already* / *yet*! I have to go, mum. Bye! Billy, has your uncle arrived ⁶*just* / *yet*?

Billy: No, he hasn't. Oh, I've ⁷*just* / *yet* seen him!

7 Make five sentences about your news and recent activities. Compare with a partner.

And **YOU**

I've already finished the History project.
I haven't … yet. I've just …

I can identify specific detail in a conversation and talk about outdoor activities.

Kayaking **A**

Snowboarding **B**

Mountain biking **C**

Surfing **D**

1 Look at the photos. Which activity would you like to do? Why?

2 🔊 4.12 Look at the photos and listen. Which activity A–D does each speaker think is the most exciting? What do you think?

1 ☐ Tony   3 ☐ Sue
2 ☐ Lucy   4 ☐ Glenn

I think mountain biking is the most exciting activity.

3 🔊 4.13 Check you understand the words below. In pairs, add each activity to the correct category – water or land.

Vocabulary A	Outdoor activities

cycling   fishing   hiking   kayaking
mountain biking   pony trekking   rock climbing
scuba diving   skiing   snowboarding   surfing
swimming   windsurfing

WATER: *kayaking, surfing, …*
LAND: *mountain biking, snowboarding, …*

4 In groups, say which activities in Vocabulary A you have/haven't tried and which are popular/unpopular in your country.

5 🔊 4.14 Listen and match statements a–e with Speakers 1–4. There is one extra statement.

1 ☐   2 ☐   3 ☐   4 ☐

a He/She says the activity can be dangerous.
b He/She is very good at the activity.
c He/She talks about the last time he/she did the activity.
d He/She talks about when he/she did the activity for the first time.
e He/She describes the good and bad sides of the activity.

6 🔊 4.15 How do you say the words below in your language?

Vocabulary B	Sporting equipment

bike   boots   compass   gloves   goggles
helmet   kayak   life jacket   map   paddle
snowboard   surfboard   wetsuit

7 🔊 4.16 Complete the sentences with the correct items of equipment from Vocabulary B. Listen and check.

• **Pony trekking** – you need a [1]*helmet* for your head and a map and a [2]_____ so you don't get lost.
• **Windsurfing** – you need a [3]_____ to float in the water and a [4]_____ to keep you warm.
• **Skiing** – you need skis, ski poles, ski boots, [5]_____ to protect your eyes and [6]_____ for your hands.

8 🔊 4.17 Listen to four people talking about sports activities. Mark the sentences T (true) or F (false).

1 ☐ Surfing started in islands in the Pacific.
2 ☐ It's easy to go the wrong way in a kayak.
3 ☐ A good mountain bike costs a minimum of €1,000.
4 ☐ Snowboarding started in the 1970s.

9 In pairs, ask and answer the questions about the different activities in Vocabulary A.

And YOU

1 Have you ever tried …?
2 When was the last time?
3 Did you enjoy it?
4 Which of the activities would you like to try?

A: *Have you ever tried surfing?*
B: *Yes, I have.*

I can ask for, give and refuse permission.

VIDEO CAN I ASK A FAVOUR?

Billy: Is it OK to put our tents up here, Uncle Ally?

Ally: I'm afraid that's not possible, Billy. There's a big bull in this field. He won't like it.

Billy: What about that field? Can we camp in there?

Ally: I'm afraid that's not a good idea, either. There's a lot of water over there at the moment. You'll wake up swimming in your tents!

Lee: So is it all right to camp next to the farmhouse?

Ally: Yes, of course. Good idea.

Krystal: Can I ask a favour? Can we dry our clothes in the house? All my things are soaking!

Ally: No problem. Let's go and have a cup of tea. You all look so unhappy!

Can I ask a favour?

OUT**of class**

1 ▶ 9.5 ◀)) 4.18 In pairs, look at the photo. Do you think the people are having a good time? Watch or listen and check.

2 Find examples of the phrases from the Speaking box in the dialogue.

Speaking	Asking for, giving and refusing permission

Asking for permission
- Can I/we ...?
- Is it OK (for me/us) to ...?
- Is it all right to ...?

Giving permission
- Yes, of course.
- No problem.
- Sure – go ahead. (informal)

Refusing permission
- I'm sorry but you can't.
- I'm afraid that's not possible.
- I'm afraid that's not a good idea.

3 ◀)) 4.19 Complete the dialogues with one word in each gap. Listen and check.

1 **Lee:** Is it OK ¹*for me* to use your toilet?
 Ally: Sure – go ² _____ .

2 **Amy:** Sorry, but can I make myself a cup of tea and a snack?
 Ally: ³ _____ problem! The kitchen's on the left.

3 **Krystal:** Is it ⁴ _____ for me to have a hot bath?
 Ally: Yes, ⁵ _____ course!
 Krystal: Oh, and ⁶ _____ I borrow a hairdryer?
 Ally: I'm afraid that's not ⁷ _____ . We haven't got one!

4 Work in pairs. Replace the highlighted phrases in Exercise 3 with another phrase from the Speaking box. Then practise reading your dialogue.

5 ◀)) 4.20 Listen to the end of the story. How many people spent the night in the tents?

6 In pairs, ask for permission. Use the ideas below or your own ideas.

borrow a pen?
leave my bag here?
use your mobile?
look at your student's book?
ask you a favour?
visit you this weekend?

A: Is it OK for me to borrow a pen?
B: Sure – go ahead.

7 In pairs, follow the instructions. Use the Speaking box to help you.

- **Student A** – Look at page 130. Choose a situation and ask your partner for permission.
- **Student B** – give or refuse permission
- Change roles. Student B, look at page 130.

I can write a postcard.

Dear Aunty Linda,
I hope you're well. **1** We're having a great time in Scotland. **2** Actually, the weather has been terrible but it hasn't stopped us! **3** We've had some lovely walks, we've visited the castle and we've helped Billy's uncle with the sheep! **4** Tomorrow we're going to try kayaking – I'm so nervous!
5 See you soon!
Lots of love
Amy
6 PS: Lee is so annoying. He wants to be with me all the time. I think Billy is nicer ;-)

Linda Jenk
Flat 23
Battenbur
19 Oxtails
Harlow M
Essex
CM20 8K

Writing — A postcard

Dear/Hi + person's name

1 **Say where you are**
I'm writing from ...
We're having a great/nice time in ...
Here we are in ...

2 **Describe the weather**
It hasn't rained yet!
The weather has been terrible.

3 **Say what you've done**
We've been to ...
We've visited/walked/swam/sunbathed/
had/seen ...

4 **Talk about your plans**
This afternoon/Tomorrow we're going to ...
We're coming home on Sunday.

5 **Ending**
See you soon!
Miss you!
(Lots of) love

6 PS: If you want, you can add a PS
(postscript) for funny information or gossip!

1 In pairs, talk about the last time you sent or received a postcard. Answer the questions.

1 Who sent it?/Who did you send it to?
2 Where was it from?
3 Did you keep it?

2 Read Amy's postcard. Is she having a good holiday?

3 Underline the phrases in the Writing box which are in Amy's postcard.

4 Read the sentences. Decide if the weather has been good (+) or bad (–).

1 [+] The weather has been amazing.
2 [ ] It's been very cold and windy.
3 [ ] It hasn't rained at all.
4 [ ] It's so cold and wet!
5 [ ] It's been lovely and warm.
6 [ ] It hasn't stopped raining.

5 Underline four activities you like doing most when you're on holiday. Compare with a partner.

buy clothes/souvenirs   eat ice cream   go to the cinema
have a barbecue   sunbathe   have a long walk
make friends with people your own age   watch the sunset
read a novel   swim in the sea   visit a museum/castle

6 Imagine you're on holiday at the moment. Write a sentence about what you've done so far. Use the ideas from Exercise 5 and the Present Perfect.

I've swum in the sea, watched the sunset …

Writing Time

7 Imagine you are on holiday at a popular tourist resort. Write a postcard to your friend:

1 **2** **3** mention the place, the weather and what you have done so far
4 write about your plans
5 include an ending

Use Amy's postcard and the Writing box to help you.

adventure /əd'ventʃə/ n
alone /ə'ləʊn/ adv
amazing /ə'meɪzɪŋ/ adj
beach /biːtʃ/ n
blow up /bləʊ ʌp/ v
boat /bəʊt/ n
(ski) boots /ˌski: 'buːts/ n
border /'bɔːdə/ n
camp /kæmp/ v
capital city /ˈkæpətl 'sɪti/ n
civilisation /ˌsɪvəlaɪ'zeɪʃən/ n
cliff /klɪf/ n
coast /kəʊst/ n
come across /kʌm ə'krɒs/ v
compass /'kʌmpəs/ n
country (state) /'kʌntri/ n
cut /kʌt/ n
cycling /'saɪklɪŋ/ n
dead /ded/ adj
desert /'dezət/ n
dry /draɪ/ adj
earth/Earth /ɜːθ/ n
(sporting) equipment
/ˌspɔːtɪŋ ɪ'kwɪpmənt/ n
faint /feɪnt/ v
farmhouse /'fɑːmhaʊs/ n
field /fiːld/ n
find out /faɪnd aʊt/ v
fishing /'fɪʃɪŋ/ n
flag /flæg/ n
float /fləʊt/ v
forest /'fɒrəst/ n
give up /gɪv ʌp/ v
gloves /glʌvz/ n
go back /gəʊ bæk/ v
goggles /'gɒgəlz/ n
gossip /'gɒsəp, 'gɒsɪp/ n
helmet /'helmət/ n
hiking /'haɪkɪŋ/ n

holiday /'hɒlədeɪ/ n
hometown /ˌhəʊm 'taʊn / n
island /'aɪlənd/ n
jungle /'dʒʌŋgəl/ n
kayak /'kaɪæk/ n
kayaking /'kaɪækɪŋ/ n
lake /leɪk/ n
land /lænd/ n
landscape /'lændskeɪp/ n
life jacket /laɪf 'dʒækət/ n
map /mæp/ n
mountain /'maʊntən/ n
mountain bike /'maʊntən
baɪk/ n
mountain biking /'maʊntən
'baɪkɪŋ/ n
natural feature /'nætʃərəl
'fiːtʃə/ n
ocean /'əʊʃən/ n
official language /ə'fɪʃəl
'læŋgwɪdʒ/ n
outdoor activity /ˌaʊt'dɔː
æk'tɪvəti/ n
paddle /'pædl/ n
passenger /'pæsɪndʒə/ n
pick sb up /pɪk 'sʌmbədi
ˌʌp/ v
pilot /'paɪlət/ n
place /pleɪs/ n
plane /pleɪn/ n
pony trekking /'pəʊni
'trekɪŋ/ n
population /ˌpɒpjə'leɪʃən/ n
rain /reɪn/ n
rainforest /'reɪnˌfɒrɪst/ n
river /'rɪvə/ n
rock climbing /rɒk
'klaɪmɪŋ/ n
rocks /rɒks/ n

sand /sænd/ n
scuba diving /'skuːbə
ˌdaɪvɪŋ/ n
sea /siː/ n
skis /skiːz/ n
ski poles /ˌski: 'pəʊlz/ n
skiing /'skiːɪŋ/ n
sky /skaɪ/ n
snowboard /'snəʊbɔːd/ n
snowboarding
/'snəʊbɔːdɪŋ/ n
soaking /'səʊkɪŋ/ adj
storm /stɔːm/ n
sunbathe /'sʌnbeɪð/ v
surfboard /'sɜːfbɔːd/ n
surfing /'sɜːfɪŋ/ n
survive /sə'vaɪv/ v
swimming /'swɪmɪŋ/ n
take place /teɪk pleɪs/ v
tent /tent/ n
(train) ticket /'treɪn ˌtɪkət/ n
tourist resort /'tʊərəst
rɪ'zɔːt/ n
travel /'trævəl/ v
visa /'viːzə/ n
volcano /vɒl'keɪnəʊ/ n
warm /wɔːm/ adj
water /'wɔːtə/ n
waterfall /'wɔːtəfɔːl/ n
weather /'weðə/ n
wet /wet/ adj
wetsuit /'wetˌsuːt/ n
windsurfing /'wɪndsɜːfɪŋ/ n
windy /'wɪndi/ adj

WORD FRIENDS

a happy ending
a true story
by a lake/a river/the sea
buy a souvenir
catch a bus/train
check a (train) timetable
climb a mountain
fly in a plane
get lost
get off a bus/train
go on holiday
go the wrong way
have a good/bad
    experience/holiday
have a good/great time
have a problem (with)
in a forest/a field/a lake/the
    mountains/the sea
lose control of (a vehicle)
make friends
miss a bus/train
on a beach/an island/the
    coast
pack a rucksack
protect your head/eyes
put up a tent
receive a postcard
send a postcard
spend the night in a tent
swim in the sea
try an activity
visit a country/museum
watch the sunset
write a postcard

VOCABULARY IN ACTION

1a Use the wordlist to find:
1 eight things you could buy in a sports shop: *boots, …*
2 ten sporting activities:
3 twelve places you could see in a nature documentary:

1b In pairs, say:
1 three things you have bought in a sports shop: *map, …*
2 three sporting activities that you enjoy and three that you don't like:
3 three natural features that you haven't seen but would like to see:

2 Complete the words in the sentences.
1 When I was kayaking, I dropped my **p** _a d d l e_ and fell in the water. Fortunately, I was wearing a **l** _ _ _ _
   j _ _ _ _ _ _.
2 We got lost in the mountains because of a bad **s** _ _ _ _ _.
   Fortunately, I had a map and a **c** _ _ _ _ _ _ _ with me.
3 There were a lot of people waiting to cross the
   b _ _ _ _ _ _ into India. Fortunately, my **v** _ _ _ _ was OK and they let us through.

3 Complete the Word Friends.
1 _write_ a postcard
2 _____ a rucksack
3 _____ a mountain
4 _____ in the sea
5 _____ a holiday
6 _____ control of a motorbike

4a 🔊 4.21 **PRONUNCIATION** Listen and write the words below in the correct column.

adventure amazing dangerous
equipment holiday museum
rainforest snowboarding volcano
waterfall

1 oOo	2 Ooo
adventure	

4b 🔊 4.22 **PRONUNCIATION** Listen, check and repeat.

Revision

VOCABULARY

1 Choose the correct option. Then write a similar text about your hometown.

> St Andrews is a university town ¹*by / in /* (*on*) the east coast of Scotland. It has a ²*border / flag / population* of about 17,000 people. The town is a popular tourist ³*hometown / landscape / resort* because of its famous golf course and its long sandy ⁴*beaches / cliffs / fields*. A few miles north of the town is a bridge over the ⁵*ocean / river / water* Tay. Edinburgh, the ⁶*capital / country / official* city of Scotland, is about fifty miles to the south.

2 Match the activities below with the groups of words. Then, in pairs say which activity you think is the most a) dangerous, b) tiring, c) difficult.

> hiking   kayaking   mountain biking   skiing
> snowboarding   ~~surfing~~   windsurfing

1 *surfing* – sea, board, wetsuit
2 _____ – goggles, mountains, board
3 _____ – helmet, cycling, countryside
4 _____ – lake/sea, board, windy weather
5 _____ – life jacket, river, paddle
6 _____ – map, forest, boots
7 _____ – mountains, poles, gloves

I think mountain biking is the most dangerous activity because you go so fast and …

3 Complete the Word Friends and phrasal verbs in the story. Use the words in the correct form.

> I went ¹**on** holiday last week. It started very badly. I ² _____ off the bus at the wrong stop! Then I went the ³ _____ way! So I arrived late at the station and ⁴ _____ my train. I had to ⁵ _____ a slower train so it was very late when I got to the hotel. Then I ⁶ _____ a BIG problem. The receptionist said there was no reservation in my name! He said, 'I can ⁷ _____ up a tent in the garden for you.' I said, 'There's no way I'm going to ⁸ _____ the night in a tent!' I almost gave ⁹ _____ and went home. But my story had a ¹⁰ _____ ending. The receptionist was joking! I ¹¹ _____ friends with him. We've had a great ¹² _____ together. Last night, we ¹³ _____ the sunset on the beach. It was so romantic!

GRAMMAR

4 In pairs, say which of the things in the story in Exercise 3 you have/haven't done.

I've got off the bus at the wrong stop before.

5 Complete the text with the Present Perfect form of the verbs in brackets.

> I ¹*haven't been* (not be) on a fitness holiday before. I hope I enjoy it.
> **6 a.m.** – We ² _____ (just/eat) breakfast! Julie says she ³ _____ (never/get) up so early!
> **10 a.m.** – We ⁴ _____ (already/run) ten kilometres and we ⁵ _____ (not/yet/finish)! I ⁶ _____ (never/feel) so tired!
> **1 p.m.** – They ⁷ _____ (just/bring) us lunch – salad and an apple! Andy ⁸ _____ (already/finish). He's still hungry. He ⁹ _____ (never/have) lunch without pudding before!

6 Make questions in the Present Perfect. Then, in pairs, ask your questions and answer with *already*, *just* or *yet*.

1 you / ever / be / to / England / ?
2 you / visit / capital city / your country / ?
3 your brother (or sister) / leave / school / ?
4 you / climb / highest mountain / your country / ?
5 you / send / text / friend / today / ?
6 you / answer / question / class / today / ?

A: Have you ever been to England?
B: No, I haven't been to England yet.

SPEAKING

7 In pairs, role play the situations. Student A, look below. Student B, look at page 131.

Student A

1 You want to go mountain biking. Student B has a better bike than yours. Ask for permission to use it. You haven't got a helmet. Try to borrow one from Student B.

2 Student B asks for permission to go on a camping trip with you. Give permission. Ask if Student B has a tent. Student B wants to share your tent. Refuse permission – it's a small tent.

DICTATION

8 🔊 4.23 Listen, then listen again and write down what you hear.

BBC

CULTURE

How many fish ...?

Sea life numbers

Fish is a popular meal for many people. It's healthy, tasty and often cheap because there are lots of fish in the sea. But are there? Perhaps you've noticed that sometimes we can't buy our favourite fish. The reason is that in the last thirty years we've taken too many fish out of the sea. Fishermen must stop catching some fish for a while and catch others instead. Man has caused lots of problems to other sea animals too.

There aren't many sea turtles left in the world. People kill them for food and many also die when they get caught in fishermen's nets. Another problem for turtles is that they lay their eggs on beaches. We have built more and more houses and hotels on the coast. When the baby turtles come out of their eggs, they need to get to the sea. But many of them don't survive, they get lost or sea birds kill them. Today in many places, like Cancun in Mexico, people help them to get to the sea.

Sea birds are also becoming rarer. Beautiful birds, like the albatross, spend nearly all their lives in the air and eat fish to live. Some types of fishing are very dangerous for these birds. Like the turtles, they get caught in fishing nets and drown. Some areas, like South Georgia, have created big protected areas to help these birds. Also conservation groups are encouraging fishermen to use new fishing techniques.

All sea birds need to catch fish to live. So for them and for us we need to control fishing.

GLOSSARY
conservation group (n phr) people who work to protect animals, plants, etc.
drown (v) to die from being under water for too long
get caught (v phr) to be in a situation that you cannot easily get out of
lay their eggs (v phr) to produce eggs
net (n) something used for catching fish, insects, or animals

EXPLORE

1 In pairs, discuss the questions.

1 Do you like eating fish?
2 Do people in your country eat a lot of fish?
3 Has the type of fish that people eat changed in recent years? How?

2 Read the article. Write T (for turtles), S (for seabirds) or B (for both).

1 ☐ People eat them.
2 ☐ Fishermen catch them accidentally.
3 ☐ Today, there are buildings in the places where they always left their eggs in the past.
4 ☐ Their young often die soon after birth.

3 In pairs, discuss the questions.

1 Is it important to know how many fish there are in the sea? Why?
2 Is it possible to count them?

EXPLORE MORE

4 You are going to watch part of a BBC programme about fishing. Read an advert for the programme. Is fishing an important industry in your country?

Coast

The series *Coast* is about different ways that humans relate to the sea. This episode asks the question, 'How many fish are in the sea?'

5 Work in pairs. What do you think 'overfishing' means?

6 ▶ 9.6 Watch Part 1 of the video and check your answers in Exercise 5.

7 Choose the correct answers.

1 What is the main job of the people on the *Scotia*?
  a to catch lots of fish
  b to get information about fish
2 Why was the *Explorer* an important ship?
  a she carried lots of scientists
  b she had new electronic equipment

EXPLORE MORE

8 Work in pairs. Do you think life on the *Explorer* was interesting? Why?/Why not?

9 ▶ 9.6 Watch the video again and correct the information in sentences 1–4.

1 Ullapool is in England.
2 They check the fish twice a year.
3 They built the *Explorer* in 1966.
4 On the *Explorer*, the scientists had to write everything.

10 ▶ 9.7 Watch Part 2 of the video and answer the questions.

1 Tick (✓) the information a–e that the scientists need about the fish.
  a ☐ how many there are
  b ☐ how big they are
  c ☐ how old they are
  d ☐ how fast they swim
  e ☐ how deep they live
2 Why do they look at a fish's ear bone?
3 Why do normal fishermen and the Scotia travel to different parts of the ocean?
4 What do the results today show?

11 Work in pairs. Do you think the future for fish is good or bad? Why?

I think it's good because scientists can change things.
I think it's bad because people are very greedy.

YOU EXPLORE

12 CULTURE PROJECT In small groups, create a presentation about an environmental problem.

1 Use the internet to research a problem connected with the sea (or an area of natural beauty) in your country.
2 Find out what people are doing about the problem.
3 Write a short script and include some photos or video.
4 Present the problem and possible answers to the class.

GRAMMAR TIME

1.2 Present Simple: affirmative and negative | Adverbs of frequency

We use the Present Simple for facts and routines.

+	I/You/We/They	live	in a small town.
	He/She/It	watches	films on TV.
−	I/You/We/They	don't (do not) live	in a small town.
	He/She/It	doesn't (does not) watch	films on TV.

Spelling rules
With *He/She/It* we add *-s*, *-es* or *-ies* to the verb:
- Most verbs, add *-s*: live – lives
- Verbs ending in *-o*, *-ch*, *-sh*, *-ss*, *-z* and *-x*, add *-es*: go – goes, watch – watches, wash – washes, buzz – buzzes
- Verbs ending in consonant + *-y*, cut *-y* and add *-ies*: study – studies

Adverbs of frequency
Adverbs of frequency go before the verb but after the verb *to be*.

always   usually   often   sometimes   never

I always listen to music on my phone.
We don't often watch films at school.

1 Order the words to make sentences.
1 the guitar / a rock group / I / in / play
   I play the guitar in a rock group.
2 American / films / often / watch / we
3 busy / she / always / is
4 go out / don't / on Mondays / usually / I
5 comics / doesn't / my / read / sister

2 Complete the text with the correct form of the words in brackets.

Sandi has a very unusual life ...
Sandi ¹*lives* (live) in an igloo in the Arctic.
She ² _____ (get) up at 4a.m. every day.
She ³ _____ (often/eat) pizza for breakfast.
She ⁴ _____ (fly) to school in a helicopter every day. After school she ⁵ _____ (study) car mechanics. She ⁶ _____ (always/go) to bed at 7p.m.

★3 Compare your life to Sandi's from Exercise 2.
I don't live in an igloo in the Arctic. I live in ...

1.4 Present Simple: questions and answers

Yes/No questions and short answers

| ? | Do | I/you/we/they | read novels? | Yes, I/you/we/they do. No, I/you/we/they don't. |
| | Does | he/she/it | live in Hollywood? | Yes, he/she/it does. No, he/she/it doesn't. |

Other questions and answers
How often do you go to the cinema?
Every Sunday. / I go to the cinema every Sunday.
I never go to the cinema.
What time does the film start?
At 8 p.m. / It starts at 8 p.m.
Where do they live?
In Harlow Mill. / They live in Harlow Mill.

Time expressions
every day/week/month
at the weekend
once/twice/three times a month
on Mondays
in the morning/afternoon/evening
at 8 o'clock

1 Make *Yes/No* questions in the Present Simple. Then ask and answer the questions in pairs.
1 like / taking photographs / you / ?
2 songs / write / your favourite singer / ?
3 music videos / on TV / watch / your parents / ?
4 dancing / like / you and your friends / ?
5 in a big house / in Hollywood / live / you / ?
6 draw / sometimes / on the board / pictures / your English teacher / ?
A: *Do you like taking photographs?*
B: *Yes, I do.*

2 Write questions for these answers. Sometimes there is more than one possible question.
1 *Where does your aunt live* ?
   My aunt lives in Italy.
2 _____ ? Jon walks to school.
3 _____ ? The concert finishes at 11.30.
4 _____ ? My parents never go dancing.
5 _____ ? No, I don't.
6 _____ ? Yes, she does.

★3 Imagine you are interviewing a favourite star/ celebrity. Write seven questions about his/her life. Use the ideas below to help you. Do you know any of the answers?

How often _____? When _____?
Who _____ with? Where _____?
What type of _____ prefer? like _____ing?

Do you like listening to music?
Where do you go on holiday?
What type of car do you prefer?

2.2 Present Continuous

We use the Present Continuous for things that are happening at the moment of speaking.

+	I	'm (am) reading a book.
	You/We/They	're (are) playing a game.
	He/She/It	's (is) sleeping.
–	I	'm not (am not) reading a book.
	You/We/They	aren't (are not) playing a game.
	He/She/It	isn't (is not) sleeping.
?	Am	I	reading a book?	Yes, I am. No, I'm not.
	Are	you/ we/they	playing a game?	Yes, you/we/they are. No, you/we/they aren't.
	Is	he/she/ it	sleeping?	Yes, he/she/it is. No, he/she/it isn't.
	Where What	are is	you he	going? doing?

Spelling rules
- Most verbs, add -ing: go – going, look – looking
- Verbs ending in -e, cut -e and add -ing: live – living
- Short verbs that end with consonant + vowel + consonant, double the last consonant:
sit – sitting, swim – swimming

Time expressions

now   at the moment
right now   today

1 In pairs, use the phrases below to describe what is happening in the picture on page 22.

read/book   sing/karaoke   sit/on the sofa   cut/pizza
talk/phone   write/text message   dance
wear/earrings   play table tennis

Leo is reading a book. Gran is ...

2 Complete the dialogue with the Present Continuous form of the verbs in brackets.

Mum: Tom! Where are you?
Tom: Hi, mum. I ¹'m sitting (sit) in the park.
Mum: What ²you doing (you/do)? ³having (you/ have) fun?
Tom: No, I ⁴'m studying. I ⁵_____ (study) for an exam.
Mum: I can hear Matt! ⁶he studying (he/study) too?
Tom: Yes, he ⁷studying
Mum: Really? We ⁸diving (drive) past the park now. You ⁹don't reading (not read)! You ¹⁰playing (play) football!
Tom: Yes, we ¹¹geting (get) ready for our PE exam!

★3 Imagine you are having a party. Use the Present Continuous to write ten sentences about what is happening.

I'm sitting on the sofa with my friend Joanna.

2.4 Present Simple and Present Continuous

- We use the **Present Simple** for facts and routines.
Bro lives in Hollywood.
Lee plays his guitar every day.
Amy doesn't tidy her room.
What time do you get up?

- We use the **Present Continuous** for something happening at the moment of speaking.
What are you doing under the table?
I'm looking for my earring!

- We also use the **Present Continuous** for something happening around now but maybe not at the moment of speaking.
Time expressions: *these days, at the moment, this week/month*
Is she enjoying school at the moment?
He isn't talking to his dad these days.

1 Complete the sentences with the correct form of the words in brackets.

1 Oh no, it *'s raining* (rain) again!
2 I living (live) in Berlin but I visiting (visit) London now.
3 He saving (save) money at the moment to buy a leather jacket.
4 Gemma _____ (often/go) to Tenerife on holiday.
5 Jim don't speaking (not speak) French but he _____ (know) a little Spanish.

2 Complete the sentences to make them true for you. In pairs, ask and answer questions about your sentences.

Free time	I always _____ [*activity*] after school. Now I'm not _____, I'm _____ .
Clothes	I often wear _____ [*item of clothing*]. I never wear _____ . At the moment I'm wearing _____ .
Music	I usually listen to _____ [*type of music*]. These days, I'm listening to _____ [*group/artist/composer*] a lot.

A: *What do you do after school?*
B: *I always run in the park after school.*
A: *What are you doing now?*

★3a Use the Present Simple to write about your typical Sunday afternoon.

On a typical Sunday afternoon, I usually sit on the sofa at home and …

★3b Now imagine you are spending an unusual Sunday afternoon. Use the Present Continuous to write about it.

This is an unusual Sunday afternoon. I'm not sitting on the sofa at home, I'm …

3.2 Past Simple: *was/were*

We use the Past Simple to talk about finished events and situations in the past. The Past Simple of *to be* is *was/were*.

+	I/He/She/It You/We/They		was at school. were at home.	
−	I/He/She/It You/We/They		wasn't (was not) hungry. weren't (were not) late.	
?	Was	I/he/ she/it	hungry?	Yes, I/he/she/it was. No, I/he/she/it wasn't.
	Were	you/ we/they	tired?	Yes, you/we/they were. No, you/we/they weren't.
	When Where	was were	she born? you yesterday?	

The Past Simple of *there is/there are* is **there was/ there were.**

+	There There	was were	a lion in a cage. two tigers.	
−	There	wasn't (was not)	time.	
	There	weren't (were not)	any people.	
?	Was	there	a gift shop?	Yes, there was. No, there wasn't.
	Were	there	many people?	Yes, there was. No, there wasn't.

Time expressions

yesterday	this evening
last Tuesday/week/month/year	at one o'clock
two days/a week ago	in June/2004

1 Complete the questions with *was/were*. Then ask and answer in pairs.

1 How <u>was</u> your last English test?
2 _____ it cold yesterday?
3 Where _____ you born?
4 _____ you at a party last weekend?
5 Where _____ you five hours ago?
6 How old _____ you in 2010?
7 _____ you late for school this morning?
A: *How was your last English test?*
B: *It was easy!*

2 Rewrite the sentences in the Past Simple.

1 'Are you bored?' 'Yes, I am.'
   'Were you bored?' 'Yes, I was.'
2 'Is it cold?' 'Yes, it is.'
3 'Are you at home?' 'No, I'm not.'
4 My neighbours are irritating.
5 'Is there a letter for me?' 'No, there isn't.'
6 We aren't very hungry.
7 There aren't any tickets.

★3 Write ten sentences about a recent day out (concert or sports game).

Last Saturday I was at a Coldplay concert. I was with … It was at … There were hundreds of fans. The weather was perfect …

3.4 Past Simple: regular verbs

+	I/You/He/She/It/We/They	watched TV.		
–	I/You/He/She/It/We/They	didn't (did not) read.		
?	Did	I/you/he/she/it/we/they	sleep?	Yes, I/you/he/she/it/we/they did. No, I/you/he/she/it/we/they didn't.
	When did	he	arrive?	
	What did	they	watch?	

Spelling rules
- Most regular verbs, add -ed: watch – watched
- Verbs ending with -e, add -d: live – lived
- Verbs ending with consonant +y, cut -y and add -ied: try – tried
- One-syllable verbs ending with vowel + consonant, double the consonant and add -ed: stop – stopped

1 Write the Past Simple form of the verbs below.

1 cook – _cooked_
2 carry – _____
3 play – _____
4 help – _____
5 drop – _____
6 marry – _____

2 Complete the sentences with the Past Simple form of the verbs in brackets.

1 Mel _tidied_ (tidy) her room.
2 '_____ (they/like) the film?' 'No, they _____.'
3 I _____ (not watch) TV last night.
4 '_____ (you/finish) your work?' 'Yes, I _____.'
5 We _____ (not talk) to her yesterday.
6 He _____ (drop) his phone and it _____ (stop) working.

3 Use the ideas below to make questions about yesterday. Then ask and answer the questions in pairs.

Did you ...?

- tidy your room
- listen to music
- cook a meal
- stay at home all day
- wash your hair
- argue with someone
- rest
- study English
- watch a film
- phone a friend

A: Did you tidy your room yesterday?
B: No, I didn't.

★4 Write five things you did last weekend and five things you didn't. Use the ideas in Exercise 3 to help you.

I tidied my room, I ...
I didn't cook a meal, ...

4.2 Past Simple: irregular verbs

+	I/You/He/She/It/We/They	took my camera.		
–	I/You/He/She/It/We/They	didn't (did not) take my camera.		
?	Did	I/you/he/she/it/we/they	take the camera?	Yes, I/you/he/she/it/we/they did. No, I/you/he/she/it/we/they didn't.
	Where did	you	put it?	

1 Write the Past Simple form of the verbs below.

1 come – _came_
2 drink – _____
3 drive – _____
4 eat – _____
5 find – _____
6 go – _____
7 leave – _____
8 make – _____
9 meet – _____
10 read – _____
11 run – _____
12 speak – _____
13 take – _____
14 write – _____

2a Use the verbs in Exercise 1 to write six sentences about last weekend.

1 *Last weekend I spoke to my gran on the phone.*

2b In pairs, ask and answer the questions about your sentences.

A: Did you speak to your gran on the phone last weekend?
B: No, I didn't. But we went to her house on Saturday.

3 Complete Amy's story with the Past Simple form of the verbs below.

| fall   feel   get   ~~have~~   hit   hurt   sit |

I was in the bathroom. I [1]*had* my MP4 player with me. On the way out I [2]_____ my head on the door. It really [3]_____ . I [4]_____ bad so I [5]_____ down on the bath and my MP4 player [6]_____ in the toilet! I didn't want to put my hand in the water so I called my dad and he [7]_____ it out for me.

★4 Write about something funny that happened to you. Use the verbs on page 129 and the story in Exercise 3 to help you.

I was in a shop with my parents. A dog ran into the shop. I …

4.4 Verb patterns

- We use the **to-infinitive** after these verbs:
  agree, decide, forget, learn, remember, need, try, want, would/'d like
  We agreed to switch off our phones.
- We use **verb + -ing** after these verbs:
  can't stand, don't mind, enjoy, finish, hate, keep, like, love, prefer, stop
  I prefer texting to emails.

1 Complete the sentences with the correct form of the verbs in brackets.

1 I'm learning *to type* (type) without looking.
2 When did you finish _____ (do) your homework?
3 Denise never forgets _____ (do) her homework.
4 Sue keeps _____ (send) me videos of cats.
5 My dad can't stand _____ (talk) on the phone.
6 We tried _____ (spend) a day without our phones.

2a Use the verbs from the lists above to write six true and six false sentences about you.

I often forget to charge my phone. (true)
I can't stand playing video games. (false)

2b In pairs, read your sentences and decide if your partner's sentences are true or false.

A: I often forget to charge my phone.
B: True.
A: I can't stand playing video games.
B: False, you love playing video games.

★3 Think of a person you know very well. Use the verbs from the lists above to write six sentences about him/her.

My best friend always tries to help other people. She enjoys …

5.2 Adverbs of manner

We use adjectives with nouns and adverbs with verbs.
- We can add *-ly* to most adjectives to make an adverb:
  She is quiet. She speaks quietly.
- With adjectives ending with *-y*, we add *-ily*:
  The rain is heavy. It's raining heavily.
- Irregular adverbs look the same as adjectives:
  hard, fast, right, wrong, early, late, high, last, best, wide
  He's a fast runner. He runs fast.
- The adverb for good is well.

We use *very*, *really* and *so* before adjectives and adverbs.
She is very slow.
Children learn really quickly.
She wakes up so slowly.

1 Complete the sentences with the correct form of the adjectives in brackets. Then, in pairs, complete the sentences with the name of someone you both know.

1 *Chris* always talks very *quickly* (quick).
2 _____ speaks English really _____ (good).
3 _____ often laughs _____ (noisy).
4 _____ speaks _____ (quiet).
5 _____ often comes to class _____ (late).
6 _____ always drives _____ (careful).

2 Complete the sentences with the correct form of the adjectives.

1 I'm a *bad* dancer. I dance so *badly*! BAD
2 Sarah's a _____ singer. She sings really _____. GOOD
3 Polly learns so _____! She's definitely a _____ learner. FAST
4 I'm sure Tim will arrive _____. He's always _____. EARLY
5 The boys are very _____ to Eva. They always laugh _____ at her. UNKIND
6 It's snowing really _____. The snow isn't usually so _____. HEAVY
7 He's a _____ baby. He smiles _____ every time I see him. HAPPY

★3 Write six sentences about what you did this morning. Use as many verbs and adverbs as possible.

I woke up late, I got dressed quickly …

5.4   Modal verbs: *can*, *have to* and *must*

Can

We use **can** to talk about rules that other people make for us.

I can go online when I want. (*It's OK/allowed.*)
I can't watch TV after 10 p.m. (*It isn't OK.*)
Can you invite friends to stay? (*Is it OK?*)

Have to

We use **have to** to say that something is necessary and **don't have to** to say that something isn't necessary.

You have to come home straight after school.
(*It's necessary.*)
You don't have to come home straight after school.
(*It isn't necessary.*)
Do I have to come home straight after school?
(*Is it necessary?*)

+	I/You/We/They He/She/It	have to help. has to clean.	
–	I/You/We/They He/She/It	don't (do not) have to help. doesn't (does not) have to clean.	
?	Do	I/you/ we/they	have to help?	Yes, I/you/we/they do. No, I/you/we/they don't.
	Does	he/she/ it	have to clean?	Yes, he/she/it does. No, he/she/it doesn't.

Must

Must has a similar meaning to *have to* but *have to* is more common.

I have to/must cook dinner.

We use **mustn't** (**must not**) to talk about what you're not allowed to do.
You mustn't stay up late. (*Don't!*)

Don't have to and **mustn't** have different meanings.
You don't have to go there. (*You can but it's not necessary.*)
You mustn't go there. (*Don't!*)

–	I/You/He/She/It/ We/They	mustn't (must not)	talk!

1 In pairs, say where you can find these signs. Then make sentences with *you have to* or *you mustn't* for each sign.

You mustn't park here.

NO PARKING

PLEASE WAIT HERE
SILENCE No Talking!

PULL

2 In pairs, choose the verb which makes the sentence true for your school.

1 You *can* / *mustn't* borrow books from the library.
2 You *can* / *mustn't* run in the corridor.
3 You *have to* / *don't have to* learn a foreign language.
4 You *can* / *mustn't* use a mobile phone in class.
5 You *have to* / *don't have to* stand up when the teacher enters the room.

3 Choose one situation below and write six sentences with rules about what you can, can't, have to and mustn't do. Write rules:

- for a visitor to your country.
- for somebody playing your favourite (video/ computer) game.
- for someone going on holiday with your family.

You don't have to have a visa.

6.2   Countable and uncountable nouns | Quantifiers

Countable	Uncountable
How many bottles of water have we got? I haven't got many hobbies. There are too many olives on my pizza.	How much water is in that bottle? I haven't got much time. There's too much ice in my drink.
I bought some bananas. We eat a lot of oranges. We don't eat a lot of apples.	She bought some popcorn. We eat a lot of cheese. We don't eat a lot of bread.
Have you got any biscuits? There aren't any eggs in the fridge.	Have you got any juice? There isn't any milk in the fridge.

1 Choose the correct option. Then discuss in pairs.

1 How *many* / *much* meals do you eat every day?
2 Do you think you eat too *many* / *much* unhealthy food?
3 Have you got *any* / *some* food in your bag?
4 How *many* / *much* time do you have for lunch on schooldays?
5 There aren't *many* / *much* places to eat near your school. True or false?

2 Complete the restaurant review with *a lot of, any, many, much* or *some*.

STEWIE'S STEAKHOUSE
★★★★★

Stewie's Steakhouse looks nice but it's very small and there are too ¹*many* tables so there isn't ² _____ space – you feel that you're eating in a phone box! There aren't ³ _____ things on the menu and they all have meat in them. There aren't ⁴ _____ dishes for vegetarians – there's no salad! The food wasn't great. I had a steak and ⁵ _____ cold chips. There was ⁶ _____ meat on my plate (about a kilo!) but it wasn't very good. And there was too ⁷ _____ salt in every dish – even the pudding was salty! Finally, they didn't have ⁸ _____ juice or cola, only water from the tap!

★3 Write ten sentences about your family's eating habits.

1 *There's a lot of yoghurt in our fridge.*
2 *My dad doesn't eat much chocolate.*

6.4	Past Continuous and Past Simple

We use the Past Continuous to say something was in progress at a precise moment in the past.

+	I/He/She/It	was watching TV.
	You/We/They	were sleeping at 9 p.m.
−	I/He/She/It	wasn't (was not) watching TV.
	You/We/They	weren't (were not) sleeping at 9 p.m.

?	Was	I/he/she/it	watching TV?	Yes, I/he/she/it was. No, I/he/she/it wasn't.
	Were	you/we/they	sleeping at 9 p.m.?	Yes, you/we/they were. No, you/we/they weren't.
	Where	was	he	going?
	What	were	you	doing?

Time expressions
at three o'clock this morning
at 5.15 last Tuesday
forty minutes ago

Past Continuous and Past Simple
We often use the **Past Continuous** with the **Past Simple**. We use the Past Simple for a short/complete action (e.g. *I broke my leg*) and the Past Continuous for a longer activity in progress at the same time (e.g. *I was playing football*). Before the Past Continuous we use **while** or **when**.

While/When I was playing football, I broke my leg.
I broke my leg while/when I was playing football.

Before the Past Simple we normally use **when**.
What were you doing when the accident happened?
When the accident happened, what were you doing?

1 Complete the sentences with the Past Continuous form of the verbs in brackets.

1 The phone rang while they *were sleeping* (sleep).
2 Anna _____ (not dance) at one o'clock in the morning.
3 Where _____ (Sue/go) when she fell?
4 We _____ (play) football when it began to rain.
5 I _____ (not listen) when the doctor told me his name.
6 What _____ (you/do) when you cut your finger?

2 Complete the story with the Past Simple or Past Continuous form of the verbs in brackets. Then compare with a partner.

Last Sunday at four o'clock I ¹*was riding* (ride) my bike home. It ² _____ (rain) a lot so I ³ _____ (put) up my umbrella. While I ⁴ _____ (go) past the station, I ⁵ _____ (see) Jennifer Lawrence! She ⁶ _____ (get) into a taxi. I ⁷ _____ (not look) where I ⁸ _____ (go) so I ⁹ _____ (ride) my bike into the back of a car! I ¹⁰ _____ (fall) and ¹¹ _____ (hit) my head. I was lucky I ¹² _____ (not break) my neck.

★3 Use the Past Simple and the Past Continuous to describe a) something surprising that happened to you, or b) a dream you had.

One day last year I was walking in the town centre with a friend when we saw an elephant. It was standing on two legs and …

7.2 Comparatives and superlatives of adjectives

We use the **comparative** form of adjectives with *than* to compare two people or things.
He's taller than me.

We use the **superlative** form of adjectives to compare one thing in a group with all the others in that group.
She's the nicest person I know.

Adjectives	Adjective	Comparative	Superlative
with one syllable	near	nearer	the nearest
with one syllable ending with -e	wide	wider	the widest
with one syllable ending with vowel + consonant	hot	hotter	the hottest
ending with consonant + -y	lazy	lazier	the laziest
with two or more syllables	intelligent	more intelligent	the most intelligent
irregular	good bad	better worse	the best the worst

We usually use *the* before superlative adjectives. But we don't use *the* after *my/your/his/her/its/our/their*.
He's their youngest son. NOT ~~He's their the youngest son.~~

We can also compare things using (*not*) *as ... as*.
This book isn't as interesting as the first one.

1 Write the comparative and superlative forms of the adjectives below.

1 fat – *fatter, the fattest*
2 easy – _____
3 late – _____
4 expensive – _____
5 young – _____
6 happy – _____

2 How much can you remember about last year? Complete the questions with the superlative form of the adjectives in brackets. Then ask and answer the questions in pairs.

1 What was *the most beautiful* (beautiful) place you visited?
2 What was _____ (happy) day you can remember?
3 What was _____ (long) journey you made?
4 What was _____ (tasty) meal you ate?
5 What was _____ (bad) film you saw?

★**3** Do you prefer shopping in a shopping centre or small shops? Use the ideas below and write five sentences to answer the question.

Price	low/high
Service	friendly/rude quick/slow
Other	busy/quiet relaxing/stressful cold/hot/warm/wet good/poor choice

I prefer shopping in a shopping centre because the prices aren't as high as in small shops ...

7.4 Going to and the Present Continuous

We use *going to* or the **Present Continuous** to talk about intentions, plans and arrangements in the future.

Going to
We use *going to* to talk about intentions and plans which will perhaps change in the future.
I'm going to get there early.
We're not going to invite them.
Are you going to watch the football?

+	I	'm (am) going to buy a new car.	
	You/We/They	're (are) going to go shopping.	
	He/She/It	's (is) going to come home.	
–	I	'm not (am not) going to buy a new car.	
	You/We/They	aren't (are not) going to go shopping.	
	He/She/It	isn't (is not) going to come home.	
?	Am	I	going to buy a motorbike?	Yes, I am. No, I'm not.
	Are	you/ we/ they	going to go to a party?	Yes, you/we/they are. No, you/we/they aren't.
	Is	he/ she/it	going to stay?	Yes, he/she/it is. No, he/she/it isn't.
	When	are	they	going to visit Gran?

Present Continuous
We use the Present Continuous to talk about arrangements. We often mention a time and/or place to show that something is more than just an intention.
The game is starting at 2.00.
My mum isn't working tomorrow.
Are you going to the party on Friday?

Time expressions:
tonight   next Monday/weekend
tomorrow   on Thursday morning/afternoon

1 Finish these New Year's resolutions with *going to* and the ideas below (or your own).

> buy   get up   revise   spend less/more time
> study   take up

1 I missed the school bus again. This year, I*'m going to get up earlier every morning*.
2 I'm not fit. This year, I _____
3 I was so horrible to my sister last year. This year, I _____
4 I feel so unfashionable. This year, I _____
5 My marks for Maths are terrible. This year, I _____
6 English is such a useful language. This year, I _____

2 Complete the questions below with the Present Continuous form of the verbs in brackets. Then use Lee's note to ask and answer in pairs.

TRIP TO LONDON – Saturday
- train from Harlow Mill to Liverpool Street Station, London, leave 8.30 a.m. and arrive 9.45 a.m.
- meet Aunty Hannah for lunch, National Gallery café, 12.30 p.m.
- train to Harlow Mill from Liverpool Street Station, 6.35 p.m.

1 What station *is Lee leaving* (Lee/leave) from? He's leaving from Liverpool Street.
2 What time _____ (he/arrive) in London?
3 What time _____ (he/catch) the train home?
4 Who _____ (Lee/meet) in London?
5 What time _____ (he/meet) her?
6 Where _____ (they/have) lunch?

★**3** Use *going to* to write three intentions you have for the next summer holidays. Then use the Present Continuous to write three plans for this evening.

This summer I'm going to help my mum decorate the kitchen.
This evening I'm watching the football match at 8 p.m.

8.2	*Will* for future predictions

We use *will* to make predictions about the future.

+	I/You/He/She/It/We/They		'll (will) win the match.	
–	I/You/He/She/It/We/They		won't (will not) lose.	
?	Will	I/you/he/she/it/we/they	win?	Yes, I/you/he/she/it/we/they will. No, I/you/he/she/it/we/they won't.
	What time How	will will	the game you	start? get there?

I think this will happen.
I don't think this will happen. NOT ~~I think this won't happen.~~

Watch OUT!

Time expressions
tomorrow
next week/month/year
in 2035/twenty years' time/the next five years/the future
by (= before) 2035/Christmas/my twentieth birthday/this time tomorrow/the end of the week

1 Complete the sentences with *will* or *won't*. Then look at your sentences with *won't* and write what *will* happen.
1 My country *won't* win the next football World Cup.
2 It _____ be bright and sunny tomorrow.
3 I _____ become famous in the next fifteen years.
4 We _____ get a surprise English test by the end of the week.
5 The world _____ end in 2035.
6 I _____ fall in love by Christmas.
7 Our English teacher _____ give us homework today.

My country won't win the next football World Cup. Germany will win it.

2 Use *I think* and *I don't think* to transform your sentences from Exercise 1. Then compare with a partner.

A: *I don't think my country will win the next football World Cup. I think Germany will win it. What do you think? Will Germany win the next World Cup?*
B: *I think …*

★**3** Look at the article in Exercise 2 on page 96 and write six sentences about life in 2035. Use the ideas below to help you.

> classrooms   a typical school timetable   popular gadgets
> travel   fashion   best and worst jobs

Classrooms will be very different in 2035. There won't be so many students and …

8.4 First Conditional

We use the First Conditional for things that will possibly or probably happen in the future if something happens.

Present Simple	will + verb
If she studies hard,	she'll pass the test.
If you don't pass,	I'll be disappointed.
If he doesn't pass,	his mum won't be happy.

We can change the order of the parts of the sentences without changing the meaning. We don't use a comma if we put will/won't in the first part of the sentence.

will + verb	Present Simple
She'll pass the test	if she studies hard.
I'll be disappointed	if you don't pass.
His mum won't be happy	if he doesn't pass.

In questions it's more usual to begin with will.

will + verb	Present Simple
Will you be angry	if you don't pass the test?
What will you do	if you get the best mark?

1 Use the verbs in brackets to make First Conditional sentences.

1 If I *become* (become) famous, I *won't forget* (not forget) my friends.

2 I _____ (tell) mum if you _____ (do) that again.

3 If my dad _____ (not get) a new job, we _____ (not move) house.

4 You _____ (not pass) if you _____ (not do) any homework.

5 If Patrick _____ (help) me, I _____ (help) him.

6 If you _____ (not panic), you _____ (get) a good mark in the test.

7 How _____ (you/feel) if you _____ (not pass) the test?

8 _____ (she/help) me if I _____ (ask) her?

2 In pairs, use the ideas below to make First Conditional sentences.

1
> pass all my exams → have a party
> we make a lot of noise → my parents tell us to be quiet → play a board game

2
> have my Maths exam → stay home to study → invite a friend to study with me → get tired of studying → play a board game

1 *If I pass all my exams, I'll have a party.*

★**3** Write five First Conditional sentences about what you will do if you don't have any homework today.

1 *If I don't have any homework today …*

9.2 Present Perfect – all forms

We use the Present Perfect to talk about completed actions in the past when we don't say when they happened.

+	I/You/We/They He/She/It	've (have) swum with dolphins. 's (has) visited Ireland.	
–	I/You/We/They	haven't (have not) swum with dolphins.	
	He/She/It	hasn't (has not) visited Ireland.	
?	Have	I/ you/ we/ they	enjoyed it?	Yes, I/you/we/they have. No, I/you/we/they haven't.
	Has	he/ she/ it	learned a lot?	Yes, he/she/it has. No, he/she/it hasn't.
	Where	have	you	been?

To form the Present Perfect, we use have/has and the Past Participle.

For regular verbs, the Past Participle is the same as the Past Simple.
I have finished.   She hasn't tried.   We've stopped.

Many Past Participles are irregular (see verb list on page 129).
They have eaten.   He's gone.   Have you slept?

Present Perfect with *ever/never*
We often use the Present Perfect with **ever** in questions. It means 'at any time before now'.
Have you ever been to Spain?

We also use the Present Perfect with ***never***. It means 'at no time before now'.
No, I've never been to Spain.

1 Complete the text with the Present Perfect form of the verbs in brackets.

ASK TODD!

Gemma ¹*has written* (write) to ask me if it's better to travel alone or with other people. Well, it depends. Some of my nicest travel experiences ² _____ (be) with my friends. My best friend, Scott, ³ _____ (travel) with me to a lot of countries and we ⁴ _____ (have) a lot of fun and we ⁵ _____ (not fall) out! But my girlfriend ⁶ _____ (never/be) abroad with me because we always argue when we're travelling!

2 Make questions with *ever* and the Present Perfect. Use the phrases below or your own ideas. Then ask and answer the questions in pairs.

> travel alone
> go to a restaurant with friends
> go on a school trip abroad
> buy clothes without your parents
> meet someone from another continent

A: *Have you ever travelled alone?*
B: *No, I've never travelled alone./Yes, I have.*

★3 Write five sentences about things you have never done but hope to do in the future.

I've never been to New York – I hope to go there in the future.

9.4	Present Perfect with *already/just/yet*

We use *already* and *just* in affirmative sentences with the Present Perfect. *Already* and *just* usually come immediately before the main verb.
He's *just* phoned. (= recently/a short time ago)
I've *already* checked the timetable. (= earlier than expected)

We use *yet* in negative sentences and questions with the Present Perfect. *Yet* usually comes at the end of the negative statements or questions.
We haven't bought all the food *yet*. (It hasn't happened but will probably happen soon.)
Have you bought tickets *yet*?

1 Complete the sentences with *just* and the Present Perfect form of the verbs below.

> make ~~do~~ tidy fix miss go

1 There's a lot of food in the fridge. I'*ve just done* the shopping.
2 I _____ my computer. It's working again!
3 Mark _____ breakfast. It's on the table.
4 Rona _____ her bedroom. It's looking better now!
5 I'm afraid you can't speak to mum now. She _____ to work.
6 We _____ the bus – we'll be late now!

2 Rewrite the underlined sentences using *yet* or *already*.

1 <u>Jason has arrived at the campsite.</u> He's putting up his tent.
   Jason has already arrived at the campsite.
2 I'm not hungry, thanks. <u>I've had breakfast.</u>
3 Hurry up! <u>Have you finished?</u>
4 Wow – you're slow! <u>We've finished.</u>
5 She can't come. <u>She hasn't done her homework.</u>
6 <u>Have they got their exam results?</u>

3 Make questions with *yet* about the things below. Then ask and answer the questions in groups.

> eat lunch   start learning for the next test
> decide what to at the weekend
> see [name of film] at the cinema
> plan your holiday

A: *Have you eaten lunch yet?*
B: *No, I haven't./Yes, I've already had my lunch.*

★4 Write five sentences with news about your favourite stars or other people you know well. Use *just*, *already* or *yet*.

Messi has just joined Dortmund but he hasn't played yet.
My sister has just started university.

IRREGULAR VERBS LIST

INFINITIVE	PAST SIMPLE	PAST PARTICIPLE
be [biː]	**was/were** [wɒz/wɜː]	**been** [biːn]
become [bɪˈkʌm]	**became** [bɪˈkeɪm]	**become** [bɪˈkʌm]
begin [bɪˈgɪn]	**began** [bɪˈgæn]	**begun** [bɪˈgʌn]
break [breɪk]	**broke** [brəʊk]	**broken** [ˈbrəʊkən]
bring [brɪŋ]	**brought** [brɔːt]	**brought** [brɔːt]
build [bɪld]	**built** [bɪlt]	**built** [bɪlt]
burn [bɜːn]	**burned** [bɜːnd]/ **burnt** [bɜːnt]	**burned** [bɜːnd]/ **burnt** [bɜːnt]
buy [baɪ]	**bought** [bɔːt]	**bought** [bɔːt]
can [kæn]	**could** [kʊd]	**been able to** [biːn ˈeɪbl tə]
catch [kætʃ]	**caught** [kɔːt]	**caught** [kɔːt]
choose [tʃuːz]	**chose** [tʃəʊz]	**chosen** [ˈtʃəʊzn]
come [kʌm]	**came** [keɪm]	**come** [kʌm]
cost [kɒst]	**cost** [kɒst]	**cost** [kɒst]
cut [kʌt]	**cut** [kʌt]	**cut** [kʌt]
do [duː]	**did** [dɪd]	**done** [dʌn]
draw [drɔː]	**drew** [druː]	**drawn** [drɔːn]
dream [driːm]	**dreamed** [driːmd]/ **dreamt** [dremt]	**dreamed** [driːmd]/ **dreamt** [dremt]
drink [drɪnk]	**drank** [dræŋk]	**drunk** [drʌnk]
drive [draɪv]	**drove** [drəʊv]	**driven** [ˈdrɪvn]
eat [iːt]	**ate** [et, eɪt]	**eaten** [ˈiːtn]
fall [fɔːl]	**fell** [fel]	**fallen** [ˈfɔːln]
feed [fiːd]	**fed** [fed]	**fed** [fed]
feel [fiːl]	**felt** [felt]	**felt** [felt]
fight [faɪt]	**fought** [fɔːt]	**fought** [fɔːt]
find [faɪnd]	**found** [faʊnd]	**found** [faʊnd]
fly [flaɪ]	**flew** [fluː]	**flown** [fləʊn]
forget [fəˈget]	**forgot** [fəˈgɒt]	**forgotten** [fəˈgɒtn]
forgive [fəˈgɪv]	**forgave** [fəˈgeɪv]	**forgiven** [fəˈgɪvn]
get [get]	**got** [gɒt]	**got** [gɒt]
give [gɪv]	**gave** [geɪv]	**given** [ˈgɪvn]
go [gəʊ]	**went** [went]	**gone** [gɒn]
grow [grəʊ]	**grew** [gruː]	**grown** [grəʊn]
hang [hæŋ]	**hung** [hʌŋ]	**hung** [hʌŋ]
have [hæv]	**had** [hæd]	**had** [hæd]
hear [hɪə]	**heard** [hɜːd]	**heard** [hɜːd]
hit [hɪt]	**hit** [hɪt]	**hit** [hɪt]
hold [həʊld]	**held** [held]	**held** [held]
hurt [hɜːt]	**hurt** [hɜːt]	**hurt** [hɜːt]
keep [kiːp]	**kept** [kept]	**kept** [kept]
know [nəʊ]	**knew** [njuː]	**known** [nəʊn]
learn [lɜːn]	**learned** [lɜːnd]/ **learnt** [lɜːnt]	**learned** [lɜːnd]/ **learnt** [lɜːnt]
leave [liːv]	**left** [left]	**left** [left]
lend [lend]	**lent** [lent]	**lent** [lent]

INFINITIVE	PAST SIMPLE	PAST PARTICIPLE
let [let]	**let** [let]	**let** [let]
lie [laɪ]	**lay** [leɪ]	**lain** [leɪn]
lose [luːz]	**lost** [lɒst]	**lost** [lɒst]
make [meɪk]	**made** [meɪd]	**made** [meɪd]
meet [miːt]	**met** [met]	**met** [met]
pay [peɪ]	**paid** [peɪd]	**paid** [peɪd]
put [pʊt]	**put** [pʊt]	**put** [pʊt]
read [riːd]	**read** [red]	**read** [red]
ride [raɪd]	**rode** [rəʊd]	**ridden** [ˈrɪdn]
ring [rɪŋ]	**rang** [ræŋ]	**rung** [rʌŋ]
run [rʌn]	**ran** [ræn]	**run** [rʌn]
say [seɪ]	**said** [sed]	**said** [sed]
see [siː]	**saw** [sɔː]	**seen** [siːŋ]
sell [sel]	**sold** [səʊld]	**sold** [səʊld]
send [send]	**sent** [sent]	**sent** [sent]
set [set]	**set** [set]	**set** [set]
show [ʃəʊ]	**showed** [ʃəʊd]	**shown** [ʃəʊn]
sing [sɪŋ]	**sang** [sæŋ]	**sung** [sʌŋ]
sit [sɪt]	**sat** [sæt]	**sat** [sæt]
sleep [sliːp]	**slept** [slept]	**slept** [slept]
speak [spiːk]	**spoke** [spəʊk]	**spoken** [ˈspəʊkən]
spend [spend]	**spent** [spent]	**spent** [spent]
stand [stænd]	**stood** [stʊd]	**stood** [stʊd]
steal [stiːl]	**stole** [stəʊl]	**stolen** [ˈstəʊlən]
sweep [swiːp]	**swept** [swept]	**swept** [swept]
swim [swɪm]	**swam** [swæm]	**swum** [swʌm]
take [teɪk]	**took** [tʊk]	**taken** [ˈteɪkən]
teach [tiːtʃ]	**taught** [tɔːt]	**taught** [tɔːt]
tell [tel]	**told** [təʊld]	**told** [təʊld]
think [θɪnk]	**thought** [θɔːt]	**thought** [θɔːt]
understand [ˌʌndəˈstænd]	**understood** [ˌʌndəˈstʊd]	**understood** [ˌʌndəˈstʊd]
wake [weɪk]	**woke** [wəʊk]	**woken** [ˈwəʊkən]
wear [weə]	**wore** [wɔː]	**worn** [wɔːn]
win [wɪn]	**won** [wʌn]	**won** [wʌn]
write [raɪt]	**wrote** [rəʊt]	**written** [ˈrɪtn]

Unit 2 — Lesson 2.1 Exercise 6

Fashion Quiz

Give yourself one point every time you have the same answer as your partner.

0–3 points – you are very different from your partner. Don't go shopping for clothes together!

4–7 points – you are not very different from your partner but you are not very similar either.

8–10 points – you and your partner have similar ideas about fashion. Go shopping together!

Unit 3 — Lesson 3.1 Exercise 6

1 T 2 T 3 F 4 T 5 T 6 T 7 T 8 T 9 T

Unit 3 — Lesson 3.4 Exercise 6

Use the prompts below to answer the questions in Exercise 6 on page 38.

1 Lee / call / police ✓
2 police / help / them ✗
3 Lee / Amy / go home ✗ *he didn't go home*
4 look / town centre / hours. then / start / rain
5 stop raining / so / return / park
6 dog / be / there ✗ *No it wasn't there*
7 he / start / panic / imagine / terrible things

Unit 5 — Lesson 5.3 Exercise 7

After dinner I went to bed but I couldn't stop thinking of the girl in the picture. I closed my eyes and tried to remember her face. When I opened my eyes, she was there. She spoke quickly. 'You have to help me! I can't do it!' She took me by the hand. But this time we went to the window. I opened the curtains and we went silently out onto the balcony. She pointed upwards. Once again, the kitten was on the roof. I began to climb.

The next morning, my gran came upstairs to wake me. When she entered the room, she stopped suddenly and pointed towards the bed.

'What is that?' she asked.

'It's a kitten,' I replied. I smiled and held the little black cat tightly in my arms.

Unit 7 — Lesson 7.1 Exercise 3

A Clothes shop	F Florist's
B Bakery	G Bookshop
C Pharmacy	H Greengrocer's
D Shoe shop	I Newsagent's
E Butcher's	

Unit 7 — Lesson 7.2 Exercise 4

Unit 7 — Lesson 7.3 Exercise 2

1 Why there aren't many places to sit down?
   If people are sitting, they aren't shopping.
2 Why do they play music all the time?
   Because then people relax and stay longer.
3 Why is it hard to find the exit?
   It's because if people can't get out easily, they stay longer and spend more money.
4 Why is the down escalator a long way from the up escalator?
   Because then shoppers walk past more shops.

Unit 7 — Lesson 7.5 Exercise 5

How important is money to you?

Give yourself 2 points for every a) answer and 1 point for every b) answer.

5–6 points

For you money is like water. When you're thirsty, you have to drink. When you have money, you have to spend it. You don't know how to save money.

7–8 points

For you money is useful and important but you don't worry about it all the time. You are generous, but intelligent with your money. You don't spend more than you have but you don't try to save every penny.

9–10 points

For you money is a wonderful thing. It is so wonderful that you don't want to spend it. Maybe you need to learn how to enjoy spending money.

Unit 9 — Lesson 9.6 Exercise 7

Student A
1 You want to check a website. Your friend has his/her laptop with him/her.
2 You're on the bus. There's a free seat next to your friend.

Student B
1 You want to check a word. Your friend has a dictionary.
2 You're on the bus. A window's open and it's very cold.

STUDENT ACTIVITIES

Student B

You work at a cinema. Use this information to answer Student A's questions.

FILMWORLD CINEMA	
Film	**Time**
X-Men: the End **Sold Out**	6.40 / 8.30
Up 2 **Row 7 – No, Row 6 – Yes**	6.50 / 8.40
Tickets	£6.95

Student B

1 Greet Student A. Say you're pleased to see him/her.
2 Give your news:
  • you're taking lots of photos with your smartphone
  • you've got two free tickets to a cool concert
  • your best friend isn't talking to you.
3 Listen and respond to Student A's news.

Student B

1 Student A started the argument but it was your fault too. You like Student A a lot and want to stay friends with him/her. Accept Student A's apology.
2 You posted an embarrassing photo of Student A on the internet. Now you feel bad about it. Apologise.

Student B

1 Listen to Student A's story.
2 Use phrases like *Awesome!/No way!* [lesson 2.6].
3 Ask questions to show you are listening: *How did you feel?/What did you do?/Why did you do that?* etc.

Student B

1 Give Student A advice on how to change the decoration in his/her bedroom. If he/she rejects your ideas, give him/her different advice.
2 You want to organise a surprise party for a friend. Ask Student A for advice. Then accept or reject the advice.

Student B

1 Answer Student A's question – you're unhappy because you've got bad toothache.
2 Listen to Student A's advice.
3 Thank Student A for his/her advice.

Student B

1 You are a shop assistant in a sports shop. Help Student A buy a new tracksuit.
2 You go to a shoe shop to buy a new pair of shoes. You can't decide between boots or trainers.

Student B

1 You are at a Student Careers office. You enjoy working with your hands, being creative, working alone and being in contact with nature.
2 You're thinking of working as an accountant.
3 Listen to Student A's advice. Say which advice you agree with: *I probably won't enjoy …/I might/may be good at working as a …*

Student B

1 Student A wants to go mountain biking tomorrow and asks for permission to use your bike. Refuse permission. You want to use the bike yourself tomorrow. Then Student A asks for permission to borrow a helmet. Give permission. You have an old helmet you never use.
2 You hear that Student A is going on a camping trip with some friends. Ask for permission to go with him/her. If Student B agrees, say you don't have a tent and ask for permission to share Student A's tent.

1 🔊 **4.24 Listen to five short conversations. For each question choose the correct answer A, B or C.**

Tip: Read the questions carefully before listening so that you know what to listen for.

Example: Which film do they want to see?

1 What is the boy's uncle?

2 How many students are in the girl's class?

3 What does the girl decide to wear for the party?

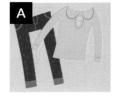 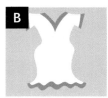 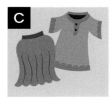

4 Which pets has the girl got?

5 When is Tina's birthday?

 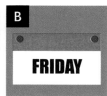 

2 🔊 **4.25 Listen to Alex talking to his friend, Lindsay, about his new hobby. For each question choose the correct answer A, B or C.**

Tip: The answers to the questions in the recording come in the same order as the questions.

Example:

Which free time activity does Alex not do anymore?
A play football
B play the guitar
C do salsa

1 Which language is he learning?
A Italian
B French
C Spanish

2 How is he learning it?
A online
B at school
C from his dad

3 How long are his lessons?
A forty minutes
B forty-five minutes
C fifty minutes

4 What is hard for him?
A the grammar
B the vocabulary
C the writing

5 What time is Lindsay's swimming lesson?
A 4.30 p.m.
B 4.50 p.m.
C 5.15 p.m.

3 🔊 **4.26 Listen to a girl, Fran, asking a friend about helping at an animal centre. Complete the gaps with the missing information.**

Tip: Read the notes carefully before listening to the recording and guess the type of information you are listening for: a number, an animal, etc.

ANIMAL CENTRE WITH FRAN
When: ¹*after school today*
Work: Feed new ² _____
Address: ³ _____
Fran's number: ⁴ _____
Return by: ⁵ _____
Wear: ⁶ _____

4   **Tip:** Listen carefully to the questions and if you don't understand, ask the examiner to repeat them: *Can you repeat the question, please?*, *Could you repeat that, please?*

Students A and B, answer the questions below.

1   What's your name? How do you spell that?
2   Where do you come from?
3   What school subjects do you like best?
4   What other subjects do you study?

Student A, answer the questions below.

1   What do you do in your free time?
2   How often do you go out with friends?
3   Do you like watching sports on TV?
4   Tell me something about your favourite celebrity.

Student B, answer the questions below.

1   What's your hobby?
2   How often do you go to the cinema?
3   Do you go to music concerts?
4   Tell me something about your favourite musicians.

5a   **Tip:** Read the prompt card information carefully so that you can answer your partner's questions.

Student A, turn to page 135 for some information about flamenco lessons and answer Student B's questions about them.

Student B, you don't know anything about the flamenco lessons, so ask Student A some questions about them.

FLAMENCO LESSONS

Who for? _____
Name / school? _____
Address? _____
Time? _____
Cost? _____

5b   Student B, turn to page 135 for some information about a school play. Answer Student A's questions about it.

Student A, you don't know anything about the school play, so ask Student B some questions about it.

BRINTON SCHOOL PLAY

Name / play? _____
Where? _____
When? _____
Cost? _____
Wear? _____

Exam Time 3, Listening and Speaking, Exercise 5a, Student A (page 137)

NEW SHOPPING CENTRE

Denby Shopping centre
Opens on Saturday, 6 May
Come along to the opening at 10 a.m.

ALL shops will have special offers for the day – free gifts and lower prices!

And children can enjoy a children's party in the entrance hall at 3 p.m.

Exam Time 3, Listening and Speaking , Exercise 5b, Student B (page 137)

BEACHSIDE HOTEL

Come and stay at our lovely five-star hotel in Blue Bay – one minute from the beach! All our rooms have sea views. Breakfast and evening meal are in the price.
Contact us:
www.beachside.com
for more information

1 🔊 **4.27 Listen to five short conversations. For each question choose the correct answer A, B or C.**

Tip: Don't decide on your answer before you hear the whole conversation, sometimes the correct answer is at the end.

Example: What is the boy's problem?

1   What is near the boy's home?

 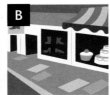 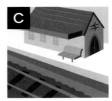

2   What did the girl do last night?

 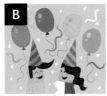 

3   How much was the girl's laptop?

4   What does the girl have to do after school?

5   When did the boy move to this town?

2 🔊 **4.28 Listen to Kenny talking to a friend about buying things for a new house. What did each person get? Match things A–H with people 1–5.**

Tip: All the options from the list A–H are in the recording, even the ones you don't need. Listen carefully to choose the correct ones.

PEOPLE

Example:

F	Dad
1	Mum
2	Kenny
3	Elsa
4	Helena
5	Harry

THINGS

A   bed
B   armchair
C   bookcase
D   games console
E   TV
F   fridge
G   rug
H   curtains

3 🔊 **4.29 Listen to Beth talking to her friend, Chris, about a concert. For each question choose the correct answer A, B or C.**

Tip: Try to answer the questions first before you look at the options.

Example:

Who went with Chris to the concert?
A   Beth
B   Ray
C   Brad

1   Which band did Chris like best?
A   Dakota
B   The Baileys
C   Blue Paper

2   Where did Beth see the band before?
A   at the Park Festival
B   at the Royal Theatre
C   on TV

3   Which band member didn't play?
A   Mike
B   Joe
C   Danny

4   Why did the band member not play?
A   He hurt his back.
B   He had a sore throat.
C   He hurt his head.

5   What time did the concert finish?
A   11.00 p.m.
B   11.30 p.m.
C   12.00 a.m.

4 Tip: Try to say more than one sentence for some of the questions. You can give a reason for your answer or maybe an example.

Student A, answer the questions below.

1 How often do you go online?
2 Which websites do you like?
3 Do you play computer games?
4 Tell me something about the house you live in.

Student B, answer the questions below.

1 How often do you watch television?
2 What are your favourite programmes?
3 Do you watch films online?
4 Tell me something about the music you listen to.

5a Tip: There isn't only one correct question for each prompt. For example, you can say *What's the name of …?* or *What's the … called?*

Student A, turn to page 137 for some information about a computer shop sale. Answer Student B's questions about it.

Student B, you don't know anything about the computer shop sale, so ask Student A some questions about them.

COMPUTER SHOP SALE

Name of shop? _____
Address? _____
What / in sale? _____
When / sale? _____
Website? _____

5b Student B, turn to page 137 for some information about a new health centre. Answer Student A's questions about it.

Student A, you don't know anything about the new health centre, so ask Student B some questions about it.

NEW HEALTH CENTRE

Name? _____
Address? _____
How many doctors? _____
When / open? _____
Phone number? _____

Exam Time 1, Listening and Speaking, Exercise 5a, Student A (page 133)

FLAMENCO LESSONS

For anyone, kids, teenagers and adults

Learn flamenco at
Dara's Dance School
3, Morris Road

Friday evenings:
5 p.m. – 8 p.m.

Cost: £80 a lesson

Exam Time 1, Listening and Speaking, Exercise 5b Student B (page 133)

BRINTON SCHOOL PLAY

Come and see your friends in *Chicago*!

In the main hall
From 25 to 27 June
at 7.30 p.m.

Tickets: **£5**

We'd like everyone to wear clothes from the 1920s!

1 🔊 **4.30 Listen to five short conversations. For each question choose the correct answer A, B or C.**

Tip: Don't decide on your answer before you hear the whole conversation, sometimes the correct answer is at the end.

Example: What are the boy and girl going to buy?

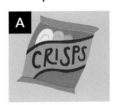 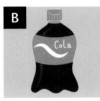 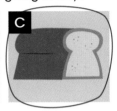

1 What is the girl's sister's job?

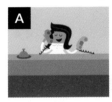 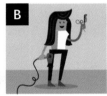 

2 What date is the school trip?

3 What was the weather like on the boy's holiday?

4 How much did the boots cost?

5 Where did the boy go on holiday this year?

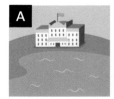  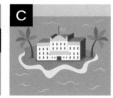

2 🔊 **4.31 Listen to Karen talking to her friend, Tilly, about what they're going to do during Tilly's visit. What are they going to do each day? Match activities A–H with days 1–5.**

Tip: The things or people 1–5 are mentioned in the same order in the recording but the items A–H are in a different order.

DAYS

Example:

	H	Monday
1	☐	Tuesday
2	☐	Wednesday
3	☐	Thursday
4	☐	Friday
5	☐	Saturday

ACTIVITIES

A go shopping
B swim in the sea
C go to the museum
D go to a restaurant
E visit the castle
F go to the theatre
G go to the cinema
H go for a walk

3 🔊 **4.32 Listen to a girl, Helen, talking to her friend, Mark, about a summer job. Complete the gaps with the missing information.**

Tip: Some information you need is a number or a name that is spelled. Make sure that you write it down correctly.

SUMMER JOB
Time: _August/September_
Place: ¹_____ shop
Where: the ²_____ Centre,
in the High Street.
Pay: ³_____
Phone number: ⁴_____
Speak to: Mr ⁵_____

4 **Tip:** The questions below are all personal questions about you, so you will know the answers.

Student A, answer the questions below.

1 How often do you go shopping?
2 What are your favourite shops? Why?
3 Who do you go shopping with?
4 Tell me something about your best friend.

Student B, answer the questions below.

1 How often do you go on holiday?
2 What are your favourite holiday activities?
3 Where would you like to go on holiday? Why?
4 Tell me something about your plans for next weekend.

5a **Tip:** If you need more time to think, use phrases such as: *Let's see …, Well, yes, …, Just a moment …*

Student A, turn to page 133 for some information about a new shopping centre. Answer Student B's questions about it.

Student B, you don't know anything about the new shopping centre, so ask Student A some questions about it.

NEW SHOPPING CENTRE

Name of centre? _____
Date / open? _____
Time? _____
Special offers? _____
Event? _____

5b Student B, turn to page 133 for some information about a hotel. Answer Student A's questions about it.

Student A, you don't know anything about the hotel, so ask Student B some questions about it.

NEW HOTEL

Name? _____
Where? _____
Rooms? _____
Meals? _____
Contact? _____

Exam Time 2, Listening and Speaking, Exercise 5a, Student A (page 135)

COMPUTER SHOP SALE

Come to the big sale at
Electronics for All
20, Garden Road
Buy PCs, laptops, printers, keyboards, etc. at very cheap prices!
From 16 – 26 October
Go on our website to check out our prices.
www.electronics4all.com

Exam Time 2, Listening and Speaking, Exercise 5b, Student B (page 135)

NEW HEALTH CENTRE

WATERSIDE DOCTORS
5, Main Road
Three doctors in the group:
Dr Mann, Dr Jones and Dr Wise.

Open every day 9 a.m. – 7.30 p.m.
(weekends 9.30 a.m. – 12.00 p.m.)

Health problem?
Phone to make an appointment: 02354378576

ART — Why is street art popular?

STREET ART

You usually see paintings and sculptures in galleries and museums. But today there is another place where you can see art. It's in the street. Street artists want their art to be in public places. Then everyone can see it.

Here are some different forms of popular street art.

1 Traditional graffiti

Artists don't usually use brushes for these pictures and they don't paint on a canvas. For them, the canvas is a wall or a pavement! Graffiti artists use spray cans or roll-on paint when they paint on walls. Traditional graffiti is usually words, names or short messages. It's always bright and colourful.

2 Stencil graffiti

Stencil graffiti artists cut shapes in card. Then they put the card on the wall before they paint. This means they can do the pictures quickly. These pictures are often permanent. They stay on the buildings for a long time.

3 3D street art

3D street art is very clever. Artists draw 3D pictures on the pavement or on buildings. There are competitions in many countries for this art form. 3D artists often use coloured chalk to draw their pictures. They look very real. You think it's a real hole in the ground or real water! These pictures aren't permanent. But the artists take photos. This keeps the pictures alive.

4 Video projections

This new street art form uses computers and lights. Artists create special pictures on buildings. These are called video projections. You can sometimes see video projections at big concerts, festivals and also at sports events. Important buildings in big cities all over the world have video projections.

A   B   C   D

1 Read the article and match photos A–D with paragraphs 1–4.

2 Read the article again and answer the questions.

1 What do graffiti artists use to paint pictures?
2 Why do some graffiti artists use stencils?
3 Where do 3D artists draw pictures?
4 Where can we see video projections?

3 Work in pairs. Choose one of the four styles of street art from the article. Describe it to your partner but don't say which one you are talking about! Can your partner guess the style? Use these words to help you.

brush	canvas	card	chalk	colourful
lights	paint	roll-on paint		
spray can	stencil			

4 Now listen to your partner. Which style is he/she describing?

5 In pairs, discuss why you like the styles you chose.

6 **PROJECT** Work in pairs to create a presentation about a street artist in your country. Make notes about:
- what sort of artist he or she is.
- where the artist works.
- why you like/don't like the art.
- any other interesting information.

7 **PROJECT** Write a paragraph about the artist. Add pictures.

Animals in fiction

There are a lot of books about animals. Many of these are books for children but some aren't. Can you think of any famous books for adults about animals?

One very famous book with animal characters is *Animal Farm* by the English author, George Orwell, published in 1945. It's quite short – only ten chapters – but it's an important classic. The story is about a group of animals who live on a farm. A pig, Old Major, dreams about a life on the farm without humans. He tells the animals that they can work on the farm and make their own decisions. There is a fight and the animals chase Mr Jones, the unkind farmer, off the farm. Then they run the farm themselves. They make some rules. An important one is: 'All animals are equal'. There are many wonderful animal characters in the book. Boxer is the big horse who is strong and works hard. There are three very clever pigs, Snowball, Squealer and Napoleon. For a while the animals work well together but then the pigs start to become powerful. Napoleon wants to be the leader and he chases Snowball away. The meetings stop and the pigs make all the decisions. They also begin to wear human clothes and behave like humans. They live in the warm farmhouse and eat and drink well. The other animals have difficult lives. They work hard but they are often cold and hungry. Now the important rule says: 'All animals are equal but some are more equal than others.' Other farmers come to the farmhouse and eat and drink with the pigs. When the animals look through the window, it's impossible to know which are animals and which are humans.

Animal Farm seems quite a simple story but George Orwell used it to give his opinions about important events at that time. It's a very clever book. It makes us think a lot about our lives and society.

---

1 Look at the covers of three books about animals. What do you know about them?

2 Read the article. Which of the books from Exercise 1 is it about?

3 Read the article again and complete the factfile.

> Title: ¹_____
> Author: ²_____
> Nationality: ³_____
> Published in: ⁴_____
> Number of chapters:
> ⁵_____
> Main characters: ⁶_____

4 Choose and read ONE of the summaries (A or B) below.

5 Work in pairs. Take turns to ask your partner questions about the summary. Use the headings from the factfile in Exercise 3 to help you.

A *Moby-Dick; or, The Whale,* is an important classic by the American author Herman Melville. It was published in 1815 and it's very long – 135 chapters! It's about a man called Ahab who works on a boat that finds and kills whales. A big whale bites off his leg! He doesn't die but he can't forget or forgive the whale. He goes on a boat to find and kill it. He is completely mad and ignores everyone's advice. In the end, they find Moby Dick but it kills everyone on the whaling boat – except the narrator, the person who is telling the story. He's called Ishmael.

B *White Fang* is a brilliant book about a wolfdog in Canada. It's shorter than *Moby-Dick* – only twenty-five chapters. It's by Jack London, another American author, and was published in 1906. For a lot of the book the narrator is the wolfdog! It's a sad story because people make White Fang fight with other dogs. But in the end everything is OK. A young hunter called Weedon Scott saves White Fang and takes him home to California.

6 **PROJECT** Use the internet to research a book about an animal written by an author from your country. Make notes about:

- the author and when he/she wrote the book.
- the story and the characters.
- why the book is important.
- any other interesting information.

7 **PROJECT** Write a factfile and a story summary about the book. Add pictures.

Beaulieu Palace House

Started by a king, destroyed by a king

There are many large old houses in England that once belonged to rich people. Beaulieu Palace House, in the south of England, is one of these. Today, this very old building from the thirteenth century is the home of the Montagu family.

In 1203, King John gave some land to a group of monks so they could build a great monastery or 'abbey'. They built Beaulieu Abbey – it was one of the biggest in the south. The building took a very long time but after four decades – in 1246 – it was finished. It had a very big church and places for the monks to live. The Abbey was very famous and very rich.

At that time, the people of England were Catholic but when Henry the Eighth was king of England (between 1509 and 1547) he decided to break with the Pope in Rome. Instead, he started the Church of England.

King Henry believed that the monasteries of England had too much money, so in 1538 he closed and destroyed nearly all of them. Beaulieu Abbey was destroyed too and now only the building where the monks had their meals is still standing. It is now the local church. In the ruins of the Abbey you can still see the lines of the old walls.

The Earl of Southampton bought the land in 1539 and used the gatehouse for his home. Builders made it bigger in the sixteenth and nineteenth centuries and today it is called Palace House. The owners are the Montagu family.

Visitors come to the small village of Beaulieu to visit Palace House every day of the year (except Christmas Day!). They also come to see the ruins of Beaulieu Abbey and the famous National Motor Museum which Lord Montagu started in 1972.

1 **Read the article and match labels 1–5 with photos A–E.**

1 ☐ Beaulieu Palace House
2 ☐ a monk
3 ☐ the National Motor Museum
4 ☐ King Henry VIII (the Eighth)
5 ☐ the ruins of Beaulieu Abbey

2 **Read the article again. What happened at these times?**

1 in 1203   4 in 1538
2 in 1246   5 in 1539
3 1509–1547   6 in 1972

3 **Work in pairs. Would you like to visit Beaulieu Palace House? Why?/Why not?**

4 **Work in pairs. Create a quiz about important events in your country. Use the notes below to help you.**

This person became king/president/prime minister in …
This war happened between … and …
This man/woman invented … in the … century.
This queen died in …

5 **Work with another pair. Ask and answer your quiz questions.**

6 **PROJECT Find out about a famous building in your country. Make notes about:**

- where it is.
- who built it and when.
- what's special about it.
- how people use it today.
- other interesting information.

7 **PROJECT Write a paragraph about the building. Add pictures.**

Antibiotics

1 _____

Antibiotics are very important medicines in our lives. Doctors use them to fight many different kinds of infections. However, before 1928 scientists didn't know about them! At that time lots of people died for unimportant reasons, for example, cuts on the skin. Alexander Fleming, a Scottish scientist, discovered an antibiotic called penicillin – just by mistake! Now, we use antibiotics all the time.

2 _____

Antibiotics are chemicals that kill bacteria and stop infections. There are many different types of antibiotics because there are different types of bacteria and infections. One type of bacterium is called Gram-positive. These bacteria have very thin cell walls and antibiotics can go through the walls easily. The second is called Gram-negative and these have very thick cell walls.

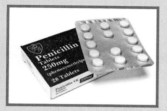

3 _____

The antibiotics kill the bacteria and stop them from making new cells. They make the cell walls weak and they break. There are 'broad spectrum' antibiotics that can fight all types of bacteria and doctors use them for lots of different infections. There are also 'narrow spectrum' antibiotics which are good for attacking special problems.

4 _____

Today doctors are worried. Many bacteria are getting resistant – that means they get stronger and a lot of antibiotics don't kill them. This is because we use them too often. Also, we should finish all our tablets but sometimes we don't do this because we feel better. Then, the bacteria which are still in our bodies get stronger. In the past, doctors had a lot of different antibiotics to give us but now many of them don't work. Scientists need to find new antibiotics but it isn't easy. If they don't find new antibiotics, people will die for unimportant reasons again.

1 **Read the article and match paragraph headings A–D with paragraphs 1–4.**

   A   How antibiotics work
   B   A problem for scientists
   C   Antibiotics and bacteria
   D   The first antibiotics

2 **Read the article again and answer the questions.**

   1   Who discovered the first antibiotic?
   2   When did he discover it?
   3   What was it called?
   4   What are antibiotics?
   5   Name two types of bacteria.
   6   Name two types of antibiotics.
   7   What is a problem today?
   8   Give two causes of that problem.

3 **Work in pairs. Do you think that doctors give antibiotics when they don't need to? Why?**

4 **Work in pairs. Look at the list of things a–g which scientists do to develop a new antibiotic drug. Put the stages in the order which you think they happen.**

Scientists:
   a   ☐ test the drug on people who have the illness.
   b   ☐ test the new drug using a computer model.
   c   ☐ test the drug on human cells in a laboratory.
   d   ☐1 find a new source for an antibiotic.
   e   ☐ test the drug on animals.
   f   ☐ stop testing if the drug damages the cells.
   g   ☐ test the drug on healthy humans.

5 **Compare your ideas from Exercise 4 with another pair. Do you agree on the order? Ask your teacher for the correct order. Who was right?**

6 **Now cover the list and take turns with your partner to give the correct stages.**

7 **PROJECT** **Use the internet to research a possible source for a new antibiotic. Make notes about:**
   ● possible places to look.
   ● animals which might be a source.
   ● why this might be a good source.
   ● what infections it might be good for.

8 **PROJECT** **Write a report and add some pictures. Present your report to the class.**

Yellowstone National Park

1 Yellowstone National Park in the USA was probably the first national park in the world. Yellowstone is very popular and very big (8,983 km²). It's a wonderful place to see wildlife and different natural features such as mountains, forests, canyons, rivers, lakes and waterfalls. But many people don't realise that this amazing park is sitting on top of something that is very dangerous – one of the biggest supervolcanoes in the world!

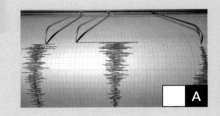

A

2 Deep under Yellowstone Park is a volcanic 'hotspot'. Heat from inside the Earth melts the rocks above it and this makes a big pool of magma. Sometimes this magma erupts and sends out huge amounts of lava, rock and ash. A really big eruption throws out nearly all the magma and then the land above the magma pool falls in. This creates a huge hole called a caldera. The Yellowstone Caldera is fifty-five kilometres wide and eighty kilometres long! Another natural feature of Yellowstone Park are the many geysers: rainwater goes down through the rocks, the magma heats it and then very hot water rises back up to the surface. The water rises fast into the air with clouds of steam. The most famous geyser at Yellowstone is called 'Old Faithful' and it erupts nearly every hour.

B

3 The Yellowstone Supervolcano has erupted several times in the last two million years (the last time about 640,000 years ago) and it's still active. It will erupt again! The ash could cover the whole of North America and make the temperatures cold for a long time. But scientists don't think that this will happen soon – maybe in one or two million years. They study the area very carefully with special equipment. They are always checking for movements in the crust that might cause earthquakes. They hope that they will be able to tell people a long time before an eruption happens.

C

1 Have you ever heard of 'Yellowstone National Park'? What do you know about it?

2 Read the article and match photos A–C with paragraphs 1–3.

3 Read the article again and answer the questions.

1. How big is Yellowstone National Park?
2. Name three natural features that you can see there.
3. What do many people NOT know about Yellowstone Park?
4. How big is the Yellowstone caldera?
5. If there is another eruption, what will happen?
6. When do scientists think this might happen?

4 Choose a diagram (A or B) below. Study the diagram. Find the part of the reading text that explains your diagram and read it again.

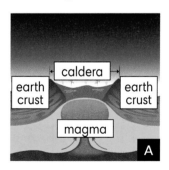

A

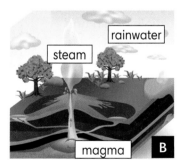

B

5 Work in pairs. Cover the reading text. Use your diagram to explain to your partner how a volcano or a geyser works.

6 PROJECT Use the internet to find out about another supervolcano. Make notes about:
- where it is.
- how it has changed the landscape.
- how dangerous it is.

7 PROJECT Write a factfile about the supervolcano you have chosen. Add pictures.

1 Read about the USA. How many states are there in the USA?

2 Read about the USA again. Answer the questions.
1 Is the USA a multicultural country? Why?
2 What is the capital of the USA? Why is this city important?
3 What is the 'Big Apple'?
4 Which famous buildings are in New York?
5 What is the weather like in LA?

3 In pairs, answer the questions.
1 What is the largest city in your country?
2 What is your favourite city in your country?
3 What other cities do you know in Europe and the USA?

4 Write a short paragraph about your favourite city in your country. Use your answers to Exercise 3 and the USA examples to help you.

The USA

The USA has fifty states and they are all different. There are many different kinds of climate, landscape, cities and culture in the USA. People from all over the world live there. It is very multicultural.

DC Washington DC is the capital of the USA. It is an important city. The President and his family live in Washington DC in the White House. The White House has tennis courts, a swimming pool and a cinema for the President's family. Inside the White House is the Oval Office. It is the office of the President. Leaders from around the world travel to the Oval Office to meet the President.

I love NYC New York city, or the 'Big Apple', has a population of 8.2 million people. The New York skyline is very famous. It has some tall buildings called skyscrapers. The Empire State Building and the Chrysler building are easy to recognise. The Statue of Liberty is in New York Harbour. It was a present from the people of France to the USA. It is a symbol of freedom and democracy.

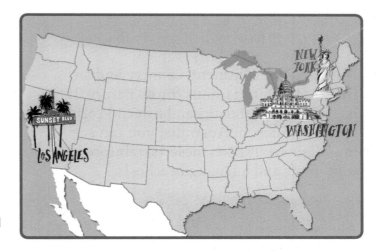

City of Angels Los Angeles (LA) is very multicultural. People from all over the world live, work and enjoy the good weather in LA. The city has many important centres of culture, science and technology and it is the movie capital of the world! You can see the famous Hollywood sign in the hills of the city. You can also walk down Hollywood Boulevard and see the handprints of famous actors.

Washington DC   New York   Los Angeles

1 Read about Australia. Is Australia a continent, a country or an island?

2 Read about Australia again. Answer the questions.
  1 How many beaches are there in Australia?
  2 What can you see from space?
  3 Do children go to school in the Outback?
  4 What are the 'Three Sisters'?

3 In pairs, answer the questions.

And YOU

  1 What country and continent do you live in?
  2 What is special about the nature in your country?
  3 Do you know an old story about your country? Tell your partner.

4 Write a short paragraph about the nature in your country. Use your answers to Exercise 3 and the Australia examples to help you.

AUSTRALIA

Australia is a continent, country and an island. It is very famous for its nature. It has 550 national parks and fifteen World Heritage Sites. In Australia, you can see mountains, salt lakes, deserts, rainforests, coral reefs and amazing beaches!

The Outback

The Outback is part of Australia where few people live. It is often dry like a desert. Many families work on big sheep farms and live hundreds of kilometres away from towns or schools. Children in these families don't go to school. They learn at home and speak to their teachers over the internet!

The coast

There are over 10,000 beaches in Australia! The Great Barrier Reef is on the north-east coast of Australia. It is a marine park that is over 3,000 kilometres long! It is longer than the Great Wall of China and you can see it from space. It is very famous for its natural beauty. The Reef has many colourful corals and is home to whales, dolphins, turtles and crocodiles!

Mountains

The Blue Mountains are in the south-east of Australia. In the Blue Mountains, there are three famous rocks called the 'Three Sisters.' The Aborigine people have a very old story about the rocks. The story is about three beautiful women. The women fall in love with three brothers. The brothers are from a different tribe and they can't get married. The brothers try to catch the sisters. A magician wants to protect the sisters and he changes them into rocks!